D1187838

ECONOMIC GROWTH IN IRELAND
The experience since 1947

70232

Economic Growth in Ireland:

THE EXPERIENCE SINCE 1947

KIERAN A. KENNEDY
and
BRENDAN R. DOWLING

GILL AND MACMILLAN · DUBLIN
BARNES & NOBLE BOOKS · NEW YORK
a division of Harper & Row Publishers Inc.
in association with
THE ECONOMIC AND SOCIAL RESEARCH
INSTITUTE, DUBLIN

First published in Ireland in 1975

Gill and Macmillan Ltd
15/17 Eden Quay
Dublin 1

and in London through association with the
Macmillan International Group of Publishing Companies

Published in the USA in 1975 by
Harper and Row Publishers Inc
Barnes and Noble Import Division

Gill and Macmillan SBN 7171 0744 2
Barnes and Noble ISBN 0 – 06 – 493631 – 7

Printed in Great Britain by
Bristol Typesetting Co Ltd
Barton Manor, St Philips, Bristol

To Finola and Dorothea

Acknowledgments

WE would like to acknowledge with deep gratitude the extensive comments and criticisms received on the various drafts of this book from the following: Professor P. Lynch, University College, Dublin; Professor Simon Kuznets, Havard University; Dr Brendan Menton, Department of Finance; Messrs J. Doherty and T. Hoare, Central Bank of Ireland; Mr T. J. Baker, Mr J. Durkan, Dr R. C. Geary, Mr J. C. Hughes, Professor R. O'Connor and Professor B. M. Walsh of the Economic and Social Research Institute (E S R I); Professor Noel Farley, Bryn Mawr College; Dr D. McAleese, Trinity College, Dublin; Mr John Martin, Nuffield College, Oxford; and Mrs Finola Kennedy.

We owe many debts to Professor M. P. Fogarty, Centre for Studies in Social Policy, London, who was Director of the E S R I when this study was initiated.

In revising earlier drafts, we were most fortunate to have available to us the services of our Institute colleagues Mr L. Ebrill (now at Harvard University) and Mr R. Bruton, who provided invaluable research assistance with data as well as making many penetrating comments.

We are deeply grateful to Mrs M. Dempsey, Assistant Director (Administration) of the E S R I, and her staff for their efficient and ready help at all times. We are especially indebted to Miss M. Maher, the Director's secretary, for her outstanding work in typing the various drafts of the study. We would also like to record our thanks to Miss B. Payne, Miss M. McElhone and Mrs P. Hughes for their work in proof-reading.

Contents

List of Tables

List of Charts

Introduction

I R E L A N D experienced a marked rise in the longer-term growth
rate of real Gross National Product (G N P) from about the end
of the 1950s or the beginning of the 1960s. The faster rate of
growth of output in the 1960s is reflected in many other social and
economic trends, the most notable, perhaps, being the arrest
of the secular decline in population. The object of this study is
to examine the nature of the changes in the Irish economy and the
major economic forces that have brought about such changes.

In undertaking this study we are conscious of the unsettled
theoretical controversies over the causes of economic growth. We
have not used Irish data to apply rigorous tests to various
theoretical models, since our object was to analyse the Irish
experience rather than verify theories of growth. Our emphasis, in
studying the Irish economy, is on the behaviour of the components of aggregate demand, changes in the structure of the
economy over time, and the short-run management of the
economy. We feel that this approach is likely to prove more
productive in a first attempt to provide a comprehensive picture.
The Irish economy presents some unique features which it would
be unwise to suppress or ignore in an effort to impose a rigid
theoretical framework that might not give such features adequate
weight.

Nevertheless, although the structure and experience of the
post-war Irish economy differs considerably from that of advanced
industrial nations, this does not mean that theoretical approaches
developed to explain the behaviour of the mature economies have
no relevance to Ireland. If, in fact, this were the case Ireland, as
a nation, would be at a considerable disadvantage since it would
be unable to reap the substantial externalities available by means
of the rapid progress in economic theory made elsewhere. We

believe, and this study is in part a reflection of such belief, that when allowance is made for important structural differences (such as the free external mobility of capital and labour, constraints on policy arising from the degree of interdependence with the U K economy, etc.), the experience of the Irish economy is amenable to analysis by tools developed from the experience of other economies.

In seeking to understand the much more rapid rate of economic progress in the 1960s compared with the earlier post-war period, there are various levels at which the change might be explained. There is a general belief that the change cannot be fully understood solely in terms of conventional economics, but that there were also important changes in social, psychological and other forces underlying the economic factors. Examples of such changes were the emergence to responsible positions of a new post-Independence generation, placing greater emphasis on solving unemployment and emigration than on ending Partition or restoring the Irish language; the assumption of a greater role in international affairs (as indicated, for example, by the participation of Irish soldiers in the Congo and of Irish diplomats in the United Nations, which Ireland joined in 1955, and Ireland's application to join the E E C in July 1961) and the sense of pride and purpose derived therefrom; and the influence of key personalities in dissipating the cynicism, born of apparent failures, about Ireland's economic prospects and in arousing enthusiasm for economic growth as a prerequisite to the achievement of more fundamental national goals. While we ourselves share the view that a purely economic explanation cannot be a complete explanation, we feel, nevertheless, that, as economists, we can make a worthwhile contribution by examining the mechanism of change in economic terms. In this way we would hope to isolate the key economic factors at work, thereby highlighting the economic variables to which might be linked the social, psychological, political, administrative and other 'non-economic' forces at work.

In this study, therefore, we investigate certain factors which are usually postulated as causes of growth and which seem related, in the Irish case, to the acceleration of economic growth. These factors are the growth of exports, both visible and invisible, the growth of fixed investment, the behaviour of the savings ratio, the effect of structural changes and policy measures on short-term fluctuations in the economy, and the relation between short-term fluctuations and longer-term growth. These are not, of course, the only relevant influences on growth, but they appeared to us to be the most relevant to understanding economic development in post-war Ireland.

In Part I we lay the groundwork for more detailed analysis by examining the longer-term economic trends in the post-war period. Part II describes in detail the behaviour of exports and examines the determinants of major components of exports—both goods and services. The argument, frequently advanced in the Irish case, that the change in the rate of growth of the economy can be attributed to exports—the so-called 'export-led growth hypothesis' —is discussed, but our conclusions on the subject are deferred to Parts IV and V after other relevant factors have been considered. Part III is devoted to an analysis of savings and investment behaviour. As we shall demonstrate later, there were powerful prejudices against the use of external capital inflows in the first decade or so after the war, and increased investment was regarded as dependent on increased saving; nor were the conditions in which saving could increase always properly understood. Our analysis of the determinants of saving in Chapter 10 has, there-fore, a wider importance in understanding the overall course of the economy. In Chapter 11 changes in the level and composition of investment, and their relation to the growth of output and productivity, are examined.

Given the nature of our investigation, we must inevitably con-sider economic policy during the post-war period. Indeed, it would be unrealistic to pretend that we could undertake a formal analysis of the Irish economy as if it were a disembodied entity separated from the myriad of policy decisions that shape its structure. Thus, throughout the work, we discuss the impact on structure and performance of various measures adopted by policy-makers. Furthermore, Part IV is devoted to an evaluation of short-term demand management in the economy and its contri-bution to the change in the rate of growth.

The concluding part—Part V—opens with a chapter giving an overview of our conclusions in regard to the post-war period up to 1968. At the time when the bulk of the research for this study was undertaken, the year 1968 was the latest for which most of the data required was available. Since then information has become available about the years 1969–72—a period of considerable economic difficulty, with an average growth rate below that for the 1960s as a whole. To ignore the performance of the economy in these years would lay us open to charges of undue optimism and pre-selection of an arbitrary cut-off date for the study. However, the economy was seriously affected in these years by the Northern Ireland situation—a factor which we all hope to be temporary—and by the exceptionally high rate of inflation—a feature of almost all advanced economies in the past few years. Nevertheless, we believe that many of the problems of the 1968–72 period can be analysed within the framework we have adopted for the rest of the post-war period. But in order to allow for special factors, and because of the provisional nature of much of the data, we discuss this period in a separate chapter in Part V.

We are conscious of the fact that there is always a danger of generals fighting the last war, or, at least, of not realising that the present war includes new aspects as well as old. As a counter to this danger, we review in a final chapter the major problems and opportunities affecting future growth prospects. Some of the problems have long been with us but as yet remain unsolved (such as the high rate of unemployment); some may have been generated in part in the very process of economic expansion itself (such as the difficulties of public finance); while others emerge as a result of changing circumstances (the challenge of E E C competition). However, our aim has not been to reach, on the model of governmental commissions, a set of clearly enunciated recommendations; and Chapter 18 might more suitably be regarded as a brief for further research.

Indeed, in undertaking so broad a task as examining the post-war growth of the economy, we are conscious that any one of the issues we discuss could well form a substantial research project in itself. Thus at times we raise more questions than we can hope to answer; we hope that this is our work's strength rather than weakness. It is possible that for many readers we will not have raised all the key questions. If such omissions provoke research, we will have felt the study worthwhile. For we have aimed, above all, at developing an overall view of the post-war economy in order to provide a framework for further discussion and research. Hopefully, we have succeeded in drawing together the results of previous research in this area; in identifying, and in some places filling, important gaps in our knowledge; and in giving policy-makers an opportunity to compare their impressions of the period, based on their own experience, with what, we hope, is an objective analysis. If we have helped to establish more clearly how we have arrived where we are, we can proceed with greater assurance for the future.

PART I

THE GROWTH OF AGGREGATE OUTPUT AND EXPENDITURE

CHAPTER 1

Growth of Aggregate Output and Productivity

O N E of the more striking features of the post-war experience of Western economies has been the ability to achieve and sustain high rates of growth of output. Indeed, governments are often judged, largely, on their ability to maintain and, where possible, increase the growth of output. While few would now argue that economic growth, as measured by changes in, say, G N P, is the only, or even an adequate, measure of the change in society's welfare, the benefits of such a sustained rise in real income would appear substantial. Over the post-war period as a whole the Irish growth rate was low by European standards: between 1947 and 1968[1] the volume of G N P grew at an annual rate of 2.9 per cent. However, not only has the year-to-year performance fluctuated a great deal around this average, but there was also a marked change in the trend of output growth from about the end of the 1950s or the beginning of the 1960s.

THE BREAK IN TREND

In Chart 1 the volume of G N P (i.e. G N P valued at constant 1958 prices) is plotted for each year from 1947 to 1968.[2] The year-to-year percentage changes in G N P are also set out in Table A.1 at the end of this chapter. It is clear from the chart and the table that there has been substantial variation from year to year in the rate of growth of output. Furthermore, it would appear that the variations were not simply fluctuations about a relatively constant growth rate. Rather, there is a distinct shift in the average slope from about the end of the 1950s. We have set out in Table 1 the average annual growth rates of G N P volume for selected sub-periods.

Since, as is well known, average annual growth rates over a short

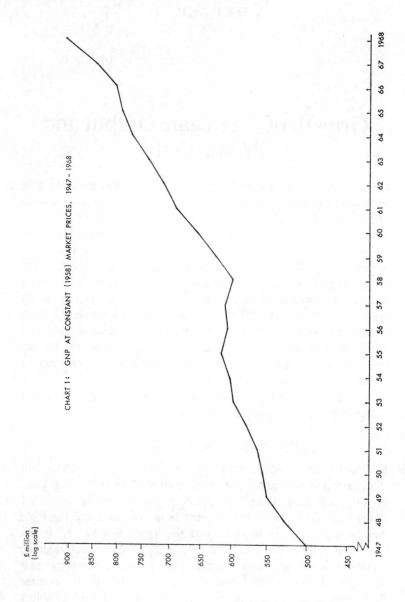

CHART 1:   GNP AT CONSTANT (1958) MARKET PRICES, 1947 - 1968

Table 1: Average annual growth rate of G N P in constant prices, sub-periods 1947–68

Sub-period	Average annual growth rate*
	%
1947–49	5.0
1949–55	1.8
1955–61	2.0
1961–68	4.1
1947–68	2.9

*These growth rates are based on the beginning and end year of each period. Trend growth rates, based on all years in each period yield the following results: 1947–49: 5.0 per cent; 1949–55: 2.0 per cent; 1955–61: 1.9 per cent; 1961–68: 3.7 per cent; 1947–68: 2.5 per cent. Thus, on this basis the 1961–68 growth rate is rather lower than shown in the table, but still nearly double that of the sub-periods 1949–55 and 1955–61.
Source: *National Income and Expenditure 1969.* The growth rates have been derived from the deflated expenditure data.

period are sensitive to the choice of beginning and end years, it is necessary to justify our selection of the particular sub-periods used in Table 1.[3] The choice of 1947 as the beginning of the post-war period is mainly due to the fact that this is the first year for which a set of national accounts statistics, entirely consistent with all succeeding years, is available. It is also likely that by 1947 the volume of national product had recovered after the war-time decline to the highest pre-war level.[4] As may be seen from Table 1, the economy grew rapidly from 1947 to 1949. On a number of grounds it seems best to view the rapid growth in 1948 and 1949 as substantially influenced by post-war recovery. Although the volume of industrial output in 1946 exceeded the highest pre-war level, many individual industries were still below pre-war output levels. Moreover, the volume of net agricultural output, which had remained high during the war, reaching a peak in 1945, declined considerably in 1946 and 1947: the substantial recovery in agricultural output in 1948 and 1949, although not sufficient to restore 1945 output levels, also contributed to the high rate of growth of G N P in those years.

In marking 1949 as the end of the post-war recovery phase, we are supported by the fact that by then aggregate real income had, for the first time since the beginning of the Second World

War, reached the level indicated by an extrapolation of the pre-war growth rate from 1931–39.[5] Thus it might be said that by 1949 total product had recovered from the interruption in growth occasioned by the war. This is not to say, of course, that recovery from the war was complete in every respect by 1949, or that recovery in some respects was not completed well before then.

After 1949 there was a marked deceleration in growth, although there was no actual decline in real G N P until 1956. The second sub-period distinguished in Table 1, 1949–55, which ends just before the major depression of 1956–58, was one in which there was an average annual rate of growth of G N P of 1.8 per cent. Although such a growth rate compares unfavourably with the rates achieved in other European economies, it does not suggest a completely stagnant economy.

The years 1956–58 were years of rather severe depression and one might expect that, for some time after 1958, part of the growth in the economy simply represented post-depression recovery. Thus, although the substantial increase in output in 1959 raised real G N P above the 1955 level, there is little doubt that recovery was by no means complete for the entire economy. In other words, the rapid growth rates for a few years after 1958, and not just in 1959 alone, can be considered as strongly influenced by recovery from a depressed phase. There are many indicators supporting this interpretation of the years 1959–61. If the growth experience from 1949–55 is taken as a norm, then only in 1961 did the actual volume of G N P exceed the volume indicated by extrapolating the growth experience of the earlier period. The 1957 level of real net output in agriculture, which fell substantially in 1958, was first surpassed in 1961. For several important groups of industries (notably building and the manufacturing industries associated with building), the volume of industrial production did not recover fully to pre-depression levels until 1961 or 1962. In addition, employment in industries covered by the Census of Industrial Production surpassed the 1955 level only in 1962, whereas prior to the 1956–58 depression it had risen in every post-war year (except 1952).[6] Finally, the volume of fixed investment did not again reach the 1955 level until 1961, while the 1955 share of fixed investment in G N P, both at constant prices, was reached only in 1962.

In the light of these factors we would judge 1961 as the most appropriate year to mark the termination of the cycle which began after 1955. Indeed, 1961 is interesting in other respects in marking the transition in the economy. Most important, perhaps, was the steady, though modest, upswing in population, which had fallen almost without interruption for over a century, reaching its nadir in 1961. This change was due to a massive reduction in net emigration which averaged 16,000 per annum in the intercensal period 1961–66 compared to 42,000 per annum for 1956–61, 39,000 per annum for 1951–56, and 24,000 per annum during 1946–51. Total employment, which had fallen throughout the post-war period, also reached its lowest level in 1961 and subsequently rose slightly, although not at a steady rate.

It is clear from Table 1 that the growth rate from 1961–68 far exceeded the growth rate in the two preceding sub-periods, 1949–55 and 1955–61. The growth rate in these two sub-periods was very similar: however, too much should not be read into this similarity since the sub-period 1955–61 was picked partly by reference to when the economy had recovered to the 1949–55 trend rate. Our main point is that from about the early 1960s the economy has sustained a rate of growth far higher than for any lengthy period since the war—or, indeed, for any period prior to the war for which data are available.[7] The change in the growth rate from 1.9 per cent (the average for the period 1949–61) to 4.1 per cent (the average for 1961–68) might seem small to some, but its significance can be appreciated better if the implications of such growth rates are considered over a longer time period. If we project the rates over a twenty-year period, the 1.9 per cent growth rate would yield an increase in output of 46 per cent while a growth rate of 4.1 per cent involves a rise in output of 124 per cent. Thus what might appear to be small differences in growth rates can lead, if sustained over a longish time period to quite large differences in output.

In marking this acceleration in growth—confirmed by many other economic and non-economic indicators—at about 1961, we do not suggest that the forces underlying the change emerged suddenly in a single year: rather we consider 1961 as the year from which the change can be unambiguously identified. Thus we do not necessarily view the years 1958–61 *solely* as a recovery phase from the preceding slump. For it is very probable that the growth from 1958 involved *both* normal recovery from a slump *and* elements of a take-off to faster growth. Furthermore, it would be foolish to ignore the contribution to growth of the many developments that took place throughout the 1950s and laid a basis for potential expansion in the 1960s. Throughout this study we are conscious of the continuity of the economy and of the long time-lag between policy action and structural change. We deal explicitly with these considerations in later chapters.

Variability of G N P Growth in the Post-War Period

Not only was the growth rate much lower in the first period, it was also relatively more variable. The impression obtained from Chart 1 and confirmed by Table 2 is that there was less fluctuation in the year-to-year growth of G N P around the longer-term trend during 1961–68 than during 1949–61.[8] It can be seen from Table 2 that the coefficient of variation of the annual percentage changes in G N P for 1949–61 was over twice as great as that for 1961–68.

Table 2: Variability of growth rate of real G N P, 1949–61 and 1961–68

| Period | Annual percentage change in real G N P | | |
	Mean	Standard deviation	Coefficient of variation
1949–61	1.9	2.2	1.13
1961–68	4.1	1.9	0.47

Source: *National Income and Expenditure 1969.*

It is sometimes held that rapid growth is likely to take place in leaps and bounds, and, therefore, involves considerable short-term fluctuations. This view does not appear, however, to receive any support in Irish post-war experience: the evidence indicates that faster growth was accompanied by less variability. There are indeed plausible reasons why faster growth might in some circumstances reduce short-term variability. If, for example, rapid growth is associated with considerable changes in the structure of the economy, and if the structural changes are such as to reduce the relative importance of sectors with a high degree of output instability, then the overall variability of G N P is likely to be reduced. Agriculture—a sector characterised by sizeable annual fluctuations in prices and output—may decline in importance while other relatively more stable sectors increase their share of total product. Thus the cyclical fluctuations of agriculture have a diminishing impact on the overall economy as the weight of the other sectors in G N P increases.

Of course, there are other factors, such as the quality of demand management or the effect of external disturbances, which influence short-term variability. Moreover, any relation between faster growth and reduced variability may also be due to beneficial effects of short-term stability on longer-term growth. For example, a high degree of fluctuation in the economy may induce great uncertainty and deter investment, thereby reducing the growth potential. It is possible that both influences, from variability to growth and from growth to variability, were at work in the post-war Irish economy.

The reasons for the relatively greater short-term stability in the second period, and its relation to longer-term growth, are further discussed in later chapters.

Growth Rates of Real Product per Capita and per Worker

Ireland's performance in regard to the growth of *per capita* and per worker product has been rather less unsatisfactory throughout the post-war period in relation to other Western countries, than in regard to growth of product. This is associated with the decline, up to 1961, in population and employment. The average annual growth rates of G N P *per capita* and per worker over the post-war period as a whole—3.0 per cent and 3.6 per cent respectively—are quite respectable in comparison with the performance of many other economies.

The cessation of the decline in total population and employment in 1961 and their subsequent rise imply that the *per capita* and per worker behaviour of output did not differ as widely between the periods 1949–61 and 1961–68. This can be seen from Table 3 where, for each of the four post-war sub-periods distinguished earlier, the average annual rates of growth of real G N P, population, employment, G N P *per capita* and G N P per worker are set out.[9] It may be noted that whereas the growth rate of output rose by 2.2 percentage points between 1949–61 and 1961–68, the growth rate of *per capita* output rose by only

Table 3: Average annual growth rates of real product *per capita*
and per worker, sub-periods 1947–68

Period	GNP at constant prices	Popula-tion	Employ-ment	GNP *per capita*	GNP per worker
	%	%	%	%	%
1947–49	5.0	0.1	—0.1	4.9	5.1
1949–55	1.8	—0.3	—1.1	2.2	3.0
1955–61	2.0	—0.7	—1.4	2.6	3.4
1949–61	1.9	—0.5	—1.3	2.4	3.2
1961–68	4.1	0.5	0.2	3.6	3.9
1947–68	2.9	—0.1	—0.7	3.0	3.6

Source: See notes to Table A.1 at the end of this chapter.

1.2 percentage points and the growth rate of per worker output by only 0.7 percentage points. In all sub-periods shown in Table 3, employment fell more rapidly, or rose more slowly, than total population and, moreover, the swing in employment movement between 1949–61 and 1961–68 was more pronounced than the swing in population change. Changes in the relation between employment and population, which are in turn related to such factors as labour force participation, the age dependency ratio and the level of unemployment, are shown later to have had important consequences for the behaviour of the personal savings ratio.

If we omit the years 1947–49 as being influenced by post-war recovery factors, it can be seen that differences in aggregate productivity growth, as measured by changes in real GNP per worker, were much smaller than differences in the growth of total product. Indeed, aggregate productivity growth was relatively constant in the post-war period, with only a weak rise in response to the rise in output growth. It is possible, however, that the high level of aggregation involved in GNP estimates tends to conceal important differences in the pattern of output, employment and productivity growth in the sectors that constitute the economy, and which we now examine.

SECTORAL CHANGES IN REAL PRODUCT AND EMPLOYMENT

Throughout the post-war period there have been considerable changes among sectors in the distribution of total product and employment. These structural shifts have tended to accelerate with the increase in the overall growth rate. In Table 4 the share of the three major sectors—agriculture, industry and services[10]— in total gross domestic product (G D P)[11] at constant 1958 prices and in total employment is set out for four years: 1949, 1955, 1961 and 1968.

On the whole, structural change is most noticeable in the case of employment. Between 1949 and 1968 the share of agricultural employment in the total declined by 13½ percentage points from 43 per cent to 29½ per cent, and this fall was matched by a corresponding rise—almost equally divided—in the shares of industrial and services employment. Industrial employment thus almost equalled agricultural employment in 1968, whereas in 1949 it was only half as great. Of course, such movements in employment shares are by no means unique to Ireland: a fall in the employment share of agriculture and a corresponding rise in the share of industry and services is a phenomenon widely experienced by economies in the course of development. What is worthy of note, however, is that in most countries these shifts take place in the context of rising employment, whereas employment was falling in Ireland up to 1961. Looking at the shifts in employment shares between sub-periods, we can see that the most sizeable shifts have occurred between 1961 and 1968—the decline in the agricultural sector's share of total employment between these years was 6.7 percentage points while the decline between 1949 and 1961, a period of twelve years, was 6.8 percentage points. It is only to be expected that faster growth is likely to involve greater structural change.

Changes in share over time indicate differences in relative growth rates. Thus the decline in the agricultural employment share indicates that employment in this sector grew less than total employment—or where total employment declined, declined more. Similarly, we can see that the share of the agricultural sector in real product declined by 8 percentage points between

Table 4: Sectoral shares in total product and employment for selected years

Sector	1949		1955		1961		1968	
	£m	% of total	£m	% of total	£m	% of total	£m	% of total
	(i) Gross Domestic Product at constant (1958) factor prices							
Agriculture	131.0	29.5	134.9	26.9	145.7	26.0	158	21.5
Industry	114.2	25.7	150.4	30.0	175.4	31.3	272	36.9
Services	198.3	44.7	216.1	43.1	240.3	42.7	302	41.6
Total	443.5	100.0	501.4	100.0	561.4	100.0	732	100.0
	(ii) Employment							
	Nos. (000s)	% of total	Nos. (000s)	% of total	Nos. (000s)	% of total	Nos. (000s)	% of total
Agriculture	526	42.9	442	38.6	379.5	36.1	313	29.4
Industry	264	21.5	272	23.7	257.2	24.4	303	28.4
Services	437	35.6	432	37.7	415.8	39.5	449	42.2
Total	1,227	100.0	1,146	100.0	1,052.5	100.0	1,065	100.0

Sources and Methods:

(i) Gross Domestic Product (GDP) at constant (1958) factor prices. All data for 1961 and 1968 taken from *National Income and Expenditure 1969*. For 1949 and 1955, total GDP estimated by multiplying 1958 GDP at current factor prices by an index of GDP at constant (1958) market prices derived from *National Income and Expenditure 1969*. GDP in agriculture estimated by multiplying 1958 agricultural GDP at current factor prices by index of volume of net output in agriculture taken from *Statistical Abstract of Ireland 1968* and *Irish Statistical Bulletin*, September 1969. GDP in industry estimated by deflating industrial GDP at current factor prices in 1949 and 1955 by the implied price of net output in industry derived from the Census of Industrial Production. GDP in services can then be estimated residually. It may be noted that these methods have been tested by estimating sectoral real GDP for 1968 and give results very close to the official figures, which are only available for 1958–68.

(ii) Employment. Data for 1961 and 1968 from *Review of 1969 and Outlook for 1970*; 1955 data from *Economic Statistics 1964*; 1949 data are estimates based on trends in various employment indicators between the Census of Population years 1946 and 1951.

A fuller description of the derivation of the above data is given in Kennedy (1968).

1949 and 1968, which again implies a lower growth rate (or faster decline). But the drop in its product share is less than in the case of its employment share. This indicates that average physical productivity in the agricultural sector grew relatively faster than for the whole economy. Likewise, the increase in industry's share of total product—over 12 percentage points—exceeded the increase in its employment share—nearly 7 percentage points— also indicating relatively faster productivity growth. On the other hand, productivity growth in services was much less than in the whole economy, as is clear from the fact that the growth in its output share fell far short of the increase in its employment share. These findings are brought out more clearly in Table 5, which shows the average annual growth rates of real product, employment and productivity for the sectors discussed above; the relevant periods are 1949–61 and 1961–68, with data also included on the sub-periods 1949–55 and 1955–61.

As may be seen from the table, the acceleration in output growth was confined to the industrial and services sectors, while the growth rate of agriculture increased only slightly from 0.9 per cent for 1949–61 to 1.2 per cent for 1961–68. The relative increase in the growth rate was greatest in the case of services, where the rate more than doubled. Likewise, the reversal of the overall decline in employment was due to the change in employment growth in industry and services. Both sectors suffered a small decline in employment from 1949 to 1961 but a significant rise from 1961 to 1968. On the other hand, in agriculture the rate of decline in employment has been substantial throughout the post-war period at a fairly constant rate of about $2\frac{3}{4}$ per cent per annum.

It is interesting to compare the relative sectoral contributions to output and employment growth. This is done in Table 6, where weighted sectoral growth rates are shown. The average annual growth rate of each sector in each period is weighted by the average of its share in G D P (or total employment) in the first and last year of the period, and this gives an indication of how much of the overall growth rate was accounted for in that sector. By comparing the 1949–61 sectoral contributions with those for 1961–68 we can get an indication of the relative importance of sectoral contributions to the acceleration in overall growth. The weighting is essential since a high growth rate for a

B

Table 5: Average annual rates of growth of sectoral product, employment and productivity, 1949–61 and 1961–68

Period	GDP at constant (1958) factor prices (%)	Employment (%)	GDP per worker (%)
	Agriculture		
1949–61	0.9	—2.7	3.7
1949–55	0.5	—2.9	3.5
1955–61	1.3	—2.5	3.9
1961–68	1.2	—2.7	4.0
	Industry		
1949–61	3.6	—0.2	3.8
1949–55	4.7	0.5	4.1
1955–61	2.6	—0.9	3.5
1961–68	6.4	2.4	3.9
	Services		
1949–61	1.6	—0.4	2.0
1949–55	1.4	—0.2	1.6
1955–61	1.8	—0.6	2.4
1961–68	3.5	1.1	2.4
	Total		
1949–61	2.0	—1.3	3.3
1949–55	2.1	—1.1	3.2
1955–61	1.9	—1.4	3.4
1961–68	3.9	0.2	3.7

Sources: As in Table 4. It may be noted that the growth rate of total product here refers to GDP at factor cost, and this accounts for the slight differences between some of the figures and those given earlier in Table 3 which refer to GNP at market prices.

sector might have a negligible impact on the overall growth rate in a given period if the sector accounted for only a small proportion of total output (or employment) in that period. For the period 1949–61 the industrial sector accounted for 1.0 percentage points, or half of the total growth rate of G D P; 0.7 percentage points can be attributed to services and 0.3 percentage points to

Table 6: Contribution of sectoral growth rates to growth rate of total real G D P and employment, 1949–61 and 1961–68

Sector	1949–61	1961–68	Change between the two periods
	G D P at constant (1958) factor prices		
	%	%	%
(a) Agriculture	0.3	0.3	0.0
(b) Industry	1.0	2.2	+1.2
(c) Services	0.7	1.5	+0.7
Total growth rate (=a+b+c)	2.0	3.9	+1.9
	Employment		
	%	%	%
(a) Agriculture	—1.1	—0.9	+0.2
(b) Industry	—0.05	0.65	+0.7
(c) Services	—0.15	0.45	+0.6
Total growth rate (=a+b+c)	—1.3	0.2	+1.5

Sources: As in Table 4. The contribution of each sector was measured by weighting its average annual growth rate in each period by the average of its share in total G D P (or total employment) in the first and last year of the period. This weighting system is an approximation, but is sufficiently accurate for our purposes given the share changes here and in other instances later where the same method is used.

agriculture. For 1961–68 industry contributed 2.2 percentage points (or 56 per cent of the total) to the overall growth rate of 3.9 per cent per annum. The fact that the relative contribution of industry increased by 120 per cent, while its own growth rate of output only increased by 78 per cent, is due to the greater weight in total output of the industrial sector in the second period. Similarly, the contribution of agriculture was the same in both periods, in spite of the slight acceleration in growth, owing to the declining share of this sector. The same effect is observed in the case of employment. The employment figures also show the impact on total employment of the fall in agricultural employment. In both periods the contribution of the agricultural sector to employment growth was negative but in the later period it was offset by positive growth contributions by the industrial and services sectors.

Looking at the differences in the contributions to total growth between the two periods, we can see that 1.2 percentage points, or over 60 per cent of the total rise of 1.9 percentage points in the output growth rate, can be attributed to the industrial sector. This is due partly to the faster growth of output, and partly to the greater relative share, in the later period. The balance of the increase in the overall output growth rate was contributed by services, with agriculture making no contribution. On the employment side, all sectors made a positive contribution to the change in the growth rate, although the improvement yielded only a small positive overall growth in employment for 1961–68. The positive contribution of agriculture is entirely due to its declining share in total employment, since the average annual decline in agricultural employment was the same for both periods. However, the most significant contribution to the change in the employment growth rate came from industry and services.

Productivity Growth in the Sectors

The comparative stability of the growth of output per worker compared with the acceleration in output growth, which was noted in Table 3, also holds true for sectoral disaggregation. As may be seen from Table 5, there was only a slight rise in the growth of productivity in all three sectors[12] between the periods 1949–61 and 1961–68. Throughout the post-war period, productivity growth in agriculture and industry was above the national rate, while in services it was substantially lower. It is noteworthy that, despite having quite different records of output growth, agriculture and industry experienced much the same rate of growth of productivity. It is often held that there is substantial 'disguised' unemployment in Irish agriculture and that the rapid rate of growth of productivity in that sector is simply a consequence of the fall in agricultural employment as workers move out. However, the withdrawal of employment from any sector will not, *ceteris paribus*, leave output unaffected in that sector unless the marginal product of the workers withdrawn was zero. This is an extreme assumption which, while it might hold in some cases, can hardly explain satisfactorily the sustained high rate of growth of agricultural productivity. It is much more likely that investment and technical change in agriculture were such that output could be maintained, or even increased slightly, in the face of falling employment. In that case, the decline in agricultural employment is not so much a cause as a consequence of increased productivity—combined, of course, with other factors such as the slow growth in demand for agricultural output, due to low income elasticities, and the attraction of higher wages in other sectors.

The low growth rate of productivity in the services sector may to some extent reflect inadequate measurement. It is widely recognised that there are considerable difficulties in measuring the output of services.[13] This is due in part to the heterogeneous nature of such services, and in part to the difficulty in defining the concept of output. For some services, such as public administration, changes in real output are effectively measured in terms of changes in numbers engaged, and this would understate output growth to the extent that productivity in such services had risen. Thus it is possible that the growth rate of services output is understated for both periods. Since there is less ambiguity in the measurement of labour input, measured productivity growth would also bear the burden of any underestimation of output growth.

Some part of the overall change in productivity may be due to changes in employment shares between sectors. This is defined as an *inter-sectoral*[14] productivity rise. The *intra-sectoral* productivity rise is an estimate of the overall rise in productivity due to productivity growth in each sector, given unchanged employment shares. We have estimated the inter-sectoral productivity rise by weighting the 1949 average products in each sector by the sectoral employment shares in 1961 and 1968 and comparing the result with the 1949 total product per head. This gives an estimate of the overall growth in productivity due to the change in employment shares between sectors, assuming no change in average productivity in each sector. The intra-sectoral productivity growth estimates are derived by dividing the index of total productivity change by the index of inter-sectoral productivity change: it thus provides an estimate of the overall rise in productivity due to productivity growth in each sector, given no change in employment shares.[15] The results of these calculations are set out in Table 7.

Table 7: Average annual rates of change in total productivity: inter-sectoral and intra-sectoral components, 1949–61 and 1961–68

	1949–61	1961–68
	%	%
Inter-sectoral change	0.3	0.5
Intra-sectoral change	3.0	3.2
Total productivity change	3.3	3.7

Source: Based on data in Table 5. The derivation of the figures is explained in the text.

As might be expected, the inter-sectoral component is somewhat greater in the second period due to the greater degree of structural change that took place during it. In both periods, however, it is clear that intra-sectoral productivity changes accounted for the bulk of aggregate productivity growth. Of course, it is possible that a greater degree of disaggregation would attribute a larger role to inter-sectoral changes, although it is unlikely that intra-sectoral changes would cease to dominate.

Perhaps the most striking feature of Table 7 is that, when inter-sectoral movements are netted out, overall productivity grew at much the same rate in both periods. It is true that inter-sectoral changes in employment may have helped to raise productivity growth more than our measurements suggest, since the rise in productivity *within* sectors might not have been so great in the absence of shifts in employment shares. But this qualification, if it could be quantified, would be likely only to reinforce the point that intra-sectoral productivity growth has shown little or no acceleration between the two periods.

INTERNATIONAL GROWTH RATES

The question arises whether the acceleration in economic growth in Ireland corresponded to an acceleration in countries generally. It is of interest, therefore, to compare the Irish experience, in relation to output and productivity growth, with the performance of other, mainly European, economies. If a similar acceleration in output growth took place in most European economies, it could be argued that the faster growth in Ireland was in some sense induced by faster growth elsewhere. Admittedly, such an induced growth would tend to show up in the behaviour of external transactions which we analyse in some detail later. But if faster growth in the 1960s, compared with the 1950s, was a common European phenomenon, we might find that explanations of this acceleration elsewhere were applicable to Ireland.

In Table 8 the average rates of growth of volume of G N P, G N P *per capita* and G N P per worker for fourteen selected O E C D countries are set out. The choice of 1950 as the first year was determined by data limitations, but the period 1950–61 is roughly comparable with the 1949–61 period chosen for Ireland. The later period, 1961–68, is the same for all economies included in the table. It is clear that in the first period the growth rate of the Irish economy was well below that of the other countries considered. Of the fourteen countries listed, Ireland ranked lowest in the growth of G N P, while the mean rate of growth of G N P was over twice that of Ireland. Although declining population in Ireland improved the relative performance of *per capita* output growth, it was still well below the mean for the fourteen countries —Ireland ranked twelfth in the growth of G N P *per capita* in the first period. If we confine our attention to European economies, the Irish growth rate of G N P was only one-third of that achieved by the E E C countries and two-fifths of the growth rate of all European O E C D economies. The relative ranking of the growth of Irish aggregate productivity (G N P per worker) was improved by the large decline in employment that took place between 1949 and 1961. Here the Irish performance was joint eighth of the twelve economies for which data were available.

Of course, our main interest here lies not in the relative performance of Ireland *vis-à-vis* other O E C D economies, but in whether these other economies have experienced an acceleration in growth. Comparing the 1961–68 performance with that of 1950–61, this would not appear to have been the case. Some countries did have significant upward shifts in the growth rate— the United States (3.1 to 5.2), Portugal (4.7 to 6.1), Norway (3.5 to 4.9), Belgium (3.2 to 4.4). However, the upward shifts in growth that occurred in some O E C D economies were offset by downward movements in other economies. Thus the growth of

Table 8: Average annual rates of growth of volume of G N P, etc. for selected O E C D countries, 1950–61 and 1961–68

Country	1950–61			1961–68		
	Real G N P (1) %	Real G N P *per capita* (2) %	Real G N P per worker (3) %	Real G N P (4) %	Real G N P *per capita* (5) %	Real G N P per worker (6) %
Austria	5.6	5.4	4.9[1]	4.0	3.3	4.5
Belgium	3.2[2]	2.6[2]	2.8[2]	4.4	3.8	3.8
Denmark	3.6	2.7	3.6[3]	4.2	3.5	3.5
France	4.6	3.7	4.7[4]	5.5	4.3	4.6
Germany	7.6	6.4	5.4	4.2	3.5	4.4
Greece	6.4	5.3	5.3[1]	6.8	6.2	6.0
I R E L A N D	1.9[5]	2.4[5]	3.2[5]	4.1	3.6	3.9
Italy	5.8[1]	5.2[1]	n.a.	5.2	4.3	6.1
Netherlands	4.6	3.3	3.7	5.2	4.0	4.0
Norway	3.5[1]	2.5[1]	3.2[1]	4.9	4.1	4.3
Portugal	4.7[6]	4.0[6]	4.2	6.1	5.3	6.2
Sweden	3.7	3.0	n.a.	4.2	3.5	3.6
United Kingdom	2.8	2.3	3.1	2.9	2.2	2.7
United States	3.1	1.4	2.3[7]	5.2	3.8	3.2
Mean	4.4	3.6	3.9	4.8	4.0	4.3
E E C	5.8	4.9	n.a.	4.7	3.8	4.7
O E C D Europe	4.8	3.9	n.a.	4.5	3.4	4.2

n.a. 'not available'.

Notes: Cols (1) 1951–61; (2) 1953–61; (3) 1955–61; (4) 1954–61; (5) 1949–61; (6) 1956–61; (7) 1950–59.

Sources: Cols (1), (2), (4) and (5) from O E C D *National Accounts of O E C D Countries 1950–68*. Employment data used in cols (3) and (6) from O E C D *Manpower Statistics 1950–62* and O E C D *Labour Force Statistics 1959–70*. The measure of employment used is the civilian labour force less numbers unemployed. The Irish data are taken from Table 3.

G N P for all E E C economies and for all European O E C D economies was lower in the period 1961–68 compared with 1950–61. This would tend to indicate that the faster Irish growth was not merely a response to faster growth in Europe. But although the change in the Irish growth rate of G N P was substantial, it was not sufficient to bring it up to the rates experienced by most O E C D countries.

An interesting point which emerges from the comparison of growth rates is the similarity between the Irish and U K performances in the first period—at least in so far as they were both very low. This broad similarity is also found between the Scandinavian countries included (i.e. Denmark, Norway and Sweden) and between Germany and Austria. But while the contiguity factor might be advanced as an explanation of the low growth rate of the Irish economy from 1949 to 1961, it hardly explains the great improvement in the later period when there was no marked rise in the U K growth rate.

Examination of developments abroad indicates that this rise in growth did not take place in the context of a general rise in growth rates of output among the O E C D countries. The comparison with other economies also shows that the turnaround, large as it was, has not been sufficient to bring Ireland's performance fully up to the level of the generality of O E C D countries. It did, however, put Ireland well ahead of the growth rate realised by the U K, which is a considerable achievement given the close trading and other relations between the two economies.

CONCLUSIONS

We have noted the marked rise in the rate of growth of output in Ireland from about the beginning of the 1960s. The acceleration in output growth was not found, however, to anything like the same extent in productivity growth, and much of the increased output growth was matched by increased employment. Thus, while the overall rise in employment from 1961 to 1968 may rightly be deemed unsatisfactory as being totally insufficient to achieve full employment, it nevertheless represented a substantial improvement upon the earlier period. Indeed, the change in employment behaviour was greater than might have reasonably been expected, as indicated by the comparatively small rise in the growth of aggregate productivity despite the considerable rise in the growth of output. Thus the employment situation did respond favourably to the rise in output growth. It seems reasonable to infer that a still larger rise in the growth of output would have ensured progress towards full employment.

As already noted, the figures, both for the total and for the sectors, suggest a fairly constant rate of productivity growth over the longer term, with only a limited tendency for productivity growth to be higher in periods when output growth was higher. This contrasts with the tendency *within any given time period*—at least in manufacturing industry—for differences in output growth among industries to exert a strong influence in determining differences in productivity growth among industries.[16] However, these contrasting findings could be reconciled on the basis that the mean rate of productivity advance in any period is determined by factors largely independent of the growth of output, whereas the distribution of productivity advance among industries is crucially dependent on the relative rates of growth of output in the industries in that period. At any rate, the comparatively stable overall rate of productivity growth in different post-war periods would seem to rule out certain 'supply-side' factors, such as a rise in exogenous technological change, as a major cause of the acceleration in output growth. The failure of output to grow sufficiently in the earlier period to sustain employment levels, let alone absorb the natural increase due to population growth, would suggest instead that we must look largely to the forces influencing the demand for output as the major stimulus to the more rapid growth of output in the second period.

Table A.1: Annual percentage changes in G N P (at constant market prices), population, employment, G N P *per capita* and per worker, 1947–68

Year G N P (1)	%	Population (2) %	Employment (3) %	GNP per capita (4) %	GNP per worker (5) %
1947–48	5.0	0.4	0.6	4.6	4.4
1948–49	5.1	—0.1	—0.7	5.2	5.8
1949–50	0.8	—0.4	0.1	1.2	0.7
1950–51	1.3	—0.3	—0.9	1.6	2.2
1951–52	2.8	—0.3	—1.8	3.1	4.7
1952–53	3.1	—0.1	—2.4	3.2	5.6
1953–54	1.0	—0.3	—0.3	1.3	1.3
1954–55	2.0	—0.7	—1.5	2.7	3.6
1955–56	—1.3	—0.8	—1.8	—0.5	0.5
1956–57	0.6	—0.5	—3.6	1.1	4.2
1957–58	—1.8	—1.1	—1.5	—0.7	—0.3
1958–59	4.3	—0.2	—0.7	4.5	5.0
1959–60	5.2	—0.5	—0.5	5.7	5.7
1960–61	5.0	—0.5	—0.2	5.5	5.2
1961–62	3.3	0.4	0.7	2.9	2.6
1962–63	4.1	0.7	0.6	3.4	3.5
1963–64	3.7	0.5	0.5	3.2	3.2
1964–65	2.8	0.4	—0.2	2.4	3.0
1965–66	1.4	0.3	—0.3	1.1	1.7
1966–67	5.4	0.5	—0.6	4.9	6.0
1967–68	7.9	0.4	0.3	7.5	7.6

Sources:

Col (1) *National Income and Expenditure 1969;*

Col (2) Census of Population reports; *Report on Vital Statistics 1966;* and *Review of 1968 and Outlook for 1969;*

Col (3) 1951–61 from *Economic Statistics 1964;* 1961–68 from *Review of 1968 and Outlook for 1969;* 1947–51 are estimates based on trends in the sectors agriculture, industry and services between the Census of Population years 1946 and 1951. A fuller explanation of the method of estimation is given in Kennedy (1971, I);

Col (4) based on cols (1) and (2);

Col (5) based on cols (1) and (3).

APPENDIX TO CHAPTER 1

THE INDUSTRIAL SECTOR AND CIP INDUSTRY

T H E finding that there was little acceleration in the growth rate of productivity in the industrial sector in 1961–68 as compared with 1949–61 may occasion some surprise. Industry is often regarded as synonymous with that portion covered by the Census of Industrial Production (C I P) and is sometimes even identified with transportable goods or manufacturing. However, 'industry' as used in the preceding chapter includes activities not covered by the C I P, which in the aggregate are of some importance.[17]

Table A.2: Average annual rates of growth of output, employment and productivity in C I P industry, 1949–61 and 1961–68

	Volume of output	Employ-ment	Output per head
	%	%	%
Transportable goods			
1949–61	4.5	1.8	2.7
1961–68	6.8	2.2	4.5
Building and utilities			
1949–61	2.4	—1.2	3.6
1961–68	6.1	2.8	3.2
Total C I P			
1949–61	4.0	0.9	3.1
1961–68	6.6	2.3	4.2

Source: C I P reports. Employment figures for building and utilities and total C I P in 1968 are estimates and exclude those building workers that have been included in the C I P since 1966 but were previously not included. The official volume of output figure for total C I P has been kept comparable with earlier years.

There has, in fact, been a big rise in the growth of productivity in transportable goods. Table A.2 gives the growth rates of volume of output, employment and productivity in industry as covered by the C I P. It will be seen that productivity growth in transportable goods rose from an average annual rate of 2.7 per cent in 1949–61 to 4.5 per cent in 1961–68. However, when account is taken of building and utilities (as covered by the C I P), where there was a slight fall in the rate of productivity growth, the rise in the growth rate of productivity in total C I P industry was considerably less, i.e. 4.2 per cent in 1961–68 as against 3.1 per cent in 1949–61. And, as shown in Table 5, productivity growth in the industrial sector as a whole rose only from 3.8 per cent in 1949–61 to 3.9 per cent in 1961–68. What accounts for the difference between C I P industry and the industrial sector as a whole?

The difference arises from the fact that the C I P does not cover all industrial firms, notably those employing less than three persons. These omissions are substantial in some industries, particularly in building and construction. In 1949 non-C I P industrial workers represented well over 20 per cent of employment in the industrial sector as a whole. Between 1949 and 1961 the number of non-C I P industrial workers fell markedly and, as C I P employment rose somewhat, the share of non-C I P workers in total industrial employment declined very considerably to about 12 per cent of the total in 1961. Thus from 1949–61 both output and employment rose less in the industrial sector as a whole than in C I P industry, as may be seen by comparing Table 5 and Table A.2. However, productivity grew more rapidly in the industrial sector as a whole than in C I P industry. This does not necessarily imply that productivity in the non-C I P part rose more than in the C I P part. Although we have only scattered information on the *level* of productivity in the non-C I P part, we do know that it was considerably below the level in C I P firms. A sample inquiry carried out by the C S O among the non-C I P firms in 1946 indicates that the average level of net output per head in such firms was less than half the average for C I P firms. The substantial shift in the share of employment between 1949 and 1961 from the non-C I P part to the C I P part would therefore tend to raise productivity more in the industrial sector as a whole than in the C I P part, even if, as is probable, productivity grew less in the non-C I P part than in the C I P part.

From 1961 to 1968 there was a reversal of the falling trend in non-C I P employment. In fact, non-C I P employment rose more

than C I P employment so that its share of total industrial employment was higher in 1968 than in 1961.[18] This, combined with the
fact that productivity growth was probably lower in the non-C I P
part than in the C I P part, explains why productivity growth was
lower in the industrial sector as a whole than in C I P industry
from 1961 to 1968.

There are other differences, probably of a minor character,
between C I P industry and the industrial sector as a whole. The
former includes laundry, cleaning and dyeing, whereas the latter
does not. The C I P volume index is based on gross output prices
for each industry, though net output weights are used in com-
bining the individual industries. On the other hand, our estimates
for the industrial sector as a whole for the years 1949 to 1957 are
based on deflated gross product. It is possible that our estimates
overstate the growth of output, and, therefore, of productivity,
in the industrial sector as a whole in the first period. However,
as mentioned earlier, our method of estimation gives results close
to the official figures that are available for the years 1958 to 1968.
At any rate, in the light of the facts mentioned above, we would
expect the disparity in the growth rate of productivity between the
periods 1949–61 and 1961–68 to be considerably less for the
industrial sector as a whole than for C I P industry.

CHAPTER 2

The Behaviour of Aggregate Demand

W E now turn to a preliminary analysis of the behaviour of aggregate demand in the post-war period. The longer-term movements in the major components of expenditure on G N P will be the main area of interest. These components are consumption, both private and government, investment and the balance on current external payments (exports less imports).

CONSUMPTION AND SAVING

The major expenditure component of G N P is, of course, consumption. We would not, however, expect consumption to be a major autonomous source of income growth. This is because it is generally accepted that consumption responds to changes in income rather than causes such changes. But if the average propensity to consume is constant, then we would expect consumption to grow in line with income. In Chart 2 we show the ratio of consumption to G N P for each year from 1947 to 1968. Total consumption is divided into private consumption expenditure and government consumption expenditure.[1] Both current and constant price ratios are shown, although most of the discussion below relates to the current price figures, with any significant differences in the constant price figures being noted. As may be seen from Chart 2, the proportion of national expenditure devoted to private consumption was extraordinarily high in 1947 (almost 84 per cent of G N P). The proportion fell rapidly to 76½ per cent in 1949 and, although it rose again in 1951 to 81 per cent, it remained in the region of 72–76 per cent of G N P throughout most of the 1950s. Since 1958 there has been a sustained fall, and in 1968 the share of private consumption in G N P was 68.4 per cent compared with 76.4 per cent in 1958. To a small extent this fall was offset by

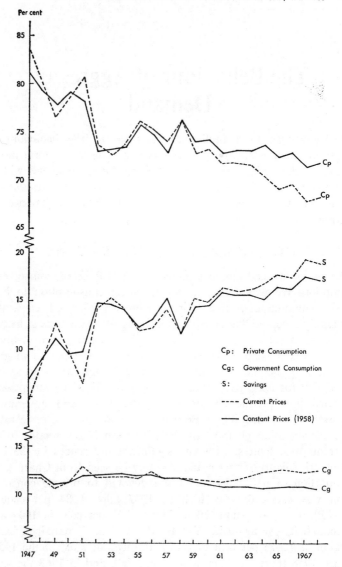

CHART 2:   SHARES OF CONSUMPTION AND SAVINGS IN GNP, 1947-1968

a rise in the share of government consumption. For most of the post-war period up to 1962, the government share was relatively stable at about 11–12 per cent of G N P (exceptional years being 1949, 1951 and 1956) but since then there has been a rise from 11.7 per cent in 1962 to 12.5 per cent in 1968. Even allowing for this slight rise, total consumption declined substantially as a proportion of G N P from about 1959 onwards.

The identity between income and consumption plus savings implies that the fall in the consumption ratio was matched by an equal rise in the savings ratio. Thus there was a substantial, and fairly steady, rise in the ratio of saving to G N P from 15.5 per cent in 1959 to 19.1 per cent in 1968.[2] The difference in the average savings behaviour in the two periods 1949–61 and 1961–68, taken as a whole, can be seen in Table 9, which shows the

Table 9: Average of annual shares of consumption and savings in G N P, 1949–61 and 1961–68*

	Current market prices		Constant (1958) market prices	
	1949–61	1961–68	1949–61	1961–68
	%	%	%	%
Total consumption	87.2	82.4	87.0	83.6
Private	75.4	70.2	75.3	72.8
Government	11.7	12.2	11.7	10.8
Savings	12.8	17.6	13.0	16.4
Total G N P	100.0	100.0	100.0	100.0

*Figures for the period 1949–61 are averages of the annual ratios in the twelve years 1949 to 1960 inclusive, while the figures for the period 1961–68 relate to the eight years 1961 to 1968 inclusive. The same procedure is followed in similar tables, following in this chapter. It might be more consistent to use for the period 1961–68 the averages of the seven years 1961 to 1967 inclusive; but, as we established, the resulting figures would not be significantly different from those given in the book.
Source: *National Income and Expenditure 1969.*

averages of the annual savings ratios in all years of each period. The average savings ratio rose considerably from 12.8 per cent in the first period to 17.6 per cent in the second. This rise reflects, of course, not only the rise in the ratio between 1961 and 1968 but also the fact that in 1961 itself the ratio, 16.5 per cent, was considerably higher than the average for the years 1949–60; thus even if the ratio were unchanged after 1961, the average for the second period would still be considerably higher than the average for the first.

An even greater contrast between the two periods is evident in the year-to-year variability of the savings ratio. Whereas in the second period the savings ratio rose fairly steadily, in the period 1949–61 there were very large year-to-year variations, and the range of variation was from as low as 6.3 per cent (in 1951) to 15.5 per cent (in 1953). These fluctuations explain why the average ratio for 1949–61, 12.8 per cent, was no higher than the 1949 ratio even though the 1960 ratio was considerably higher at 15.0 per cent.

Abstracting from short-term considerations, it is generally accepted that a rise in the savings ratio, in so far as it permits increased investment, will tend to increase longer-term growth. Of course, in an open economy investment need not be constrained by the domestic supply of savings. But if investment were to exceed domestic savings over an extended period, the dependence on capital inflows would be considerable. In Ireland, as we discuss later, there was strong official reluctance in the earlier period to rely on capital inflows from abroad, and the availability of domestic savings tended to be viewed as the ultimate constraint on domestic capital formation. In addition, a prior increase in savings was often seen as a necessary precondition to increased investment and income, without adequate advertence to the dependence of increased savings on increased income. The causes and consequences of variations in the savings ratio are therefore highly relevant to our purpose and are examined in some detail in Chapter 10.

Comparing the current price shares of consumption and savings in G N P with the constant price shares, significant differences in trend emerge from about 1958. In the case of private consumption, the fall of $4\frac{1}{2}$ percentage points in the constant price share between 1958 and 1968 was substantially less than the fall of 8 percentage points in the current price share. Moreover, the average share in constant prices in the period 1961–68 was only 2.5 percentage points lower than the average for 1949–61—much less than the fall of 5.2 percentage points in the current price share. We show later, in a more detailed analysis of savings behaviour, that the larger fall in the current value consumption share than in the real consumption share in the second period (or, alternatively, the larger rise in the current value savings share) was chiefly accounted for by changes in the terms of trade. These were much more favourable in the second period than in the first; and, in Part III, we develop the argument that, when the terms of trade improve, a higher proportion of income can be saved without any reduction in the share of real output devoted to consumption.

In the case of government consumption, the constant price share fell relative to the current price share. From 1958 to 1961 the constant price share declined from 11.7 per cent to 10.8 per cent and subsequently remained remarkably constant at about that level, in contrast with the current price share, which rose in this period. This difference is probably partly due to the statistical difficulties involved in measuring the volume of government activity. In practice, the measure used takes no account of possible productivity growth in the public sector. Therefore, to the extent that productivity growth has taken place, the volume of government activity is understated.

INVESTMENT

We might, *a priori,* expect investment to be a major source of increased growth in the economy. This is because rising investment increases both aggregate demand and the productive capacity of the economy. Of course, the extent to which increased investment has an immediate impact on aggregate domestic demand depends to a large degree on the type of investment undertaken. Investment in new aircraft imported from abroad would have a negligible short-run impact on domestic demand in the economy. By the same token the increases in output flowing from such investment may be forthcoming quite rapidly. A similar expenditure on, say, housing or road construction would have a much larger impact on domestic activity in the short run, but the sustained long-term increase in output flowing from the investment might be generated only over a considerable time period. There are, therefore, significant differences among different types of investment in regard to the short-run impact on output and employment and long-run output and productivity effects. For

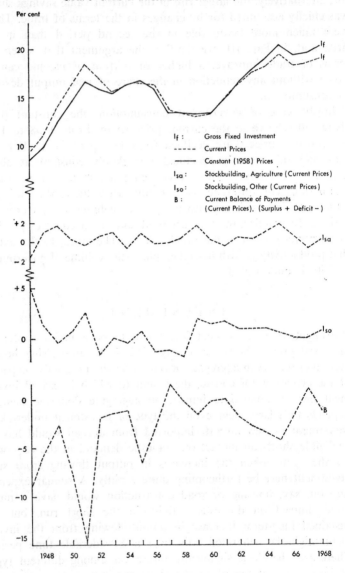

CHART 3: SHARE OF INVESTMENT ETC IN GNP, 1947-1968

Per cent

I_f : Gross Fixed Investment
---- Current Prices
——— Constant (1958) Prices

I_sa : Stockbuilding, Agriculture (Current Prices)
I_so : Stockbuilding, Other (Current Prices)
B : Current Balance of Payments
(Current Prices), (Surplus + Deficit −)

this, as well as for other reasons, it is important from our point of view to consider changes in the composition of investment as well as in its volume.

In regard to the aggregate, we can see from Chart 3 that gross fixed capital formation (or investment) as a proportion of G N P, both in current values, rose continuously and substantially from 9.5 per cent in 1947 to 18.5 per cent in 1951. Although it declined in the next two years, the share of investment in G N P up to and including 1956 was always about 16 per cent or more. There was a substantial fall in the share in 1957, and for the four years 1957–60 the share remained between 13 and 14 per cent. Only in 1961 did recovery begin and it was not until 1963 that the 1955 share of fixed investment in G N P was surpassed. The share continued rising, except in 1966, and was over 19 per cent in 1967 and 1968. Faster growth in the period 1961–68 was thus accompanied by a fairly steady rise in the fixed investment

Table 10: Average of annual shares of gross investment, etc., in G N P, 1949–61 and 1961–68

| | Current market prices | | Constant (1958) market prices | |
	1949–61	1961–68	1949–61	1961–68
	%	%	%	%
Gross fixed capital formation	15.3	17.8	14.8	18.6
Stockbuilding	0.7	1.4	0.7	1.4
Of which:				
Agriculture	0.5	0.5	0.5	0.5
Other	0.1	0.9	0.1	0.9
Total physical capital formation	16.0	19.2	15.5	20.0
Resources provided from:				
Domestic savings	12.8	17.6	13.0	16.4
Current balance of payments deficit	3.2	1.6	2.4	3.6
Total	16.0	19.2	15.5	20.0

Source: *National Income and Expenditure 1969*. Breakdown of stockbuilding (i.e. the change in stocks) for 1949–57 kindly supplied by the Central Statistics Office (C S O).

share of G N P—indicating that fixed investment grew faster than G N P for this period—but the rise took place contemporaneously with, rather than led, the more rapid growth of output. In Table 10 the average fixed investment share for the two periods 1949–61 and 1961–68 is set out. As can be seen, there has been a rise in the average ratio in the second period, the increase being about 2½ percentage points.

Stockbuilding represents a fairly small proportion of G N P in all years, but a highly volatile one that can swing rapidly from a positive to a negative value. Because of its substantial short-term fluctuations, the behaviour of stockbuilding is of considerable importance in analysing the short-term movements of the economy. Over the longer term, we might expect the share of G N P devoted to stockbuilding to remain fairly constant; indeed, if there were economies of scale in maintaining stocks, it is possible that the share of stockbuilding might decline. In fact, Table 10 shows that the average proportion of G N P devoted to stockbuilding doubled between 1949–61 and 1961–68. This increase was entirely due to the rise in the share of non-agricultural stockbuilding from 0.1 per cent to 0.9 per cent.

The combined effect of the increases in the share in G N P of fixed investment and stockbuilding between 1949–61 and 1961–68 was to raise the average share of total physical capital formation by over 3 percentage points. We noted earlier that in an open economy like Ireland domestic savings may fall short of (exceed) investment; and this shortfall (excess) is, of course, equal to the deficit (surplus) on the current balance of payments. Thus, if investment increases without a corresponding rise in savings, the balance of payments deficit will rise. The deficit will also rise if a fall in savings is not matched by a similar reduction in investment. In Chart 3 it will be noticed that for the first period (1949–61) most of the large balance of payments deficits relative to G N P were associated with actual *declines* in the savings ratio; in the second period such deficits were associated with the fact that investment increased relatively faster than savings, although both were increasing. The balance of payments position is usually related to total trade or to the level of external reserves rather than to G N P. But given the relation between consumption, savings, investment and the balance of payments, it is instructive to look at the behaviour of the ratio of the current balance of payments to G N P. Perhaps the most marked point, as may be seen from Chart 3, is the large reduction in the second period in the variability of this ratio. The largest deficit (in current values) in the period of 1961–68 was in 1965 when the ratio was 4 per cent, whereas in the period 1949–61 there was a deficit of no less than 14.7 per cent of G N P in 1951 as well as deficits of 7.6 per cent in 1950 and 6.5 per cent in 1955. Thus in the later period the economy operated within a far narrower range of fluctuations in the current balance of payments relative to G N P. This has important implications (to be discussed later) for economic management, as can be understood by imagining the possible policy responses to a balance of payments deficit of about 15 per cent of G N P.

In Table 10 we can see that, in current price terms, the balance of payments deficit as a percentage of G N P declined substantially between the two periods, falling from 3.2 per cent on average for 1949–61 to 1.6 per cent for 1961–68. Thus the rise in the savings ratio of 4.8 percentage points more than offset the rise in the investment ratio of 3.2 percentage points and so the balance of payments ratio was reduced. The faster growth of investment in the second period was not achieved through relatively greater dependence on foreign disinvestment.[3] However, as we shall see later, the greater net inflow of capital on private account in the second period enabled official reserves to be built up, and this encouraged greater confidence in the country's ability to sustain a high growth rate in the face of temporary balance of payments difficulties. Of course, the *absolute* size of the average deficit increased slightly between the two periods but, since G N P was growing, the size relative to G N P declined.

Looking at the shares of investment, savings and the balance of payments in G N P at constant prices, it may be seen from Table 10 that the rise in the average investment share in constant prices between the two periods was 1.3 percentage points greater than the rise measured in current prices. Furthermore, the increase in the savings ratio in constant prices was less impressive than in current values—a point noted earlier. Thus, whereas the average ratio of the balance of payments deficit to G N P in current values *fell* between the two periods by 1.5 percentage points, it actually *rose* in constant prices[4] by 1.4 percentage points. These differences in the movements of the current and constant price shares are due to the more favourable terms of trade in the second period, as is explained in Part III.

Table 11: Average annual rates of growth in volume of investment
1949–61 and 1961–68

	1949–61	1961–68
	%	%
Fixed investment	3.3	8.9
Total physical investment	3.1	8.2

Source: *National Income and Expenditure 1969.*

The average annual growth rates of investment in constant prices from 1949 to 1961 and from 1961 to 1968 are given in Table 11. It will be seen that in volume terms the growth rate of fixed investment nearly tripled and the improvement in the growth of total physical investment was of the same order of magnitude. It should be borne in mind, however, that in 1961 the volume of fixed capital formation had just recovered to the pre-depression level of 1955, while the volume of physical capital formation was slightly less than the 1955 volume. The choice of sub-periods in this case therefore tends to exaggerate the difference in the growth rates. However, the average annual rates of change in volume of fixed investment and total physical investment from 1949 to 1955 (6.8 per cent and 6.4 per cent respectively) were also substantially lower than the 1961–68 rates, although they compare more favourably than the rates for 1949–61.

In Chapter 11, following an examination of trends in the composition of investment, we explore further the relation between investment and changes in output and productivity.

EXPORTS AND IMPORTS OF GOODS AND SERVICES

The relatively low ratio of the balance of payments to G N P for most years tends to disguise the importance of foreign trade for Ireland. Exports of goods and services as a proportion of G N P (in current values) were quite high and reasonably steady in the period 1949–61, ranging from 35 to 39 per cent. Although there

CHART 4 : RATIO OF EXPORTS AND IMPORTS TO GNP, 1947 - 1968

has not been a sustained rise in the ratio in the later period, as may be seen from Chart 4, the average ratio was higher—the range of variation being from 37 to 41 per cent of G N P. Table 12 shows that the average ratio of exports of goods and services to G N P for the period 1961–68 (38.9 per cent) was only slightly higher than the average for 1949–61 (37.1 per cent). This constancy, however, applies only to the current price ratio of exports

Table 12: Average of annual ratios of exports and imports to
G N P, 1949–61 and 1961–68*

	Current prices		Constant (1958) prices	
	1949–61	1961–68	1949–61	1961–68
	%	%	%	%
Exports of goods and services**	37.1	38.9	34.8	44.0
Of which:				
Visible	19.6	22.9	17.8	26.0
Invisible**	17.5	16.0	17.0	18.0
Imports of goods and services**	40.2	40.5	37.2	47.7
Of which:				
Visible	34.8	34.9	32.0	41.5
Invisible**	5.4	5.6	5.2	6.2
Current balance of payments deficit	3.2	1.6	2.4	3.6

*In the official figures prior to the revision of the balance of payments statement (*Irish Statistical Bulletin*, Jun. 1970), the *net* exports (i.e. exports less imports) of the Shannon Industrial Estate (a duty-free industrial zone adjoining Shannon Airport) were classified as exports of services. Since then, Shannon trade is included in the balance of payments table on a gross basis as merchandise exports and imports. Only in the 1970 national accounts was Shannon trade treated on a gross basis; and then only from 1965. The procedure adopted here is to include the net exports of Shannon for all years and to classify them as visible exports.

**Includes gross factor income flows.

Source: *National Income and Expenditure 1969*. Data for visible and invisible trade (gross of factor income flows) were derived from *Irish Statistical Bulletin* (Jun. 1970); *National Income and Expenditure 1962* and *1969;* and *Irish Statistical Survey*, 1950–51, 1951–52 and 1953. Shannon trade for years prior to 1956 kindly supplied by the C S O.

to G N P. Looking, in Chart 4, at the behaviour of constant price exports relative to G N P, we can see that up to 1956 the ratio was fairly stable in the region of 33–35 per cent, but thereafter rose in most years, reaching 48.9 per cent in 1968. This rise in share is in marked contrast to the current price ratio, indicating a significant fall in export prices relative to G N P prices. For the period 1961–68, the average of the annual volume ratios, 44 per cent, was substantially above the average for the period 1949–61, 34.8 per cent—again a marked contrast to the small rise in the current price share noted earlier.

Whether measured in current or in constant prices, there were quite different movements in the visible and invisible components as a ratio to G N P (Chart 4). Up to about the mid-1950s the ratio of invisible exports to G N P fell markedly. Thereafter the ratio was reasonably stable in current prices, with a slight upward movement in the constant price ratio. However, the invisibles ratio in 1968, measured either in current or in constant prices, was substantially below the immediate post-war level as a result of the substantial fall in the first post-war decade. On the other hand, the ratio of visible exports to G N P increased substantially in the post-war period. The constant price ratio rose most—from 11.7 per cent in 1947 to 30.3 per cent in 1968. The periods of most rapid increase were from 1947 to 1952 and from 1959 to 1968, with a sluggish phase in between.

Chart 5 shows the value and volume of exports for each year for 1947–68 and Table 13 compares the actual growth rates of exports in the two periods 1949–61 and 1961–68. There was a marked acceleration in the rate of growth of total exports in current values from 6.4 per cent per annum in the first period to 9.2 per cent in the second period. In volume terms, the acceleration was even greater: the average annual growth rate of export volume for 1961–68 was over 75 per cent higher than the rate for the first period. But perhaps the most striking feature of Table 13 is the fact that when total exports are disaggregated into visibles and invisibles, the latter had by far the greater degree of acceleration. In current values, the growth rate of invisibles from 1961 to 1968 was twice as high as from 1949 to 1961, whereas there was only a modest rise in the growth rate of visible exports.[5] Indeed, the contrast is greater in constant price terms. There was only a negligible increase in the growth of volume of visible

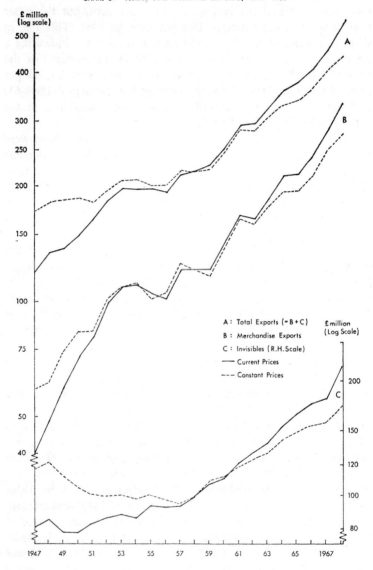

CHART 5: VISIBLE AND INVISIBLE EXPORTS, 1947 - 1968

Table 13: Average annual rates of growth of exports and imports, 1949–61 and 1961–68

	Current prices		Constant (1958) prices	
	1949–61	1961–68	1949–61	1961–68
	%	%	%	%
Total exports of goods and services*	6.4	9.2	3.7	6.5
Visible exports	9.1	10.2	7.0	7.4
Invisible exports*	3.7	7.8	0.5	5.2
Total imports of goods and services*	5.8	9.8	3.0	7.6
Visible imports	5.8	9.9	3.2	8.0
Invisible imports*	5.5	8.5	2.3	4.9

Contribution of visible and invisible exports to growth rate of total exports (at constant prices)

	1949–61	1961–68	Change between the two periods
	%	%	%
Visible exports	3.5	4.5	+1.0
Invisible exports*	0.3	2.1	+1.8
Total growth rate*	3.7	6.5	+2.8

*Includes gross factor income flows.

Sources: As for Table 12. The derivation of the contribution of visibles and invisibles to the growth rates of total exports is explained in the text. See also note to Table 6.

exports,[6] whereas the rise in the growth of invisibles was very marked involving an improvement from a virtually stagnant growth rate of 0.5 per cent per annum from 1949 to 1961 to 5.2 per cent from 1961 to 1968. It is of interest to note, in the context of our choice of periods, that 1961 was the first year in which the volume of invisible exports surpassed the 1949 level, and that only in 1962 did the volume exceed the post-war peak of 1948. Moreover, invisible exports reached their lowest volume in 1957, and since then rose in every year up to 1968, although at varying rates.[7]

It would appear, then, that the outstanding contrast in export growth between the two periods lies in invisible, rather than visible, exports, and the slower overall growth of exports in the first period could be attributed primarily to the slow growth of invisibles in this period. Of course, it can be objected that since there is no law requiring any category of exports to grow at any particular rate, it would be just as valid to say that the slower overall growth of exports in the first period was due to failure of visible exports to compensate for the slow growth of invisibles. However, the implication of this argument is that the required growth of visible exports from 1949 to 1961 to secure as high a growth rate of total exports as from 1961 to 1968 would have been very high—in volume terms $11\frac{1}{2}$ per cent per annum. In any event, the fact remains that over the longer term the growth rate of visible exports was relatively constant throughout the post-war period. Moreover, from the point of view of timing, it could be argued that the faster growth of invisibles led the increased growth of the economy, since the acceleration in the growth rate of invisibles seems to have commenced around 1957. Of course, the volume of visible exports grew at a much faster rate than invisibles in both periods and also at a faster rate than G N P. Since this implies a rising share of visibles in total exports and in aggregate output, even a constant rate of growth of visibles exerts a larger influence on total exports and output due to its increasing weight. Thus, in our endeavour to isolate factors that could account for the break in the growth trend of G N P, we do not wish to lose sight of the strong performance of visible exports throughout the post-war period.

The foregoing points are brought out clearly in Table 13, which shows the contribution of the growth of visibles and invisibles to total export growth for both periods. The contribution of the growth rate of each class to the total in each period is measured by weighting the average annual growth rate of that class by the average of its share in the first and last year of the period. Thus we see that for 1949–61 visible exports were responsible for almost all of the total growth, accounting for 3.5 of the 3.7 per cent average growth rate of total exports. For 1961–68, visibles continued to be the main contributor, accounting for 4.5 percentage points of the total growth rate of 6.5 per cent. But if we look at the *rise* in the total export growth rate of 2.8 percentage points between the two periods, we can see that the greater part of this, 1.8 percentage points, was due to faster growth of invisible exports. The remaining part, 1.0 percentage points, is attributable to visible exports and arises mainly because, even though the growth rate of visibles was much the same in both periods (7.0 per cent per annum in the first period as against 7.4 per cent per annum in the second), the weighting of visibles was much higher in the second period. The increase in the weighting of visibles, in turn, is mainly due to its more rapid growth than invisibles in both periods, but more particularly in the first.

The role of exports in the economic growth of Ireland is clearly important. For exports are a source of demand for domestic supplies both directly and through multiplier effects; and for a small country like Ireland they are also a way to escape the confines of a small domestic market. In Chapter 4 we discuss these points in greater detail. But it is well to remember that one of the most important functions of exports in the growth process may be indirect. Given a high marginal propensity to import, increasing domestic demand inevitably means increasing imports. Unless the authorities feel that exports will increase to offset this demand-induced drain on the balance of payments, or that capital inflows will cover any import excess, they are likely to take action to restrain domestic demand. Thus, even where the main impetus to growth comes from increasing domestic demand, the extent to which home demand can be allowed to expand is strongly influenced by the behaviour of exports and the balance of payments. The failure of exports to grow at an adequate rate is likely to lead to recurrent balance of payments difficulties and instability in the pressures of demand.

Turning to imports, it may be seen from Table 12 that the average ratio of imports of goods and services to G N P in current prices has varied only fractionally between the two periods 1949–61 and 1961–68. The ratio was far more variable in the first period, however, ranging from as low as 36 per cent (in 1957) to as high as 54 per cent (in 1951); the range in the second period was from 39 to 42 per cent (Chart 4). In constant prices there was a sustained upward movement during the 1960s in the ratio of total imports to G N P. The average for 1961–68 was 47.7 per cent, some 10½ percentage points higher than for 1949–61. The large divergence between the current and constant price import ratios in the second period reflects the much smaller rise in the price of imports than in the GNP price.

As may be seen from Table 13, the growth rate of imports, whether measured in value or in volume terms, was much higher in the second period. It would, however, scarcely be valid to attach much causal significance to this fact in accounting for the faster growth of the economy. It is quite true, of course, that growth could be seriously retarded if access were denied to certain categories of imports—in particular, capital equipment and materials for further production that could not be produced at home. There were, in fact, scarcities of key imports in the early post-war years, but by 1949 the significance of this factor was considerably diminished. The introduction in 1956, on balance of payments grounds, of special import levies on, *inter alia*, materials for further production did have a serious effect in retarding the growth of industrial output; this factor, however, is best considered later in the discussion of short-term economic policy. But, by and large, the much more rapid growth of imports in the second period is more appropriately viewed chiefly as a consequence, rather than a cause, of faster growth in the economy. In the several excellent studies[8] of Irish imports, changes in aggregate demand and in its composition emerge as the major determinants of the behaviour of imports.

We may briefly summarise the main causes of the large rise in volume of merchandise imports relative to GNP based on the analysis in McAleese (1970), where this question is considered. McAleese found an elasticity of import volume with respect to GNP volume well above unity—in fact, in the region of 2. With any given elasticity above unity, the faster the growth rate of GNP in any period the greater will be the rise in the ratio of imports to GNP. He concluded that 'Income/output elasticities greater than unity combined with a rapid growth of total output during the decade (i.e. 1956 to 1966) have, therefore, been the most important factors underlying the rise in the import/GNP ratio in real terms.' For each of the three major categories of imports distinguished (producers' capital goods, materials for further production and consumer goods ready for use) the output/income elasticities were well above unity. In the case of the largest category of imports, materials (mainly for use in industry), the elasticity with respect to industrial output was in the range 1.0 to 1.3; and, given that industrial output grew much faster than G N P, an industrial output elasticity of even unity would suffice to raise the ratio of such imports to G N P. As is well known, the import content of total domestic investment is relatively high, chiefly because most classes of machinery and transport equipment are not produced at home. Thus a rising ratio of investment to G N P tends to raise the ratio of imports to G N P. McAleese found that relative price changes were a comparatively minor factor in accounting for the rise in the import ratio, chiefly because materials and investment goods, which together constitute about three-fourths of total merchandise imports, are not very sensitive to relative price movements.

GROWTH OF EXTERNAL TRADE IN OTHER COUNTRIES

In the previous chapter it was shown that the rise in the Irish growth rate did not take place in the context of a general rise in growth rates among O E C D countries. It is conceivable, however, that trade among European economies grew faster in the later period even if output did not. This might arise, for example, due to the breakdown of trade barriers that occurred in the late 1950s. If so, then the impact of such increased growth in trade on a highly open economy like Ireland might be relatively greater than elsewhere. In order to examine whether any such acceleration in trade did in fact occur, we have set out in Table 14 the average annual growth rates of exports and imports for twelve O E C D countries for 1950–61 and 1961–68. Ireland and the U K stand out in the first period as having a very low growth of exports and imports. The Irish growth rate of exports of goods and services and the U K growth rate of imports of goods and services are almost identical for 1950–61. However, this similarity tends to hide the fact that Irish merchandise exports grew more rapidly than U K merchandise imports, while Irish invisible exports grew more slowly than U K invisible imports. In fact, though it is not shown in Table 14, the performance of Irish merchandise exports in the first period was quite creditable, the growth rate being close to the mean for European economies, and the poor overall

C

Table 14: Average annual rates of growth of volume of exports and imports for certain O E C D countries, 1950–61 and 1961–68

	Exports of goods and services		Imports of goods and services	
	1950–61	1961–68	1950–61	1961–68
	%	%	%	%
Austria	11.1	7.5	9.8	7.5
Denmark	6.9	7.4	6.6	8.0
France	6.3	7.5	6.0	9.6
Germany	15.6	9.4	16.3	9.0
Greece	9.0[1]	10.2	12.3[1]	9.1
I R E L A N D	3.7[2]	6.5	3.0[2]	7.6
Italy	14.6[3]	12.2	12.8[3]	9.6
Netherlands	9.1	8.1	7.4	9.3
Norway	6.4[3]	8.9	6.0[3]	7.4
Sweden	5.4	6.5	6.3	6.9
United Kingdom	2.5	4.2	3.8	4.3
United States	5.0	7.2	4.8	10.2
Mean	8.0	8.0	7.9	8.2
E E C	11.0	9.0	9.9	9.0
O E C D Europe	7.3	7.8	7.4	7.8

Notes: (1) 1956–61; (2) Ireland 1949–61; (3) 1951–61.

Sources: O E C D *National Accounts of O E C D Countries 1950–1968* for all non-Irish data. Irish data as for Table 13.

growth was due to virtual stagnation in invisible exports.

Although the growth rate of Irish exports of goods and services was substantially higher from 1961 to 1968 than in the earlier period, it was still below the mean growth rate for the countries included in Table 14 and also below the growth rate for European O E C D countries and the E E C. However, the improvement was achieved in spite of the continued slow growth of U K imports, and in the absence of any marked rise in the growth of European imports in the second period. This would suggest that the rise in total Irish exports cannot be explained by a correspondingly large upswing in imports by the countries accounting for the bulk of Irish exports.[9]

The degree of change in output and trade growth rates does not, of course, exhaust the extent to which foreign influences were important for Irish growth. It could be argued that the high growth rates achieved elsewhere, particularly with respect to trade, established the economic environment in which the Irish economy could potentially operate. The extent to which the potential was achieved would then depend substantially on domestic forces. This view implies that the factors which inhibited growth in the first period were, for the most part, purely of domestic origin. Once they were overcome, the economy could operate nearer the upper bounds established by international growth in output and trade. This is not to deny the powerful influence of international developments in conditioning the acceleration in growth once the domestic problems were overcome. But since we have shown that the international environment, as measured by the growth of output and trade, did not improve much between the two periods, it is plausible to suggest that the basic explanation of the change in the Irish growth rate lies in domestic policies and activity. Admittedly, the international environment changed considerably in other respects that had important implications for Ireland. In particular, we might mention the dampening of international short-term fluctuations in the 1960s as compared with the 1950s, and the much more favourable terms of foreign trade experienced by Ireland. These factors are later considered in greater detail.

CONCLUSIONS

In this chapter we have taken a broad look at the behaviour of aggregate demand in the post-war Irish economy. By examining trends in the shares of the main components in G N P, and the differences in growth rates between the periods 1949–61 and 1961–68, certain areas appear to warrant a more detailed study. These include the growth of exports, especially invisible exports, the significant change in the savings ratio, the increased level of investment, and the more advantageous movements in the terms of trade. We have also noted the relatively greater stability that accompanied the increased growth rate.

The rest of the book is devoted to the analysis of these topics. But before we conclude the introductory examination of the economy, we discuss in the next chapter the behaviour of the balance of payments and of prices since the war.

CHAPTER 3

The Balance of Payments and Prices

I F the amount of public discussion on a subject were taken as an index of its importance, then the state of the balance of payments and the behaviour of prices would seem to be of overwhelming importance in the post-war Irish economy. Maintenance of the external and internal value of the currency are, of course, legitimate areas of concern in economic policy. But the priority accorded, particularly in the 1950s, to the preservation of external balance seemed disproportionately greater than concern for output and employment. This tendency is sometimes attributed in part to the speed with which data become available on the balance of payments and prices compared with many other economic series. However, it was also rooted deeply in official thinking, and perhaps the greater speed with which the data are collected is itself largely a reflection of the prior importance attached to such variables. In Part IV we shall examine at some length the policy developments and the thinking underlying them. In this chapter we present a picture of the actual movements of the balance of payments and prices in the post-war period.

THE BALANCE OF PAYMENTS

Concern with the balance of payments should properly take into account the overall position on capital as well as on current account. Even a large current balance of payments deficit does not normally imply a weakening of the external position or a threat to the exchange rate, provided it is matched by long-term capital inflows. This is now well understood and generally accepted in Ireland, but for much of the period with which we are concerned, the major focus of attention seemed to be the balance of payments on current account.

The Current Account Balance of Payments

The current balance of payments is, of course, a summary figure derived from the behaviour of two aggregates—total current exports and imports of goods and services. Thus, in a formal sense, variations in the balance of payments may be due to variations in the volume of exports and imports, the price of exports or imports, or some combination of price and volume movements. Since total exports and imports can be sub-divided into merchandise (visible) exports and imports and invisibles, we can equally decompose the overall balance of payments into the balance on visibles and the balance on invisibles. This is usually done because the factors affecting merchandise trade may not be relevant to the behaviour of invisibles.

Chart 6 shows the current balance of payments in current prices for each year from 1947 to 1968, together with the balance on visibles and invisibles. It will be seen that a deficit was incurred in most post-war years: in fact, in only three of the twenty-two years shown (1957, 1961 and 1967) was there a surplus. Throughout the post-war period there has been a large deficit on visible trade and a significant surplus on invisibles. Chart 6 clearly illustrates the very considerable contribution of the rise in the invisibles surplus since 1957 towards offsetting the rapid rise in the deficit on visibles and thereby maintaining a manageable overall deficit on current account. Fluctuations in the current balance of payments were considerable and were mainly determined by fluctuations in the size of the deficit on visible trade. This was because the surplus of invisibles remained roughly constant between 1947 and 1957 and increased at a reasonably steady rate after 1957.

The current balance of payments deficit is equivalent to net foreign disinvestment, i.e. the combined extent to which the economy relies on foreign borrowing and on reducing foreign asset holdings. In looking at the post-war period from this point of view, it may be noted that the first five years after the war, 1947–51, had the heaviest reliance on foreign disinvestment: the annual average in these years was £30.2 million compared with £16.8 million for the whole post-war period up to 1968. As we discuss later in Part IV, the experience of these years, particularly following the large deficit of over £60 million in 1951, stiffened opposition to reliance on foreign disinvestment: in the following

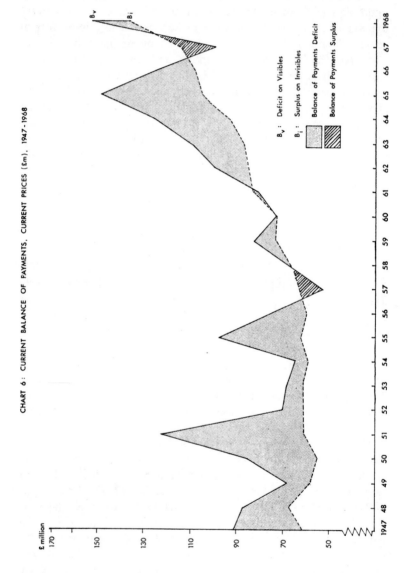

CHART 6 : CURRENT BALANCE OF PAYMENTS, CURRENT PRICES (£m), 1947-1968

B$_v$: Deficit on Visibles
B$_i$: Surplus on Invisibles

Balance of Payments Deficit
Balance of Payments Surplus

decade, apart from the two years 1955 and 1956, there was very little foreign disinvestment. This was followed by a deliberate acceptance of a moderate degree of foreign disinvestment, which in the years 1962–68 averaged £17½ million per annum.

External Reserves and Capital Inflow

The current balance of payments position is not necessarily a good indicator of the strength of the economy's external situation. Any deficit on current account must be matched by an inward movement on capital account, and what matters most in this context is whether this inward movement involves a fall in external reserves or a net capital inflow.[1] The justification for reserves is basically the need to protect the external value of the currency. In the absence of any other inward movement of capital the reserves will clearly bear the burden of the current deficit. But if there are capital inflows, the reserve position may be unaffected by what is happening on current account. Indeed, it is quite possible that reserves will move inversely to the current balance, rising, for example, when there is a current deficit. It may be seen from Table 15, which sets out the current balance of payments, external reserves and net capital inflow from 1947 to 1968, that in ten of the twenty-two years external reserves rose in spite of deficits on current account. This inverse movement of reserve changes and the deficit is due to the customary effect of the net capital inflow, which in these ten years exceeded the current balance of payments deficit. In fact, it can be seen that in only three years (1955, 1956 and 1957) was the capital movement outwards on balance, increasing the reserve loss due to a current deficit or reducing the reserve accretion due to a current surplus.

In the years 1949 to 1954 there were sizeable net inflows which meant that reserves were £14 million higher at the end of 1954 than at the end of 1948 in spite of very large deficits on current account. However, of the total net capital inflow of £137 million in the six years 1949 to 1954, over one-third represented European Recovery Programme (E R P) funds (or Marshall Aid) comprising a loan of £40.8 million and a grant of £6.5 million; the bulk of these funds came in 1949, 1950 and to a lesser extent in 1951. In 1955 there was both a current deficit, of a quite sizeable amount, and a net outflow of capital so that reserves fell

Table 15: Current balance of payments, changes in external reserves and net capital inflow, 1947–68

Year	Current balance of payments (Deficit — Surplus +)	External reserves[1] Total	External reserves[1] Annual change (Increase + Decrease —)	Net capital inflow[2] (net inflow + net outflow —)
	£m	£m	£m	£m
1946		248.7[3]		
1947	—29.8	232.5[3]	—16.2	+13.6
1948	—19.6	231.1	—1.4	+18.2
1949	—9.7	256.3	+25.2	+34.9
1950	—30.2	260.5	+4.2	+34.4
1951	—61.6	221.5	—39.0	+22.6
1952	—8.9	226.9	+5.4	+14.3
1953	—7.0	240.8	+13.9	+20.9
1954	—5.5	245.0	+4.2	+9.7
1955	—35.5	197.7	—47.3	—11.8
1956	—14.4	183.0	—14.7	—0.3
1957	+9.2	189.9	+6.9	—2.3
1958	—1.0	205.8	+15.9	+16.9
1959	—8.7	210.2	+4.4	+13.1
1960	—0.8	209.9	—0.3	+0.5
1961	+1.2	224.5	+14.6	+13.4
1962	—13.4	234.0	+9.5	+22.9
1963	—22.1	236.9	+2.9	+25.0
1964	—31.4	242.1	+5.2	+36.6
1965	—41.8	230.7 (224.1)[4]	—18.0	+23.8
1966	—16.1	253.1	+22.4	+38.5
1967	+15.2	299.4	+46.3	+31.1
1968	—16.3	291.5	—7.9	+8.4
Annual averages				
1949–54	—20.5		+2.3	+22.8 +(14.9)[5]
1955–60	—8.5		—5.9	+2.7
1961–68	—15.6		+9.4	+25.0

1. Figures relate to 31 December each year.
2. The net capital inflow is defined as Annual Change in External Reserves minus Current Balance of Payments.
3. The official figures for 1946 and 1947 have been adjusted to allow for the estimated amount of departmental funds (other than the Post Office Savings Bank) held in external assets, which were not included in the published figures for these years.

by £47.3 million, the largest decline since the war. If the capital movements in that year had been the same as the average for the previous eight years (excluding E R P grants and loans), there would have been a net inflow of £15.2 million which would have meant a reserve loss of £20.3 million. This, though sizeable, would have involved a decline of only 8 per cent in reserves compared with the 19 per cent fall that actually occurred. In 1956 and 1957 there were further small net outflows of capital, although the surplus on current account in 1957 ensured that there was a slight increase in reserves for that year. Significant net inflows of capital took place in all years from 1958 to 1968 with the exception of 1960 when the net inflow was negligible.

At the bottom of Table 15 the average annual position for three periods (1949–54, 1955–60 and 1961–68) is set out. The average annual net inflow of capital in the six years 1949 to 1954 (£23 million) was almost as large as the inflow for the period 1961–68 (£26 million). If we exclude the effects of the E R P capital movements, the average for the 1949–54 period reduces to £15 million, which is still a substantial inflow—in real terms it would probably be quite close to the inflow for 1961–68. During 1955–60 the net inflow was very small as there was a three-year period (1955–57) when there was a net outflow.

The net capital inflow is the sum of different movements of capital, some of which might normally be expected to be outflows (such as life assurance payments) and others inflows (such as direct investment in new plants in Ireland). A breakdown of capital movements is available but, unfortunately, since 1961 the C S O publish only the net flows. Table 16 gives annual averages for the main capital flows (including changes in external reserves) on a net basis of three periods (1949–54, 1955–60 and 1961–68). The largest item in Table 16 is 'other capital transactions' which provided an average net inflow of £11.5 million per annum for the years 1949 to 1954, £4.7 million per annum for 1955–60 and £24.8 million for 1961–68. Only from 1961 do we have a break-

---

4. A modified concept of external reserves was introduced in 1965. The figure on the old basis is given in brackets, and the change in 1965 is measured by reference to the old figure.
5. Excluding E R P loans and grants.

Sources: *Irish Statistical Bulletin*, various issues, and *Annual Report of the Central Bank of Ireland*, various years.

down of this item—and for the period 1961–68 the largest
component was foreign direct investment in Ireland which averaged some £10½ million per annum.

Table 16: Breakdown of net capital flows (incl. changes in external
reserves): annual averages, 1949–54, 1955–60 and 1961–68*

	1949–54	1955–60	1961–68
	£m	£m	£m
1. Payments to international institutions	—	—0.7	—2.5
2. E R P loans and grant	+7.9	—0.3	—1.0
3. Changes in government funds	+1.8	+2.1	+2.1
4. Changes in net external assets of Central Bank and Associated Banks	—4.7	+2.5	—10.0
5. Purchase and sale of securities	+2.9	—0.4	+0.1
6. Capital issues by companies	+0.3	+1.1	+4.2
7. Net capital payments in respect of life assurance	—0.6	—1.0	—2.8
8. British Post Office Savings Bank and Savings Certificates	+0.5	+0.5	+0.6
9. Other capital transactions	+12.5	+4.7	+24.8
Of which:			
(a) External subscriptions to Irish Government loans, etc.	n.a.	n.a.	+5.1
(b) Borrowing by semi-state companies	n.a.	n.a.	+2.1
(c) Changes in net external assets of non-associated banks, etc.	n.a.	n.a.	0.0
(d) Other direct investment	n.a.	n.a.	+10.5
(e) Other transactions	n.a.	n.a.	+7.1
Total capital items (= current balance of payments deficit)	+20.5	+8.5	+15.6

*Net capital inflow +; net capital outflow —.

Source: *Irish Statistical Bulletin*, various issues.

It has often been suggested that the capital inflow is likely to
be adversely affected by the unfavourable reactions of investors
to a large current account deficit. If so, this would mean that at
a time when the capital inflow was most needed to bolster
reserves in the face of a large current deficit, the reserves would

be even more vulnerable due to a weakening of inward capital movements and an increase in outward movements. In fact, there were some instances which might support this view. As noted earlier in regard to 1955 and 1956, when fairly large current balance of payments deficits occurred, there was a net outflow of £8 million on 'other capital transactions' in 1955 (compared with a net inflow of £8 million in 1954) and only a relatively small net inflow of £2 million in 1956. In 1965 and 1966 there were significant falls in direct investment; these years were marked by considerable short-term difficulties following the large current balance of payments deficit in 1965, which was the highest since 1951. It is possible that in these cases the confidence of investors was affected by the state of the current balance of payments. However, there are other possible explanations which we shall deal with later in discussing the short-term management of the economy.

Over the post-war period there has been a real reduction in the reserves when considered in relation to the level of imports. Total reserves increased by 26 per cent over the period end-1948 to end-1968 while imports had increased by 273 per cent. The ratio of reserves to imports of goods and services declined from 1.73 in 1949 to 0.52 in 1968. The 1968 ratio represents reserve cover for over six months' imports—still quite high by international standards, given that most European O E C D economies have reserves to cover only four to five months' trade. The appropriate level of reserves also depends on other factors, such as the degree of fluctuations in imports and exports and the extent to which recourse can be had to short-term borrowing from the I M F or other international bodies for reserve protection. On this score it seems likely that there has been a sufficient improvement in international monetary cooperation in the 1960s to justify a lower level of reserves relative to trade than might have been warranted in the 1950s.

THE BEHAVIOUR OF PRICES

Table 17 shows the average annual rates of change in the more important price indices for the periods 1949–61 and 1961–68. It may be seen from the table that all internal prices, such as the prices of consumption, capital and gross domestic expenditure,[2]

Table 17: Average annual rates of change in certain prices,
1949–61 and 1961–68

	1949–61	1961–68
	%	%
Consumer price index	3.5	4.2
Total consumption[1]	3.5	4.4
Fixed investment[2]	2.5	3.5
Gross National Product[3]	3.4	4.6
Gross domestic expenditure[4]	3.4	4.3
Merchandise exports[5]	2.0	2.6
Merchandise imports[6]	2.6	1.7
Merchandise terms of trade[7]	—0.6	0.9
Exports of goods and services[8]	2.6	2.7
Imports of goods and services[9]	2.7	2.0
Total terms of trade[10]	—0.1	0.7
Agricultural price index	2.0	3.9

1. Implied price of combined personal and government consumption in the national accounts.
2. Implied price of gross domestic fixed capital formation.
3. Implied price of G N P (not including the external trading gain).
4. Implied price of gross domestic expenditure.
5. Export unit value index.
6. Import unit value index.
7. Export unit value index divided by import unit value index.
8. Implied price of exports of goods and services (excluding factor income flows).
9. Implied price of imports of goods and services (excluding factor income flows).
10. Price index for exports of goods and services divided by price index for imports of goods and services.

Sources: *Irish Statistical Bulletin*, various issues; and *National Income and Expenditure 1969.*

rose somewhat more in the period 1961–68 than in the period 1949–61, even though import prices rose less in the more recent period. If we broke the earlier period at 1955, we would find that in the period 1949–55 all internal prices, with the exception of investment prices, rose as fast as, or faster than, the period 1961–68. However, the rapid rate of rise in internal prices in 1949–55 was strongly influenced by the large increases in import prices: the average annual rate of increase in the price of merchandise imports was 4.7 per cent from 1949 to 1955 as against 1.7 per cent from 1961 to 1968. It therefore seems fair to say that domestically generated price inflation has been greater in the period of more rapid growth. Prices generally rose less in the period 1955–61 than in either of the other two periods. This would tend to give added weight to our belief that the source of the increased growth in the 1960s was the expansion of total demand. It should be pointed out that the three years preceding the 1961–68 period (i.e. 1959–61 inclusive) were years of comparative price stability, the average annual rate of increase of most price series being less than 1½ per cent. Since much of the growth in that period was due to recovery from the slack caused by the 1956–58 stagnation, there was probably far less pressure on prices from demand factors until resources were more fully utilised.

Import prices rose more in the period 1949–61 than in the period 1961–68, whereas in the case of export prices the reverse was true. Most of the rise in the price of merchandise exports and imports in the first period, however, took place from 1949 to 1951 under the impact of devaluation and the Korean War. Although the prices of merchandise exports and imports fluctuated a good deal after 1951, there was no sustained rise again until after 1962. In both periods the prices of exports and imports rose less than internal prices, substantially so in the more recent period. The overall terms of trade improved at an average annual rate of 0.7 per cent from 1961 to 1968, as compared with an average annual decline of 0.1 per cent per annum from 1949 to 1961.

The overall terms of trade position in 1961–68, compared with 1949–61, was even more favourable than is represented by these figures. The reason may best be explained by a simple example. Suppose the terms of trade index (to any base, say 1949=100) were exactly the same in 1949, 1961 and 1968, then clearly the rates of change for the periods 1949–61 and 1961–68 would be zero and it would appear at first sight that there was no difference between the two periods. But if in the second period the terms of trade index was above 100 in all years from 1962 to 1967, whereas it was below 100 in all years from 1950 to 1960, then clearly the terms of trade position would be more favourable in the second period. In other words, in the second period there would be a gain, relative to the base year, in most years due to the terms of trade, whereas in the first period there would be a loss, relative to the base year, in most years.

This example roughly corresponds to the actual position. In eight of the eleven years 1950 to 1960 the terms of trade index was below the 1949 level, whereas in all seven years 1962 to 1968 the index was above it. A better way of measuring the average annual difference in the terms of trade between the two periods is to take the difference between the geometric averages of the terms of trade index for all years in each of the two periods. The difference amounts to 6.1 per cent per annum; this means that in each year in the period 1961–68 the terms of trade were on average about 6 per cent higher than in each year of the period 1949–61. Clearly this is a very substantial difference.

Of course, such an improvement in the terms of trade cannot be considered entirely fortuitous and outside of domestic control. The improved arrangements for the marketing of agricultural products, secured in the Anglo-Irish Free Trade Area Agreement, is one obvious means by which the terms of trade were favourably influenced by policy measures. Moreover, a changing composition of exports, giving greater weight to higher priced goods, and those likely to increase in price, could also have helped improve the terms of trade. Some part of the improvement attributed to the terms of trade may simply reflect a failure to measure quality change. This is particularly plausible in the case of tourism. If, by providing better accommodation, tourist services can be sold at a higher 'price', this should really appear as a volume increase in tourist receipts, whereas, in practice, it may appear as a price change due to the difficulties in measuring the quality change element. But in so far as some of the improvement in the terms of trade might be due to improvements in the quality of domestic exports, not adequately measured in volume indices, this improvement can hardly be considered wholly determined outside the control of the Irish economy. However, even allowing for these and other related factors, the terms of trade position was, on average, considerably more unfavourable in the first period due to circumstances outside of the economy that could not be influenced by Irish policy.

Agricultural prices rose much faster in the period 1961–68, and this was an important element of the improved terms of trade. Since a significant share of agricultural output is exported, and agricultural exports form a large proportion of merchandise exports, there is a close link between the agricultural price index and the merchandise export price index.[3] Although agricultural prices rose on average by 2 per cent per annum from 1949 to 1961, the rise was by no means uniform. From 1949 to 1955 agricultural prices rose substantially in most years, the average annual rate of increase in this period being 4.6 per cent. The 1955 level was not surpassed again, however, until 1964.

Since one of our concerns is whether or not short-term management of the economy improved in the period 1961–68, it is of considerable interest to look at the variability of price changes as well as the average values. Table 18 shows the range of price changes for the main economic series for 1949–61 and 1961–68, together with an indication of the overall variability as measured by the mean absolute deviation. As may be seen from this table, the annual changes in all prices fluctuated within a much wider range and, with the possible exception of agricultural prices, varied much more on average in the first period than in the second. The greater instability in external trade prices and in the terms of trade is particularly marked. The range or variation in the overall terms of trade in the first period was from −8 per cent to +8 per cent, while the mean absolute deviation was about 4 per cent. The magnitude of such variation is best understood when it is realised that at 1968 trade volume a favourable change of 4 per cent in the terms of trade would involve an improvement in the current balance of payments of £25 million and an unfavourable change of 4 per cent would involve a worsening of the current balance by a similar amount.

The high degree of instability in prices in the first period must have presented severe problems in any attempt at planning at industry or firm level. It also greatly complicated the task of short-term economic management. Undoubtedly, a considerable part of the fluctuation was due to factors outside the control of the economy. As we mentioned earlier, the extremely large rise in import prices in 1950 and 1951 and their subsequent fall in 1953 was to a large extent associated with the temporary boom in prices caused by the Korean War, a factor clearly beyond the control of policy in Ireland or, indeed, in most countries. Some of the price fluctuations were caused by factors nominally, but perhaps not effectively, within Irish control, such as that part of the import price rise in 1950 attributable to the 1949 devaluation.

There is no doubt, therefore, that in the first period the economy

Table 18: Variability of annual percentage changes in certain prices, 1949–61 and 1961–68

	Range	Aver-age*	Mean absolute deviation (+)
Consumer price index:	%	%	%
1949–61	0.0 to 8.7	3.5	2.3
1961–68	2.5 to 6.7	4.2	1.1
Fixed capital:			
1949–61	—1.2 to 6.6	2.6	2.0
1961–68	2.1 to 6.2	3.5	0.8
Gross domestic expenditure:			
1949–61	0.1 to 8.3	3.4	1.7
1961–68	2.7 to 7.6	4.3	1.0
Merchandise exports:			
1949–61	—5.4 to 13.4	2.1	3.3
1961–68	0.0 to 7.2	2.6	2.1
Merchandise imports:			
1949–61	—6.2 to 22.1	2.8	4.8
1961–68	—0.6 to 8.3	1.8	2.0
Merchandise terms of trade:			
1949–61	—7.2 to 7.3	—0.5	4.1
1961–68	—1.1 to 4.6	0.9	1.4
Exports of goods and services:			
1949–61	—2.5 to 11.7	2.7	2.6
1961–68	0.5 to 6.4	2.7	1.7
Imports of goods and services:			
1949–61	—5.3 to 21.1	2.9	4.6
1961–68	—0.7 to 8.0	2.0	1.9
Total terms of trade:			
1949–61	—7.8 to 8.3	0.1	4.1
1961–68	—1.5 to 3.6	0.7	1.2
Agricultural price index:			
1949–61	—9.3 to 10.0	2.1	3.9
1961–68	—1.5 to 10.7	4.0	3.7

*The figures here are the *arithmetic* averages of the annual percentage changes in each year; hence the slight difference in some cases from the figures in Table 17, which are average annual percentage changes between the beginning and end year, these latter, of course, being equivalent to the *geometric* average of the annual indices (to base 1 in the previous year).

Source: As for Table 17.

faced short-term problems, arising from external circumstances, of a degree far greater than those encountered in the second period. As we shall try to show later, the response to these problems limited longer-term growth in the earlier period. Some of the instability was also due to the structure of the Irish economy at that time, and the structural changes that took place during the early period made for greater stability in the later period. In this connection, the relation between fluctuations in agricultural prices and in merchandise export prices, mentioned earlier, is of interest. The price of agricultural exports fluctuates much more than the price of industrial exports, and fluctuations in the overall merchandise export price are strongly influenced by fluctuations in the price of agricultural exports. However, although agricultural price changes varied nearly as much in the second period as in the first, the variation in export price changes was considerably reduced.[4] The greatly reduced variability in export price changes, despite the continued large variability in agricultural prices, was due partly to the diminished share of agricultural exports in total merchandise exports.[5] Or putting the matter another way, the rise in the share of industrial exports helped to stabilise changes in export prices. This is an interesting example of how structural change helped to secure greater stability.

Indeed, a significant part of the reduced variability in both the price and balance of payments series is probably a result of structural changes affecting export volume and prices. If the value of exports varies less, then, *ceteris paribus,* the balance of payments will show a smaller degree of fluctuation. The dominant impression is that the 1961–68 period has had less dramatic swings in prices, the balance of payments or capital inflows. This facilitated the task of short-term economic management and helped to provide more favourable conditions for sustained expansion of demand and output. Apart from structural changes affecting the balance of payments, there were also important changes in official attitudes towards deficits on the current account and the use of foreign capital. These factors are explored later in greater detail.

PART II

AN ANALYSIS OF EXPORTS

CHAPTER 4

Exports and Economic Growth

WE saw in Chapter 2 that the rise in the growth of G N P was
paralleled by a rise in export growth. In Chapters 4–9 we analyse
further the growth of exports and its relation to the growth of
G N P. We concentrate particularly on two questions: first, what
is the relation between the growth of exports and economic
growth?, and, second, what determines the growth of exports?
These questions may not be unrelated. For example, if the answer
to the first question is that faster economic growth generates a
faster growth of exports, then economic growth becomes one of
the determinants of export growth.

In this chapter we take up the first question and discuss the
arguments in relation to export-led growth and the influence of
domestic demand expansion on export performance. The determinants of export growth are best examined in relation to more
narrowly defined, and somewhat more homogeneous, categories
of exports. Accordingly, in Chapter 5 we discuss changes in the
composition of merchandise exports. In Chapters 6 and 7 we
examine in more detail the determinants of two major categories
of merchandise exports—manufactured exports, and cattle and
beef. In Chapter 8 we examine changes in invisible exports,
already shown to be very important for Ireland, and we focus
attention particularly on the two major categories of invisibles—
investment income and tourism. Finally, in Chapter 9 we give
some tentative conclusions, though our final conclusions on the
role of export growth in Ireland are deferred to our general
overall view (Chapter 16) after we have examined other important
variables.

EXPORT-LED GROWTH

In Ireland the conventional economic wisdom lays heavy stress on the role of export growth in the 1960s in promoting faster economic growth. As the 1950s progressed, increasing emphasis was laid on expansion of exports as a necessary precondition for more rapid economic expansion generally. In retrospect, the faster rate of growth of total exports in the 1960s, as shown in Part I, has come to be regarded generally as the most crucial determinant of faster output growth. Whether or not the facts fit in with this view for Ireland is a question which we shall examine later in greater detail. But let us look first at the general arguments why a faster rate of growth of exports might be expected to lead to faster output growth.

There is, indeed, evidence that the rate of growth of industrial output is closely correlated with the rate of growth of manufactured exports in developed countries.[1] Maizels, for example, found a very close relationship over the past sixty years for each of the main industrial countries between the movements in their share of world production and in their share of world exports of manufactures. Furthermore, in post-war Europe, as is well known, the countries with rapid growth rates (such as Italy and Germany) tended to increase their share of world trade, whereas slow-growing countries (such as the U K) had a declining share of world trade. Such a correlation, however, tells us nothing about causation. Leaving aside chance factors, exports and economic growth could be correlated because (a) export growth stimulated economic growth, or (b) economic growth favoured the growth of exports, or (c) both were jointly influenced by some common factors. Hence, the view that (a) represents the basic chain of causation must depend on some plausible reasons why exports should play a leading role. What are these reasons?

Firstly, there is the balance of payments argument. A rapid rate of growth of output is likely to involve rapidly rising imports. If so, and in the absence of large capital inflows or a very high level of external reserves, a rapid rate of growth of exports is required to avoid balance of payments difficulties. This argument has a number of different strands. In a large developed country the rise in imports in response to growth may come about as a result of a high marginal propensity to import, say, consumer goods. This import increase could, perhaps, be restrained by import restrictions, but if trade restrictions are being reduced generally—as in developed countries in the post-war period—then exports must grow fast enough to balance the rise in imports. In an underdeveloped country the requirement for imports may be even more acute and import restrictions may be of little use. Underdeveloped countries need to import factors of production such as capital equipment, raw materials and technological knowledge that are simply not available, or cannot readily be provided, at home. In this case, one might say that it is really imports that matter for growth, and that exports are the chief means of getting foreign exchange to purchase imports. With regard both to developed and undeveloped countries, the thesis centres on changes in the *value* of total exports relative to changes in the value of total imports. It makes no difference whether the foreign exchange is earned by means of agricultural, industrial, or invisible exports. And an improvement in the terms of trade at which exports exchange for imports is as good as, if not better than, a rise in the volume of exports.

Secondly, it is generally recognised that a rapid rate of growth of aggregate demand is important for rapid output growth. Exports are a component of total demand, so that an autonomous rise in exports will generate a multiplier increase in real income and employment to the extent that there are unemployed resources. Idle capacity will be brought into use with possibly beneficial effects on unit costs, and new investment in productive capacity may be generated through the 'accelerator' process. But these effects depend not only on the degree of unemployed resources, but also on the importance of exports as a component of total demand. Obviously, if exports are a small component of total demand, the effect is likely to be slight. Moreover, the effect as described so far can be achieved by autonomously expanding any component of demand or by restricting imports that can be produced at home. However, expansion of aggregate demand arising from increased exports will normally have different implications for the balance of payments from domestically generated expansion via, for example, increased government spending. For the balance of payments effect in the former case will be the increase in exports less the increase in imports induced by the export change, while in the latter case the effect will be wholly negative—at least, in the short run[2]—being the increase in imports induced by the change in government spending. While it is theoretically possible for the balance of payments to deteriorate in the export expansion case (i.e. induced imports exceeding the increase in exports), it is almost certain that the balance of payments implications of expanding government expenditure would be less favourable. Thus there are two distinct aspects of the relation between exports and aggregate demand. One is the direct impact of exports on output and employment (including multiplier effects). The other is the influence it may have on the authorities' demand management policies, since the degree to which the authorities stimulate home demand by fiscal and monetary measures may be strongly influenced by the balance of payments situation. If exports are not keeping pace with imports, home demand may be restricted to curb the rise in imports in order to bring external payments back into balance. This may lead to stop-go policies in the management of demand, with adverse consequences for growth. It may be noted that this is not a necessary consequence, since there are other policy instruments (such as currency devaluation or import controls) that could, in principle, be used to restore external balance. To the extent that the authorities regard the maintenance of a satisfactory growth of home demand as conditional on the growth of exports, this is another aspect of the balance of payments argument mentioned above. But is there something else about export expansion that is important for economic growth—apart from its role in maintaining a sound balance of payments?

It is possible to argue that export demand plays a special role in relation to the composition of aggregate demand in ways that are important for growth. One aspect of this is that it would be difficult for an underdeveloped country to raise the savings and investment ratios unless outlets could be found abroad for some of the goods produced. The type of output produced by an underdeveloped country is generally not suitable for conversion to investment. If it is not sold abroad, the alternatives are either a deficiency of demand for native production (with adverse consequences for future production) or else the output must be sold at home as consumer goods. This would make it difficult to raise the savings ratio, which is important for financing a higher level of investment. Another aspect is the specialisation factor. The domestic market in a small economy, even with a relatively high level of income *per capita*, is necessarily too small to permit efficient production of many types of goods. Only by achieving a rapid increase in exports will it be possible to specialise in certain activities and reap economies of large-scale production.

There is a further aspect to export growth which is particularly relevant to Ireland. No economy is likely to be a perfect textbook example with ideal resource allocation and optimum specialisation in the production of goods where there is an international comparative advantage. In the case of Ireland, after an extended period of protection designed to encourage greater domestic production of a large number of different goods, it seems probable that there was considerable misallocation of resources, from the point of view of international markets and minimum cost output, by the end of the Second World War. Not the least of the costs associated with restructuring output and reallocating resources is incurred in acquiring information on areas where the economy has a comparative advantage. Exports, apart from yielding profits and increased demand for output, are one method of obtaining such information relatively cheaply. If government grants for investment in plant and training of workers tend to be devoted to export-oriented industries—and we shall see later that such an export-consciousness developed among policy-makers in the 1950s—the result may be a movement towards greater efficiency and a better allocation of resources.

Another reason why exports are singled out from other components of demand relates to their postulated effect on enterprise investment. Beckerman (1965),[3] for example, has argued that a high level of demand is not enough to induce a fast rate of increase in capacity. It must be accompanied by *expectations* of a sustained rapid increase in the level of demand. A crucial determinant of such expectations, especially where foreign trade is an important component of final demand, is the buoyancy of exports. Given these confident expectations, capacity will expand both because of a higher rate of investment and because of increases in the productivity of labour and capital. A higher rate of gross capital formation will itself tend to raise the productivity of net capital formation, because of technological progress incorporated in new machines. In addition, if output does expand rapidly, productivity per unit of factor (labour and capital) is likely to rise due, for example, to economies of scale and improved organisation of production. Thus, in this argument, exports are important not simply to avoid the 'stop-go' associated with balance of payments difficulties: they are seen as important in themselves through their effect on investment via expectations. Moreover, since rising productivity will tend to reduce relative costs and prices, rapid growth can be maintained while preserving a sound balance of payments position. In short, export-led growth, once started, is self-sustaining. This is what is known as a virtuous circle model of growth.

A related model is that of Lamfalussy (1963), who provides two variations on this theme. To add further support to the view that increased capital formation will raise productivity he introduces the concept of defensive investment. With a low level of capital formation, investment tends to be defensive—that is to say, it involves the piecemeal addition of new equipment in existing plants. This raises output per unit of investment (i.e. the productivity of investment) less than when, in the context of a rapid rate of capital formation, a wholly new plant layout is introduced. He also argues that exports will affect the distribution of income in a manner beneficial to the balance of payments. A high rate of growth of exports tends to shift the distribution of income in favour of companies; since the propensity to save out of company income is high, this will raise the savings ratio. Furthermore, the savings ratio will tend to rise because the public authorities' surplus will increase due to higher tax receipts resulting from faster growth. Lamfalussy argues that the savings ratio will rise at least as much as the investment ratio, thereby preventing a worsening of the balance of payments.

Much of the research into the question of the virtuous circle type of export-led growth has come from attempts to explain why some, mainly European, economies grew faster than others during the post-war period. These studies were thus concerned with explaining inter-country differences in growth rates of output over the same time period rather than within-country differences in growth over different time periods. Central to the argument is the role of exports in creating confident expectations about demand that induce rapid growth in investment and output, with favourable effects on productivity and unit costs. It is of interest to consider these propositions briefly in relation to the kind of evidence available to support or reject them. Most of the evidence concerns the industrial sector and manufacturing in particular.

The argument that demand expectations are crucial in determining investment seems to be reasonably well-established—a review of the evidence is given in Beckerman (1965). There is less general support for the view that demand expectations are chiefly determined by exports.[4] The importance of exports as a direct source of aggregate demand depends partly on the share of exports in total demand—a factor which varies with the size and level of development of the country. The permissive role of a sound balance of payments in allowing the authorities to expand domestic demand depends not only on the growth of the volume of exports but also on the growth of import volume and the behaviour of the terms of trade. It also depends on the level of external reserves, the possibilities of supporting the reserves by external borrowing, and the degree to which the authorities are prepared to use other policy instruments (such as exchange rate adjustments). The share of domestic value added in exports differs from one country to another, and within a country it differs significantly between different categories of exports. Yet the greater the share of value added, the greater will be the impact on domestic activity of any given rise in exports. Furthermore, in regard to the economies of scale argument, the same total rate of growth of exports may have different implications depending on whether it is achieved through a roughly equal rate of growth of all categories of exports, or exceptionally rapid growth in a specialised group of exports. The size of the domestic market is also crucial: with a large home market, expansion of home demand may provide an adequate market for achieving economies of scale in the production of goods that could only be efficiently produced in a small country by exporting the bulk of the output.

If the argument is extended to less developed countries, the required linkages may not be present, so that a rapid rate of growth of exports may not automatically induce greater investment and faster economic growth unless other policy instruments are adopted to provide the necessary linkages. The institutional and socio-cultural framework may be such that non-export firms fail to respond to profitable opportunities created by the export sector. The production function of the products exported (e.g. whether skill-intensive or not), the degree of processing before export, and the type of infrastructure required (e.g. pipeline *versus* railroad), all help to determine the nature and extent of the linkages that are likely to develop. Moreover, if the distribution of income is such that a substantial part of export income comprises profits that are either spent on luxury imports or are remitted back home by foreign enterprises, a thriving export market may do little for internal growth.[5]

If it were established that exports generate a faster rate of growth of capacity and output, it would still be necessary, in order to complete the virtuous circle, to show that faster output growth leads to faster productivity growth[6] and a greater decline (or lower increase) in unit costs and prices, thereby maintaining the country's competitive advantage. There is now a great deal of evidence for several countries showing that in cross-sections of manufacturing industries there is a high correlation between the longer-term rates of growth of output and productivity, whether productivity is measured in relation to labour input alone or combined labour and capital input.[7] The same relation has also been shown to hold in cross-sections relating to manufacturing industry as a whole among countries, though the evidence here is generally confined to labour productivity.[8] This relationship has become known as the Verdoorn Law.

If we accept that the correlation arises primarily because a faster rate of output growth generates a faster rate of productivity growth,[9] it is then necessary to show that relatively rapid productivity growth is reflected in relative unit costs and price of output—in other words, that it is not offset by relatively large increases in factor prices. For individual industries within a country, the evidence is clearcut: the dispersion of average earnings increases among industries tends to be small, and earnings increases are not strongly correlated with productivity increases. Hence, a strong negative correlation exists between changes in productivity and unit wage cost and also between output and unit wage cost.[10] For manufacturing industry as a whole in different countries, the evidence is not so clearcut. Although the degree of variation in earnings increases among different countries may be less than in the case of productivity increases, earnings increases do tend to vary among countries much more than among industries in the same country. Moreover, there is some evidence that they are significantly correlated with productivity increases. Hence, the correlation across countries between changes in productivity and unit wage cost in manufacturing, though generally negative, is not always significantly so, while the correlation between changes in output and unit wage cost is even lower.[11] There is little or no cross-country evidence available on the relation between changes in output (or productivity) and changes in other components of unit cost. Relative changes in unit wage cost are, of course, an important determinant of relative changes in export price, but the evidence available in relation to the association between relative output changes and relative changes in unit wage cost is, as noted, inconclusive.

It is worth noting that relationships between changes in output, productivity, unit costs and prices that have been established across industries in a given country need not necessarily hold for manufacturing as a whole across countries; nor, if they do hold, need the explanation be the same. Thus, for example, within a country a rapid rate of growth of productivity in an industry may have little or no effect on the size of wage increase in that industry if trade union pressures tend to secure roughly equal increases in all industries; on the other hand, the overall rate of growth of manufacturing productivity may be important in influencing the size of earnings increase that will be generally sought and agreed. A decline in an individual industry's price relative to other industries in the same country may do little to raise demand for its output (unless, of course, its price declines also relative to the same industry in other countries), whereas for the country as a whole a general decline in its manufacturing price relative to other countries producing a similar range of manufactures may secure a substantial increase in output through exports. A country can devalue, whereas an individual industry cannot. Moreover, it is conceivable that while relative rates of growth of productivity among industries are substantially determined by relative demand pressures (as reflected by relative output growth rates), the overall rate of growth of productivity might be more limited by supply considerations (such as the general level of education, the number of inventions, etc.). These possibilities suggest that intra-country findings should not automatically be drawn on to support theories in relation to inter-country behaviour.

Kaldor (1966), although accepting that the Verdoorn Law operates across countries, draws a rather different conclusion from the export-led growth view. He argues that where there are labour shortages in the manufacturing sector—the leading sector, in his view—a higher rate of growth of output may not be attainable even with a higher rate of growth of export demand. The Verdoorn Law suggests not only that every 1 per cent rise in the growth rate of output will generate roughly a $\frac{1}{2}$ per cent rise in productivity growth but will also require roughly a $\frac{1}{2}$ per cent rise in the growth rate of manufacturing employment.

In a fully-employed economy, such as post-war Britain, where the labour force as a whole is growing slowly and the level of income per head is broadly similar in all major sectors, there is no assurance that manufacturers will be able to secure an increase in labour sufficient to permit rapid growth. Thus a higher rate of growth of exports alone would not raise the growth of total output. Kaldor argues that, unlike the U K, manufacturing industry in the rapidly growing European economies was able to draw on substantial numbers of workers from agriculture because the share of the total labour force engaged in agriculture was relatively large at the start of the post-war period, and the average income per head in agriculture was still well below that in manufacturing.

While these points may throw some doubt on the universality of exports as the leading factor in growth, they, nevertheless, allow to exports an important role, though not necessarily as the sole causal factor. However, even this qualified view of the role of exports has been challenged by those who see the correlation between export growth and economic growth as arising from the stimulating effect of economic growth on export growth.[12] In this view, rapid export growth is a consequence, rather than a cause, of rapid economic growth or, at the very least, the forces that generate rapid economic growth are the same as those that generate rapid export growth. If trade is to contribute to a country's economic growth, 'a *domestic* engine of growth must be built first, to enable the country to make good use of growth opportunities offered by foreign trade... In case this domestic growth engine is missing—or not functioning properly—foreign trade cannot be a good substitute for it, and potential sources of gains offered by trade opportunities will not be realised.'[13] It is argued that far too much emphasis has been laid on foreign demand for exports, without sufficient regard to supply considerations at the production end or even to the importance of the import aspects of trade in the production process. None of this is to deny that a fast rate of export growth will reinforce economic growth generally; however, export growth itself is seen chiefly as a consequence of economic growth.

This view can be regarded partly as an attempt to develop a dynamic version of traditional trade theory. In the classical model, trade occurs because different countries have comparative advantages in the production of different goods, so that trade will lead to a more efficient allocation of world resources, and benefit all countries. To this general law certain exceptions were admitted— somewhat reluctantly—such as the infant industry argument for protection; nevertheless, free trade was the general ideal of theory, and trade was seen as determined by comparative advantage. In turn, the Heckscher-Ohlin model explained comparative advantage in terms of differences in relative factor endowments. Put simply, countries with a relative abundance of labour and a relative scarcity of capital would tend to have a comparative advantage in the production of labour intensive goods.

This theory of trade was both supply-oriented and essentially static. Though demand considerations must be introduced to explain the level of trade, the primary focus is on the supply conditions in different countries. The static nature of the theory arises from the fact that it explains trade on the basis of given factor proportions and emphasises the effect of trade on efficiency rather than on growth. Of course, it was recognised that relative factor endowments may change, but the model could then be applied to the new situation so that trade is still explained in static (or, at most, comparative static) terms. Increased efficiency was achieved not through increased exports or increased imports, separately, but through the process of mutual exchange. Of course, certain dynamic aspects were admitted which could be important for growth. It was recognised that economies of scale could result when trade enabled countries to specialise. Imports could have a demonstration effect which would produce an important reaction in the pattern of domestic consumption and a stimulus to a re-thinking of domestic production methods. But such considerations did not achieve a central place in the theory.

In the 'growth-generated trade' model, factor proportions (in the traditional sense of land, labour and capital) alone do not determine the pattern of comparative advantage. Comparative advantage can be influenced by development of technical skills in workers, by building up entrepreneurial and organisational ability and by the employment of technology (whether developed at home or borrowed from abroad). But 'a general environment of persistent slow growth is unlikely to stimulate innovation, or to be associated with improvements in quality, or with widening the range of products available, to the same extent as an economy enjoying a fast rate of growth.'[14] In other words, changes in levels of skill and technology, which are regarded as crucial determinants of foreign trade, are seen as the result and/or the cause of previous growth experience. The learning effect of producing for the home market is also regarded as important in developing entrepreneurial ability. Moreover, given that knowledge is imperfect in marketing, entrepreneurs can most readily produce for the domestic market first, and only later as they became aware of profit opportunities abroad will they be able to export. Üstünel argues that 'Changes in technology or the introduction of new products will usually generate a *domestic growth* first, and after their success at home they will generate better sales opportunities across the national boundaries and thus contribute to the export performance of a firm or a country.'[15] Thus the engine of growth is not the growth of exports due to the existence of favourable demand conditions abroad or the holding of a comparative advantage in certain products; it is, rather, the creation first of an efficient society through development of social infrastructure, education and technical and entrepreneurial skills, which then generate a successful export performance.

An exception to this might be the use of foreign enterprise geared to export markets. It might be possible, for instance, to attract industry to a country which would be required to export all its output. Presumably the foreign firm would not merely supply the technology but would also be well informed about foreign markets and would, perhaps, even possess secure market outlets with its own branches in other countries. In such circumstances, it might be possible to launch growth based on exports. Indeed, as we shall show, this is the thinking underlying much of Ireland's industrial development policy. However, the question whether this type of export-led growth *alone* can make a profound impact on overall growth is another matter. It may not develop the essential linkages with the rest of the economy and, if not based on domestic raw materials, the share of domestic value added may be small. Moreover, the profit element of value added is not owned or controlled domestically, and the degree to which profits are remitted back to the parent firm is important both for the balance of payments and growth.

The 'growth-generated trade' thesis does not necessarily rest solely on successful supply-side measures. The role of domestic demand has also been stressed as an important determinant of a country's exportable products. Export is seen as 'the end, not the beginning, of a typical market expansion path',[16] so that the growth of home demand will be important in enabling producers to develop the experience and skills, and in providing the initial base, required for successful entry into the more uncertain territory of export markets. This view, if taken to the extreme that expansion of home demand will raise exports sufficiently to improve or maintain the balance of payments, would represent an even more virtuous circle than the export-led growth model. We now consider in greater detail the arguments bearing on the relation between exports and the pressure of home demand.

EXPORTS AND THE PRESSURE OF DEMAND

While the empirical studies undertaken on the relation between the pressure of domestic demand and exports, most of which deal with the short-term situation, do not yield conclusive results, the general conclusion seems to be that exports are adversely affected by a high pressure of demand.[17] Why should a high pressure of domestic demand—interpreted either as the level or rate of growth of demand—be expected to slow down the growth of exports?

It is generally believed that reducing the pressure of home demand releases goods for export which would otherwise be sold at home. Alternatively, when home demand is expanded, exporters may be tempted to sell at home rather than export. This view implies that selling at home is easier or, in other words, more profitable. It may also mean that, though no less profitable, less is known about export markets, and that as long as an inducement to sell at home remains, firms will continue to do so and not bother much about export markets. While this view is

D

plausible, there are a number of objections which would, at least, limit its generality. Firstly, a cut-back in demand will do nothing to expand exports—at least, in the short run—in those industries where goods are not suitable for export. In other words, there may be imperfect substitution between home and export markets. Secondly, overseas marketing may involve investment of a long-term nature, which a firm may be reluctant to undertake precisely at a time of difficulty in the home market. Firms exporting a high proportion of output are already largely insulated from changes in home demand, while those exporting little or nothing may be unwilling to enter untried export markets at a time of uncertain prospects at home. This implies also that the temptation for those already engaged in exporting to divert a greater proportion of output to the home market when pressure of home demand rises, may be countered by the desire to protect marketing investment abroad. Thirdly, it is possible that while the policy of cutting home demand will operate to increase export sales in the short term, it may reduce export potential in the long term. Thus, while firms may shift to export markets in the short run, the cut-back in home demand may affect investment incentives. Export potential in the longer term could then be adversely affected by reductions in either capacity-increasing, or cost-reducing, investment. This is the basis of the view that satisfactory expansion of exports requires as a cushion the steady growth of home market demand. Fourthly, if an economy is operating already below full capacity, a rise or fall in domestic demand may, within certain bounds, have no impact either way on exports. In other words, there may be a threshold effect, and only when the pressure of home demand rises above this threshold does it begin to have adverse effects on exports.

Another reason why reduced pressure of home demand is considered to be favourable to exports is that it may reduce the rate of increase in wages and in prices and so increase competitiveness. It is generally believed that wages and prices are, to some degree at least, a positive function of the pressure of aggregate demand. However, if home demand were reduced and exports rose (or imports fell) sufficiently to take up the slack thereby created, there would be no reduction in aggregate demand. Thus for this effect to be operative it would seem that output must fall. But if productivity is a positive function of output, then whether costs and prices will fall (or rise less) depends on whether the reduction in the rate of increase in money incomes is greater than the reduction in the rate of growth of productivity. This is something that might vary from one time to another or from one country to another. It may also vary with the level of pressure at which the cut in demand is enforced. If, for example, there was already a significant level of unemployment, then a further cut in demand might have little impact on money wages but might still significantly affect productivity.

It could also be argued that deflation of demand will expand exports by releasing labour from non-exporting to exporting firms. This presupposes that the exporting firms have had difficulties in getting adequate labour, so that the effect may not operate if there is already a high level of unemployment. Moreover, the effect depends on the released labour possessing the required skills and being available in the appropriate regions, otherwise a large cut-back in demand may be required to secure a modest rise in exports. Furthermore, the cut in demand must be expected to continue, since otherwise firms may simply hoard labour in anticipation of a revival in demand, with adverse effects meantime on productivity.

To sum up, there are reasons for expecting exports to be inversely related to the pressure of demand, but these, no more than the available empirical evidence, are by no means conclusive. The circumstances in which a cut in demand is least likely to help exports are as follows: when firms already have unemployed capacity; when the level of unemployment is already high; when some firms sell the bulk of output at home while others sell the bulk of output abroad; when cost-reducing or capacity-increasing investment is adversely affected by deflation of home demand; when there is very imperfect substitution between home and export markets; when a major marketing investment is required to enter export markets; and when money incomes fall little and productivity falls a lot in response to a demand cut. In fact, in certain circumstances, expansion of home demand may favour exports by increasing investment, raising productivity, and providing a cushion for entry into riskier export markets. The effect of a demand cut could be favourable to exports in the short run but unfavourable in the longer term. It should be said that even if deflation had an adverse effect on exports, it is much less likely that it would adversely affect the balance of payments in the short run, since deflation would normally tend to reduce imports more quickly than it would, even pessimistically, reduce exports. Over the longer term, restriction of home demand could conceivably be unfavourable to the balance of payments if it seriously retarded the development of enterprise, productive capacity and technological advance. If it were true that expansion of home demand is adverse to the balance of payments in the short run but favourable in the longer term, then a lower level of reserves could operate as a severe constraint on longer-term growth, as has often been argued in the case of the post-war British economy.

CONCLUSIONS

The conflicting theories that have been considered in this chapter are all plausible, and it is fair to say that the evidence in the literature is not sufficient to resolve the issues conclusively. As yet, we should not neglect the possibility that there are elements of truth in all the theories. There is no *a priori* need to have a uni-causal view of growth, however attractive it may be to identify one unique source. It should also be remembered that in different circumstances different factors may be important for growth. Rather than further surveying the evidence for other countries, the most appropriate course for us would seem to be to examine the facts of the Irish case and see which set of ideas accords best with Irish experience.

CHAPTER 5

Merchandise Exports: Growth Fluctuations and Changes in Composition

A s the previous chapter implies, disaggregation is helpful in understanding the growth of exports and their impact on G N P. In this chapter we consider further the behaviour of total merchandise (or visible) exports[1] and changes in their composition.

GROWTH AND VARIABILITY OF MERCHANDISE EXPORTS

It was pointed out in Chapter 2 that there was much the same rate of growth of visible exports in the two periods 1949–61 and 1961–68. The average growth rate for export value was 9.1 per cent per annum from 1949 to 1961 and 10.2 per cent per annum from 1961 to 1968, volume growth being 7.0 per cent annually in the first period and 7.4 per cent in the later period.[2] Thus, since there was no substantial increase in the growth rate between the two periods, it might be argued that, as far as visible exports are concerned, there was nearly as much stimulus to growth in the first period as in the second. However, a number of qualifications must be made.

Firstly, the volume of visible exports recovered from the effects of the war later than the volume of total output. Only in 1950 did the volume of exports surpass the 1939 level, whereas total real product had surpassed the 1939 level in 1947. Not only that, however, but the 1939 level of exports was itself a comparatively low figure, since exports were seriously disrupted in the 1930s as a result of the depression, the 'Economic War' and the shift towards economic nationalism. In fact, so profound was the change in the economy in the 1930s that, despite the rapid rate of growth of exports in the post-war period, it was only in 1960 that the volume of visible exports first exceeded the 1929 or 1930 levels. Even more striking, perhaps, is the fact that only in 1967 did the ratio of volume of visible exports to G N P surpass the 1929 ratio.

Thus the ratio of visible exports to G N P at the start of the post-war period may be said to be historically low, and, of course, the impact of any given growth rate of exports on the growth of output will be less, the lower the ratio of exports to output. Since the volume of visible exports has grown, on average, much faster than real G N P, the ratio of volume of visible exports to G N P has risen substantially, from 13.5 per cent in 1949 to 24.4 per cent in 1961 and 30.3 per cent in 1968, all measured at 1958 prices. Clearly, a given rate of growth of exports starting from 1961 would, *ceteris paribus,* make a larger contribution to aggregate demand than the same rate starting from 1949.

Secondly, as may be seen from Chart 5 in Chapter 2, visible exports fluctuated more in the first period than in the second. Indeed, it might be argued that since the year 1961 was an exceptionally good year for cattle and beef exports, following three years in which such exports did not expand, this tends to exaggerate the 1949–61 growth rate compared with 1961–68. However, Chart 5, which gives volume figures for every year, suggests a fairly steady *long-term* rate of growth in the volume of

Table 19: Variability of annual percentage changes in visible exports, 1949–61 and 1961–68

	Range	Average	Mean deviation (+)
	%	%	%
Current value:			
1949–61	—4.9 to 24.3	9.6	9.3
1961–68	—2.9 to 18.0	10.4	6.4
Volume:			
1949–61	—7.7 to 21.6	7.5	10.2
1961–68	—3.8 to 17.6	7.6	5.4
Price:			
1949–61	—5.4 to 13.4	2.1	3.3
1961–68	0.0 to 7.2	2.6	2.1

Source: As for Table 12. See also note to Table 18.

visible exports throughout the post-war period. However, there was a pause from 1953 to 1956 and again from 1957 to 1959, both of which were more serious and prolonged than any set-back in the later period. Table 19 summarises the extent of the fluctuations observed in Chart 5, by setting out the range of year-to-year percentage changes in volume, value and prices for visible exports for the relevant sub-periods, together with the average year-to-year percentage change and the mean absolute deviation. It is clear that annual changes in the volume and prices of visible exports varied far more in the first period. Fluctuations in the value of exports were also greater in the first period, although the difference was less marked than for export volume. This was due to a slight tendency for export volume and price to move inversely in the period 1949–61, whereas there was no such association in the period 1961–68.[3]

The greater instability may have contributed to the slower rate of output growth between 1949 and 1961. Export instability may lead to short-term balance of payments difficulties since a fall in exports may not be accompanied by a similar decline in imports. In the absence of some assurance that the decline in exports is temporary and will be offset by a large increase the following year, the authorities may seek to protect external reserves by cutting home demand, with adverse consequences for output growth. And at the micro level, instability in exports, like instability in the growth of output generally, tends to impede planning and increase uncertainty, thereby adversely affecting investment and innovation. Moreover, with the free movement of Irish labour to the UK—an adjacent and large alternative labour market—instability of output and employment tends to lead to high labour turnover and a possible permanent loss of skilled manpower.

MAJOR COMPONENTS
OF MERCHANDISE EXPORTS

A third possible factor influencing the role of exports is their composition, which changed considerably in the post-war period. Table 20 shows the shares of the components in total domestic exports in 1950, 1961 and 1968, together with the average annual rates of growth from 1950 to 1961 and from 1961 to 1968.

Table 20: Major components of domestic exports (current values):
shares in 1950, 1961 and 1968 and average annual growth rates
1950–61 and 1961–68

SITC No.		Percentage shares of total domestic exports			Average annual growth rates	
		1950	1961	1968	1950–61	1961–68
		%	%	%	%	%
0.0	Live animals*	37.5	29.3	17.1	6.2	1.1
0.1	Meat and meat preparations	11.9	19.3	18.2	13.5	8.3
	Total 0.0 and 0.1	49.3	48.6	35.4	8.5	4.3
0.2	Dairy products and eggs	10.9	3.7	6.7	—1.4	18.8
0.3–0.9	Other food and food preparations	12.4	8.7	7.8	5.2	7.5
	Total Section 0	72.6	61.0	50.0	6.9	6.1
1	Beverages and tobacco	7.0	4.3	3.6	3.9	6.6
2–4	Crude materials, fuels, oils, fats	8.1	8.7	8.1	9.3	8.1
5–8	Manufactures	6.0**	17.8	33.2	19.9	19.3
9	Parcel post and special transactions*	6.3**	8.2	5.1	11.3	2.0
	Total	100.0	100.0	100.0	8.6	9.2
Value of domestic exports		£m 70.49	£m 175.29	£m 323.34		

*Temporary exports and re-exports of live animals are included in section
9 rather than in section 0.0.
**Temporary exports estimated at £0.6 million deducted from the published
figures for Sections 5–8 and included in Section 9.

Sources: *Trade and Shipping Statistics* and *Irish Statistical Bulletin*. The
figures do not include exports from the Shannon Industrial Estate.

Domestic exports differ from merchandise exports in that the
former excludes re-exports. It should be noted also, however, that
the figures in Table 20 exclude Shannon exports as no details
are published on the composition of Shannon trade. The choice
of the year 1950 here is dictated by the fact that it is the first
year for which the components of exports were classified according to the United Nations Standard International Trade Classification (S I T C), which has been the sole basis of classification

since 1963. The data are shown at current prices, as volume figures for all of the separate components are not available.

It will be seen from Table 20 that the average annual rate of growth of live animals, meat and meat preparations was about twice as great in the period 1950–61 as in the period 1961–68. The share of these categories declined only slightly from 49.3 per cent in 1950 to 48.6 per cent in 1961, but between 1961 and 1968 there was a fall in the share of over 13 percentage points. In both periods there was a marked shift from the live animals category to meat and meat preparations accounted for by the rise in domestic slaughtering of cattle for export.

The growth rate of total food products, which includes the live animals and meat categories, however, was not so markedly different in the two periods: 6.9 per cent per annum for 1950–61 and 6.1 per cent per annum for 1961–68. The reason is that other categories of food exports rose far more rapidly in the second period. Dairy produce and eggs fell at an annual average rate of 1.4 per cent from 1950 to 1961 but rose by 18.8 per cent per annum from 1961 to 1968. The fall in this category in the first period was to a large extent the result of a decline in exports of eggs, which fell drastically in 1954 and 1955 and had practically disappeared as an export by 1961. On the other hand, the rapid rise in the second period was comprised of exports of dairy produce. Exports of other food products rose by 7.5 per cent per annum from 1961 to 1968 as against 5.2 per cent per annum from 1950 to 1961. As we shall demonstrate later, the average growth rate for 1950–61 for this and the dairy products category conceals considerable fluctuations in the year-to-year behaviour.

Over the whole period 1950–68 food and food products have declined markedly as a proportion of domestic exports: from 72½ per cent in 1950 to 50 per cent in 1968. There has been an even larger proportionate decline in exports of beverages and tobacco from 7 per cent in 1950 to 3.6 per cent in 1968. Most of the fall occurred between 1950 and 1961, when exports grew by only 3.9 per cent per annum as against 6.6 per cent per annum from 1961 to 1968. Until recently tobacco accounted for only an insignificant proportion of this item, but the faster growth rate in the second period is substantially accounted for by relatively large exports of tobacco products in 1967 and 1968. Crude materials, fuels, oils, fats, etc. (S I T C Sections 2–4) have remained a relatively constant share of the total in the three years, 1950, 1961 and 1968, being in the region of 8 to 9 per cent.

The most striking feature of the table is the extremely rapid growth of manufactured exports in both periods. The generally accepted definition of manufactured exports (S I T C Sections 5–8) has been adopted here.[4] It should be noted, however, that it does not include manufactured food, drink and tobacco or petroleum products; otherwise it includes all of what are generally regarded as manufactured articles. The growth rate in the two periods has been almost identical,[5] and the share of manufactures in total domestic exports has risen from 6 per cent in 1950 to 17.8 per cent in 1961 and 33.2 per cent in 1968. Of course, rapid growth in the early period assumes less significance when considered in relation to the small initial base in 1950. In such circumstances it is axiomatically true that comparatively small *absolute* increases in manufactured exports involved large percentage rises. As we shall show, the contribution of manufactured exports to the growth of total exports was much greater in the more recent period than in the earlier period; thus, even though the growth rate of manufactured exports itself was unchanged, it assumed greater importance in contributing to the growth of total exports. But on the other hand, it should not be forgotten that there are considerable difficulties attached to starting an operation and that once it was shown that some manufacturers could successfully export, this was a great encouragement to others to try also. O'Driscoll (1955), discussing the report of a firm of American consultants prepared in 1951 in regard to difficulties facing export expansion in Ireland, defined the problem thus: 'One of the real obstacles to export that they found here was what they called "fear of the unknown". Firms not previously on an export basis would be reluctant to enter an export market because of lack of knowledge.' It would be unwise to play down excessively the growth of manufactured exports in the 1950s, since it laid a basis for the further expansion of such exports even before the process was greatly helped by the export tax incentives of 1956.

Thus in both periods manufactured exports substantially increased their share of total domestic exports relative to agricultural exports. The relative importance of manufactured exports was, therefore, far greater in the second period than in the first, partly as a result of their rapid growth in the first period. The role of different categories of exports in the growth process has not been subject to systematic research, although it is felt that different categories may exert a widely different impact on growth.[6] In Ireland, manufactured exports tend to have a relatively high import content, whereas agricultural exports have a relatively low import content.[7] On this criterion alone, therefore, a given absolute rise in manufactured exports would imply a smaller direct contribution to G N P than the same rise in agricultural exports. Thus, given the same overall rate of export growth, and the same ratio of exports to G N P in two periods, exports would make a larger direct contribution to G N P in the period when the weighting of agricultural exports was largest. However, the share of domestic value added in agricultural and manufactured exports themselves may have changed, either because of variations in the import content of production or because of composition changes within these classes involving goods with different import shares. Unfortunately, we do not have the necessary input-output data, ranging over the post-war period, that would enable us to examine such matters in detail. There are possibly important indirect differences also in the impact of different categories of exports on output connected with the external benefits (or costs) created by their production (e.g. the build-up of skilled labour or the development of new technology), the extent to which they mobilise resources for which there are no competing demands, and the manner in which the domestic incomes earned through exports are used (e.g. how much goes back into investment). These are all matters that would require considerable research which we cannot hope to pursue further in this work.

Fluctuations in Components of Merchandise Exports

Chart 7 shows the annual values of the major components of domestic exports. One of the most marked features is the reduction in year-to-year variability of almost all series in the later period. Exports of live animals, meat and meat preparations is an exception in that it seems to be unstable throughout the entire post-war period; because of the large influence of cattle and beef exports in causing this instability, we will examine this category of exports in greater depth later. Due to its large share in the total, fluctuations in live animals and meat exports exerted

CHART 7
MAJOR COMPONENTS OF DOMESTIC EXPORTS, 1950-1968 (£M., current values)

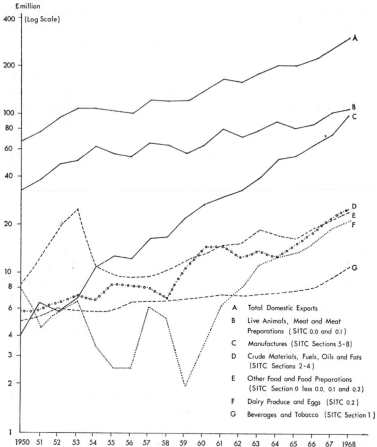

£ million

400 (Log Scale)

A   Total Domestic Exports
B   Live Animals, Meat and Meat
    Preparations (SITC 0.0 and 0.1)
C   Manufactures (SITC Sections 5-8)
D   Crude Materials, Fuels, Oils and Fats
    (SITC Sections 2-4)
E   Other Food and Food Preparations
    (SITC Section 0 less 0.0, 0.1 and 0.2)
F   Dairy Produce and Eggs (SITC 0.2)
G   Beverages and Tobacco (SITC Section 1)

1950 51 52 53 54 55 56 57 58 59 60 61 62 63 64 65 66 67 1968

a strong influence on the overall instability of exports. But the rising share of manufactured exports, a category which has exhibited a relatively small degree of fluctuation throughout, has imposed greater stability on the growth of total exports, and this is a major cause of the reduced instability of the total in the second period.

Another reason for the greater instability in total exports in the 1950s was the very pronounced fluctuations in the two other food categories shown on the chart (dairy produce and eggs, and other food (apart from live animals, meat and dairy produce)). The former accounted for almost 12 per cent of domestic exports in 1950, and of this, eggs represented about two-thirds. The great decline in 1954 and 1955 was caused to a large extent by a reduction in egg exports due to changes in the agricultural policy in the U K and the increased ability of U K domestic egg producers to meet overall demand. The increase between 1956 and 1957 and the subsequent decline in 1958 and 1959 was due mainly to changes in exports of butter. In the post-war period, prior to the 1960s, Ireland did not have an assured regular surplus of butter for disposal abroad. This meant that in some years exports of butter were negligible. Gradually over the 1950s and the early 1960s the milk surplus began to expand, mainly due to improved guaranteed prices for dairy produce. The surplus can be explained by a combination of increased yields and the expansion of the cow population. Average annual milk yield per cow, which for long had fluctuated around 400 gallons per annum, rose rapidly from 1952 (413 gallons) to 1957 (497 gallons). There was little further advance until towards the end of our period when the average rose from 493 in 1966 to 529 in 1968. The number of milch cows, which was almost stationary for over a hundred years in the region of 1.2 million, began to rise from 1956 (1.19 million) and reached 1.32 million in 1963. Expansion of the cow population received a new impetus from the calved heifer subsidy scheme,[8] introduced in January 1964, and by 1968 the number of milch cows had risen to 1.61 million. It was possible to export the growing milk surplus, however, only at an increasing cost of subsidisation both absolutely and per unit exported.[9] The burden of subsidisation per unit exported was alleviated to some extent by the market quota for butter provided in the Anglo-Irish Free Trade Area Agreement, which was signed in December 1965 and became operative from the middle of 1966. Thus the strong rise in dairy exports from 1959 was due largely to increased milk production over and above domestic requirements. The emergence of a permanent surplus did allow for orderly marketing of Irish dairy produce abroad and probably improved its price relative to other competitors in the market.

The other food items advanced rapidly in the first three years of the 1950s, rising from 12½ per cent of total domestic exports in 1950 to 23 per cent in 1953. These exports, however, were largely of a temporary nature. They consisted of such items as chocolate and sugar confectionery, mincemeat, sweetened fat, etc., and depended to a considerable extent on loopholes in the British import quota controls and rationing system. Given this basis, it is not surprising that instability in the behaviour of the other food component was far greater than for most export components. As FitzGerald (1968) put it: 'Up to £10 million worth of an individual product was sometimes exported within a twelve-month period; but in the following twelve months this item might have disappeared from the export list as British regulations were tightened, only to be replaced by another.'[10] Nor was it surprising, at least in retrospect, that such exports eventually ceased; this occurred in 1954 and 1955, a time when several other categories of exports suffered declines or at least a slowing down in growth. While such exports manifested a degree of enterprise and adaptation on the part of some Irish manufacturers at that time, with which they are not often credited, clearly it did not provide a satisfactory basis for longer-term growth. The effect of the elimination of these exports was not inconsiderable in balance of payments terms, and the dislocation at industry level was substantial. Since 1957 there has been a fairly strong and steady rise in other food products, though the 1953 level had not been surpassed by 1968. The composition of this item is now, of course, very different from what it was in the early 1950s and is generally much more soundly based from a longer-term viewpoint.

Drink and tobacco exports have shown little fluctuation and slow growth, remaining in the region of £6–£8 million in all years from 1952 to 1966. The most significant increases have come in the last two years of our period, due largely to exports of tobacco products. Crude materials, fuels, etc. have shown a strong, if not very steady, rise, starting from 1958. Three groups of products account for the vast bulk of the rise here: hides and skins, metal ores and petroleum products. The steep rise in 1959 and 1960 was due mainly to petroleum products and textile fibres (including wool), the latter, however, having since fallen back. The strong rise from 1964 to 1968 owes much to the very substantial rise in exports of metal ores which grew from only £1.4 milion in 1964 to almost £11 million in 1968. All of the commodities mentioned exhibit a fair degree of short-term fluctuation which is partly reflected in the total shown in Chart 7.

Manufactured exports have shown a strong upward trend in the entire period since 1950, though there was some fluctuation in the rate of expansion prior to 1958. The steadiness of the strong rise since 1958 is, indeed, remarkable; in no year since then has there been a decline, and even in 1965, the year of least expansion, manufactured exports still rose by 5½ per cent. However, the rise in the period up to 1958, though not so steady, was also noteworthy. The average annual rate of growth from 1950 to 1958 was 19.4 per cent, much the same as from 1958 to 1968, even though 1958 was a relatively depressed year for manufactured exports.

CONCLUSIONS

While there was no appreciable upward shift in the growth of total merchandise exports in the period 1961–68 compared with the earlier period, there have, however, been substantial changes in the relative importance of merchandise exports in GNP and in the components of merchandise exports. The ratio of visible exports to GNP more than doubled between 1949 and 1968, suggesting that, *ceteris paribus,* visible exports contributed increasingly to the growth rate of output. Much of the increased share of visible exports in GNP was due to the very rapid growth of manufactured exports throughout the post-war period. In so far as the rising ratio of merchandise exports to GNP increased the impact of any given growth rate of exports, this creates a link between the two periods, since the share of exports in the second period was higher than in the first, partly because exports rose rapidly in the first period.

Total merchandise exports had a steadier rate of expansion in the second period. For certain components, the degree of fluctuation in the first period was very considerable. The greater variability in the first period may have had adverse consequences for growth both because of balance of payments uncertainty and disruption at industry and firm level.

We now examine in greater detail the determinants of two of the major categories of Irish merchandise exports—manufactures and cattle.

CHAPTER 6

The Growth of Manufactured Exports

W E have seen that manufactured exports grew at a very high rate, around 19 per cent per annum, throughout the post-war period. There was no evidence of any long-term acceleration in the growth rate, although fluctuations about the growth trend were less in the period 1961–68. However, in 1950 manufactured exports amounted to only £4½ million or 6 per cent of domestic exports. Thus the contribution of the high growth rate of manufactured exports to the overall growth of visible exports would have been quite small for much of the 1950s. Of course, given that manufactured exports continued to grow at a much faster rate than any other major component of domestic exports, its share in the overall total increased considerably. Thus by 1961 manufactured exports represented almost 18 per cent of visible exports and by 1968 the share had risen to 33 per cent. Clearly

Table 21: Contribution of manufactured exports to growth rate of total domestic exports, 1950–61 and 1961–68

Domestic merchandise exports (current values)	Average annual growth rate		Contribution to total growth rate*	
	1950–61	1961–68	1950–61	1961–68
	%	%	%	%
Manufactures	19.9	19.3	2.3	4.9
All other	7.3	6.0	6.4	4.4
Total	8.6	9.2	8.6	9.2

*The contribution in each period is measured by weighting the average annual growth rate by the average of the shares in the total in the beginning and end year of each period. See also note to Table 6.

Sources: *Trade and Shipping Statistics*; *Irish Statistical Bulletin*.

the sustained faster growth of manufactured exports tended to accelerate the growth of total domestic exports over the post-war period and the impact of the faster growth was greatest in the period 1961–68.

We can attempt to quantify the contribution of manufactured export growth to the growth of overall domestic exports by weighting the average annual growth rates of manufactured exports and non-manufactured exports by the average of their shares in the total for the beginning and end year of each period. In this way, we can obtain a measure of the contribution of the growth of manufactured exports and other exports to the total growth rate. The results of the calculations are set out in Table 21. Although non-manufactured exports grew at a slower rate during 1961–68 compared with 1950–61 and manufactured exports grew at about the same rate in both periods, the overall growth rate of domestic exports was slightly higher in the second period. This was due to the greater weight of manufactured exports in the total in 1961–68, so that maintenance of the high growth rate of manufactured exports involved a larger contribution to the overall growth rate of exports. In fact, manufactured exports accounted for over half the total growth rate of domestic exports in the period 1961–68 compared with little more than a quarter for 1950–61.

MANUFACTURED EXPORTS AND MANUFACTURING OUTPUT

The importance of manufactured exports does not lie solely in their relative contribution to total exports, but also in their impact on the performance of manufacturing output. To relate manufactured exports to manufactured output, we need a measure of output compatible with the definition of manufactured exports. This requires adjustment of the usual output index for manufacturing, since the food and drink and tobacco groups are not included in manufactured exports and, moreover, certain inter-industry transactions are double-counted in the output index.[1]

In Chart 8 the annual movements in the volume of manufactured output and exports are plotted. Variations in the movements of the output and exports curves are similar, allowing for the much more rapid growth of exports. Particularly noticeable is the strong upsurge in volume of output and exports from 1958.

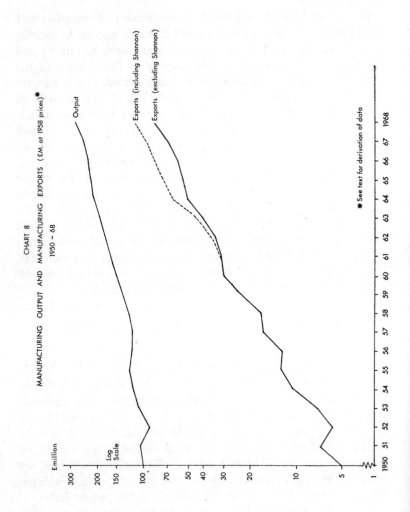

CHART 8

MANUFACTURING OUTPUT AND MANUFACTURING EXPORTS (£M. at 1958 prices)*

1950 – 68

* See text for derivation of data

By 1958 output had recovered to the 1955 level, having declined in 1956 and 1957, and although the very strong growth rate of output from 1958–61 included recovery factors, it also undoubtedly incorporated elements of the longer-term accelera- tion in output growth. It will be noted that this expansion in output was accompanied by a strong expansion of exports in 1959 and 1960, and it is tempting to assign a leading role in the process to exports. However, it should be mentioned that there was also a very marked rise in volume of domestic sale (i.e. output less exports) and that, in fact, the rise in domestic sale accounted for the greater proportion of the rise in output in these years, as is shown in Table 22.

Table 22: Gross value of output, exports and domestic sale in manufacturing (1953 prices) in selected years*

	1950	Change 1950 –58	1958	Change 1958 –61	1961	Change 1961 –68	1968
	£m	£m	£m	£m	£m	£m	£m
Gross value of output	99.8	+23.1	122.9	+42.0	164.9	+88.1	253.0
Exports	4.9	+12.1	17.1	+13.6	30.7	+54.5	85.3
Domestic sale	94.9	+11.0	105.8	+28.4	134.2	+33.5	167.7

*The figures here exclude the output and exports of the Shannon Industrial Estate because of their different composition and determinants. Shannon output has been excluded on the assumption that it is equal to Shannon exports, since almost all of the output of Shannon is exported. Domestic sale is equivalent to gross value less exports.

Sources: *Irish Statistical Bulletin* and *Trade and Shipping Statistics.* The derivation of the figures is explained in note 1, Chapter 6.

Table 22 gives data on output, exports and domestic sale for the four years 1950, 1958, 1961 and 1968. It is clear that slightly over one-half of the comparatively small increase in output between 1950 and 1958 was accounted for by the rise in exports. In the years 1958 to 1961, which in the case of manufacturing seem to incorporate the transition to a higher longer-term growth rate, only 32 per cent of the rise in output was due to the rise in exports. This would suggest that the expansion of both domestic demand and exports was important in initiating faster growth. It does not, of course, tell us which, if either, was the primary causal factor. Over the period 1961–68, exports took over as the more important contributor, accounting for 62 per cent of the rise in output.

Table 23: Average annual rates of growth of gross value of output, exports and domestic sale in manufacturing (1953 prices), 1950–58, 1958–61 and 1961–68

	1950–58	1958–61	1961–68
	%	%	%
Gross value of output	2.6	10.3	6.3
Exports	16.8	21.6	15.7
Domestic sale	1.4	8.2	3.2

Source: Based on data in Table 22.

The average annual growth rates implied in the figures in Table 22 are given in Table 23. The figures show clearly that, because of the low initial ratio of manufactured exports to manufactured output, the rapid rate of growth of exports from 1950 to 1958 was not sufficient to secure a high rate of growth of output, given the very low rate of growth of domestic demand, which was particularly badly affected by deflationary measures in 1952 and 1956–57. The very much larger growth of output from 1958 to 1961, which comprised both recovery factors as well as the transition to a higher long-term growth rate, was partly due to a higher growth rate of exports and the larger weight of exports in output, but was mainly due to the very substantial rate of growth of domestic sale. Of course, the impact of exports on output comes not only from direct stimulation of demand but also in generating, via multiplier effects, a faster rate of growth of domestic demand. However, there is no reason to expect that the magnitude of the export multiplier was any greater in this period than earlier, so that the larger increases in manufactured exports in this period could scarcely account for more than a small part of the much larger increase in domestic demand. Domestic demand for manufactured output is also affected by the expansion of total exports both through multiplier effects and its influence on the authorities' use of stimulatory policies, but consideration of these aspects is deferred until Part IV, which discusses the course of demand more comprehensively.

In the period 1961–68 a high growth rate of output was maintained as a result both of rapid expansion of exports and a moderate rate of growth of domestic sale. Comparing 1950–58 with 1961–68, we find that although the growth of volume of exports was slightly lower in the second period, its impact in raising output was greater because of the increasing weight of exports; the faster growth of domestic demand was also a significant factor in lifting the growth rate of output.

The correlation between the annual first differences in volume of manufacturing output and manufactured exports for the eighteen observations from 1950 to 1968 is 0.75, significant at the 0.01 per cent level. However, it must be pointed out that increased exports formed a substantial part of the increase in output volume throughout, and clearly this 'numerical' fact alone forms part of the reason for the correlation apart from any dynamic interaction between exports and growth of output. Changes in the volume of output were also closely related to changes in the volume of domestic sale (i.e. output less exports), the correlation between the first differences being 0.91. But it is of interest to note that the correlation between the annual changes in domestic sale and in exports was also positive, though its value (0.42) was significant only at the 0.1 level.

A positive correlation between changes in domestic sale and in exports could arise due to forces operating in either direction. It could be argued, for instance, that large increases in manufactured exports encourage a more rapid expansion of domestic demand for manufacturing output, both because increased incomes are generated in the industries producing exports and because the authorities tend to be more willing to tolerate, or even stimulate, an expansion of domestic demand. In so far as domestic demand is curbed because of inadequate export expansion, the more relevant criterion is, as mentioned earlier, total exports of goods and services rather than manufactured exports alone. For much of the period it is unlikely that, despite their rapid rate of growth, variations in manufactured exports alone could have had a major influence on home demand, given the low initial level of such exports. It might be argued, however, that movements in manufactured exports were closely related to movements in exports as a whole, because of the great dependence of all categories of exports on the U K market. There is some truth in this but it is hardly the whole of the story, as may be seen from the exports charts shown earlier.

The stimulus to demand and domestic output arising from an increase in manufactured exports, or any other export category, depends also on the import content of such exports. It would be necessary to have information on the import content of exports and domestic sale in order to assess their relative contribution to domestic activity rather than to gross value of output, which includes imported materials. The necessary data are unavailable except for a few years in the 1960s. It is of interest to note, however, that the direct and indirect import content of manufactured exports, as defined earlier, amounted to 47.5 per cent in 1964 and rose to 53.3 per cent in 1968.[2] About half of the rise was due to more rapid growth of classes of exports with relatively high import content and the rest to increases in the average import content of manufactured exports. These import shares compare with 19.2 per cent and 20.8 per cent for the import content of other merchandise exports for 1964 and 1968 respectively. The import content of household expenditure was about 27 per cent in both years, while the import content of another important demand category, building and construction, was 25.5 per cent in 1964, rising slightly to 27.6 per cent in 1968. The high average import content of manufactured exports combined with the rise between 1964 and 1968 means that about 59 per cent of the increase in manufactured exports from 1964 to 1968 was absorbed directly and indirectly by imports. Only 25 per cent of the increase in other merchandise exports was so absorbed, while only 32 per cent of the increase in investment in building and construction represented imports. While these figures are based on values for only two years and may not reflect true marginal propensities to import, they indicate that a given absolute increase in domestic demand can have a greater stimulative impact on output than the same rise in manufactured exports.

The causation underlying a positive correlation between changes in domestic sale and exports could operate in the opposite direction —from domestic demand to exports. This could be due to increased incentives to invest when demand is rising, to the creation of a stronger domestic base capable of absorbing more of the overhead costs and providing a cushion against the greater risk and competition of export markets, and to productivity gains and reductions in cost (or in the rate of increase in costs) due to output growth. What is clear is that the evidence does not support the view that manufactured exports were held back when domestic demand for manufactured goods was expanding relatively fast. Had the growth of domestic demand been faster in the earlier period, it is unlikely that the growth of exports would have been reduced. It is reasonable to conclude that the low growth rate of output in the earlier period was largely due to a demand deficiency which the rapid growth of manufactured exports alone could not remove.[3] Thus the dependence of the Irish economy on exports does not minimise the importance of a satisfactory growth of domestic demand in achieving a high growth of output.

DETERMINANTS OF GROWTH OF MANUFACTURED EXPORTS

Even if domestic demand expansion was of considerable importance in ensuring faster output growth, there is no doubt that the rapid growth of manufactured exports was an important source of demand expansion. We now consider further the forces underlying the rapid growth of manufactured exports, focusing particularly on exports to the U K, which was by far the largest market.

Table 24 shows the average annual rate of growth of Irish-manufactured exports in comparison with the growth rates of world exports of manufactures and U K manufactured imports for the three sub-periods given in Table 23. The growth rate of Irish manufactured exports was markedly faster than that of world manufactured exports for all three sub-periods. The Irish growth rate also exceeded the growth of U K imports, although the relationship between the two was closer than between Irish exports and world exports. However, a relationship between U K imports and Irish exports is hardly surprising since a substantial, though declining, share of Irish manufactured exports go to the U K.[4] In 1953 80 per cent of Irish manufactured exports went to the U K. By 1958 the proportion had declined only slightly to 78½ per cent. Since then there has been a substantial fall to 71½

Table 24: Average annual growth rates of world manufactured
exports and U K manufactured imports, 1950–58, 1958–61
and 1961–68

	1950–58	1958–61	1961–68
	%	%	%
World manufactured exports:			
Value ($)	10.0	8.7	10.7
Volume	7.3	8.0	9.6
U K manufactured imports:			
Value (£)	10.1	16.1	14.5
Volume	n.a.	14.6	9.0
Irish manufactured exports (excluding Shannon):			
Value (£)	19.4	21.3	19.3
Volume*	16.8	18.0	15.8
Irish manufactured exports (including Shannon):			
Value (£)	19.4	23.3	23.4
Volume	16.8	20.0	20.8

*The difference between these figures and those given in Table 23 is that
here manufactured exports refer to S I T C Sections 5–8 whereas the figures
in Table 23 include also exports of petroleum products.

Sources: Irish data from *Trade and Shipping Statistics* and *Irish Statistical
Bulletin*. World exports figures from United Nations, *Yearbook of International Trade Statistics*. U K value figures from *The British Economy: Key
Statistics 1900–1966* (London and Cambridge Economic Service), Table K
and *Overseas Trade Accounts of the United Kingdom*. U K volume figures
derived by deflating the value data by the import unit value index for
manufactured goods given in *Annual Abstract of Statistics* and *Monthly
Digest of Statistics*.

per cent in 1963 and 64 per cent in 1968.[5] It is clear, therefore,
that Irish exports of manufactures to places other than the
U K have been growing faster than exports to the U K market.
But if the share of Irish exports going to the U K has been
declining, this is not because of a decline in the Irish share of
the British market. In fact, the Irish share of U K imports has
been rising. For example, the ratio of Irish manufactured exports
to the U K to U K manufactured imports in each of the years
1963 to 1968 is as follows:[6]

	1963	1964	1965	1966	1967	1968
Irish Share (%)	1.74	1.74	1.67	1.75	1.84	1.82

However, the rise in the share from 1963 to 1968 (0.08 percentage points) must be regarded as small. In that period Irish manufactured exports to the U K (in current values) rose by £39.2 million from £29.6 million to £68.8 million. If in 1968 Ireland had merely maintained the 1963 share of the U K market, the rise would still have been £36 million. The balance of the total rise (£3.2 million) is due to the overall rise in the share of the U K market.

Ireland's overall share of the U K market may change either because of the commodity composition of exports or because of changes in competitiveness in the widest sense.[7] The first effect arises because U K imports of different commodities grow at different rates, so that even if there is no change in the Irish share for every commodity, the overall share could rise (fall) if those imports in which the initial share was largest grew most (least). On the other hand, the overall share may change due to changes in Ireland's relative competitive position, which we here regard as being shown by a change in the share of the market for a given commodity. It should be noted that competitiveness, in this sense of the term, must be taken to denote, not merely price competitiveness, but also all of the other factors (such as better delivery dates, more aggressive selling, special arrangements with associated companies, etc.) that may be expected to raise the market share of a given commodity.

In order to assess the relative importance of changes in the commodity composition of U K imports as against changes in competitiveness, we have broken down the annual data for the years 1963 and 1968 into S I T C two-digit categories. The share of Irish exports in U K imports for each category in each of the years 1963 and 1968 is shown in column (1) of Table 25. Of the twenty-five classes distinguished, in only six was there a fall in the Irish share. In the remaining nineteen classes, the Irish share rose and, in all but one of these, the rise was far greater than the rise in the aggregate share. An estimate of the change in Irish exports due to changes in competitiveness was derived as follows. The Irish share of U K imports of each class in 1963 was applied to U K imports of this class in 1968, the results being given in

Table 25: Shares of Irish manufactured exports to the UK in UK manufactured imports in 1963 and 1968

SITC No.		(1) Irish share 1963	(1) Irish share 1968	(2) Hypothetical exports in 1968 using 1963 share £000	(3) Actual Irish exports in 1968 £000	(4) Column (3) minus column (2) £000	(5) % Change in UK imports 1963-68
		%	%	£000	£000	£000	%
51	Organic and inorganic chemicals	0.05	0.21	84	350	266	120.7
53	Dyeing, tanning, etc, materials	0.42	0.78	112	205	93	129.3
54	Medicinal and pharmaceutical products	2.96	8.01	576	1,560	985	208.8
55	Essential oils, toilet preparations	0.45	2.19	94	455	361	60.1
56	Fertilizers, manufactured	0.03	0.02	8	6	−2	45.4
58	Plastic materials, etc.	0.31	0.56	255	464	208	90.5
52, 57, 59	Mineral tar, etc.; explosives; chemicals n.e.s.	0.39	0.97	261	657	395	94.0
61	Leather, leather manufactures	11.13	12.41	3,736	4,167	431	25.8
62	Rubber manufactures, n.e.s.	0.95	2.42	263	669	405	228.3
63	Wood manufactures (excl. furniture)	1.34	1.44	1,284	1,444	160	81.8
64	Paper and paper manufactures	1.87	1.94	3,460	3,602	142	62.7
65	Textile yarn, fabrics, etc.	4.15	6.02	9,583	13,920	4,337	59.7
66	Non-metallic mineral manufactures	0.98	1.13	3,296	3,804	509	113.3
67, 68	Metal, wrought and unwrought	0.24	0.31	1,740	2,237	496	133.4
69	Manufactures of metal n.e.s.	2.91	5.89	2,060	4,162	2,102	124.6
71	Machinery (non-electric)	0.54	0.37	3,432	2,366	−1,065	149.4
72	Electrical machinery	3.39	2.99	8,022	7,094	−929	155.6
73	Transport equipment	0.48	0.22	1,525	711	−814	429.1
81	Plumbing, heating etc., fixtures	2.90	5.20	228	410	181	53.1
82	Furniture	2.88	3.52	404	495	91	136.7
83	Travel goods, handbags etc.	7.50	6.32	436	367	−69	71.5
84	Clothing	6.47	9.60	7,119	10,561	3,442	70.0
85	Footwear	8.95	7.30	2,937	2,398	−539	67.8
86	Scientific instruments etc.	0.05	0.71	58	783	725	103.8
89	Miscellaneous manufactures n.e.s.	2.75	3.21	5,044	5,890	846	99.7
	Total manufactured exports	1.74	1.82	56,017*	68,777	12,759	121.5

*This is the sum of the items in column (2).
Sources: Trade and Shipping Statistics, Trade Statistics of Ireland, Overseas Trade Accounts of the United Kingdom.

column (2) of Table 25. This shows what exports would have been in 1968 if competitiveness (in our sense of the term) had not improved or disimproved. Actual Irish exports of each class in 1968 are given in column (3). The difference between column (3) and column (2), which is shown in column (4), gives a measure of the change in exports due to changes in competitiveness.

It emerges that, of the total rise in Irish manufactured exports of £39.2 million, almost one-third (£12.8 million) was, on balance, due to increased competitiveness. While there was a marked decline in competitiveness in the case of a few commodities, notably machinery and transport equipment and footwear, in the vast majority of commodities there have been substantial gains. We have carried this analysis only as far as the S I T C two-digit level, but it is possible that at a further level of disaggregation the proportion of the increase in exports due to improved competitiveness would be greater. Moreover, the decline in competitiveness in the case of machinery and transport equipment is to a large extent more apparent than real since it is due to very substantial increases in imports by the U K of items (e.g. aircraft) that are not manufactured in Ireland at all.

Why, then, given the large improvement in competitiveness at the commodity level, did the overall share rise so little? The reason is that those items in which Ireland held a relatively large share of the U K market in 1963 grew more slowly than total U K imports of manufactures. This may be seen by comparing column (5) of Table 25, which gives the percentage change in U K imports from 1963 to 1968, with column (1) which shows the Irish shares in 1963. It is especially notable that in the case of manufactures of leather, textiles, travel goods, clothing and footwear, where Ireland had a comparatively high share of the U K market, the growth of U K imports was well below the overall growth of U K imports. Thus, only by increasing substantially the market shares at the commodity level was it possible to maintain, and increase slightly, the overall share. If in 1968 Ireland had simply maintained the 1963 commodity shares, then the overall share would have fallen from 1.74 per cent (in 1963) to 1.48 per cent (in 1968). Thus the commodity composition of U K imports changed in a manner unfavourable to Irish exports and offset most of the gain in competitiveness at the commodity level.

The position from 1963 to 1968 may be summarised as follows.

The total rise in Irish manufactured exports to the UK was £39.2 million. Of this, £36 million can be attributed to the overall growth of UK imports. This figure represents the rise in Irish exports assuming no change in the overall share of the UK market. The balance (£3.2 million) is the amount of the rise due to the increase in the Irish overall share of the UK market. The rise in market share can, in turn, be divided into the rise (fall) due to improved (reduced) competitiveness, and the rise (fall) due to changes in the commodity composition of UK imports. A rise (fall) in competitiveness is here equated with a rise (fall) in the market shares of individual commodities. As already shown, improved competitiveness in this sense would, *ceteris paribus,* have added £12.8 million to Irish exports. The difference between this figure and the amount of the rise in exports due to the rise in the overall share gives an estimate of the effect of changes in the commodity composition of UK imports. The resulting figure (−£9.5 million) indicates that adverse changes in commodity composition of UK imports tended to offset most of the gains from improved competitiveness in this period.

It would appear from this analysis that a proper understanding of developments in Irish manufactured exports requires a considerable measure of disaggregation. It may also be noted that the aggregate relation between Irish exports and British imports is likely to alter somewhat as time goes on. For one thing, there were relatively rapid increases between 1963 and 1968 in the Irish share of some categories of UK imports which have grown, and probably will continue to grow, at a high rate, so that the drag on the overall share imposed by the concentration in slowly-growing categories is likely to diminish.

The results of similar analyses for two earlier five-year periods (1953–58 and 1958–63) are set out in Table 26. For convenience the results for the period 1963–68 are also given in the table. The overall growth of UK manufactured imports was a factor of major importance in the two periods 1958–63 and 1963–68 but was relatively less important in the period 1953–58. This is immediately clear from the percentage increases in UK imports, which were 40 per cent, 74 per cent and 122 per cent in the periods 1953–58, 1958–63 and 1963–68 respectively. The corresponding increases in Irish manufactured exports in these periods were 140 per cent, 116 per cent and 133 per cent respectively.

Table 26: Sources of growth in Irish manufactured exports to the U K, 1953–58, 1958–63, 1963–68*

Changes in exports due to	1953–58	1958–63	1963–68
	£m	Current	values
Growth of U K imports	2.3	10.2	36.0
Changes in commodity composition of U K imports	3.2	3.6	—9.5
Competitiveness	2.5	2.1	12.8
Total change	8.0	15.9	39.2

*The derivation of the figures for 1963–68 has already been explained in the text. The figures for 1953–58 and 1958–63 were derived on a similar basis, using for each period the market shares of the initial year of the period.

Sources: As for Table 25. Irish exports to the U K, were reclassified on a S I T C basis for 1953 and 1958 with the aid and advice of officers of the C S O.

As is implied in these two sets of figures, the proportionate rise in the Irish overall share was greatest in the first period (70 per cent) and least in the last period (4½ per cent); the rise in the second period was 24 per cent (from 1.40 to 1.74 per cent).

In the first two periods, changes in the commodity composition of U K imports favoured Irish exports. In other words, the U K imports that grew fastest were those in which Ireland had, on balance, a relatively high share at the beginning of the period. This position was reversed in the period 1963–68, when the commodity composition of U K imports altered unfavourably for Ireland. In all periods there was a relatively substantial increase in exports due to improved competitiveness, the rise being lowest, both absolutely and relatively, in the period 1958–63.

If it is granted that an increase in the Irish share of U K manufactured imports of individual commodities is an indication of greater competitiveness in the widest sense, to what can we attribute the sustained improvement in the competitiveness of Irish manufactured exports? One possible factor could be a fall in unit wage cost in Irish manufacturing industry relative to the U K or to other countries exporting to the U K.

Unit Wage Cost and Price Competitiveness

In Table 27 we compare, *inter alia*, changes in unit wage cost

Table 27: Changes in unit wage cost, etc., in manufacturing industry
for various countries, 1953–58, 1958–63 and 1963–68

	1953–58	1958–63	1963–68
	% Change in each period		
Ireland:			
Unit wage cost	16.8	12.5	15.8
Unit wage cost excluding food, drink and tobacco	8.0	5.7	12.8
Export price of manufactures (£)	2.3	5.6	19.1
United Kingdom:			
Unit wage cost	24	9	12
Import price of manufactures (£)	—7	5	34
Export price of manufactures ($)	9	8	4
United States:			
Unit wage cost	2	—6	2
Export price of manufactures ($)	13	4	13
Japan:			
Unit wage cost	1*	15	5
Export price of manufactures ($)	—8	—7	0
West Germany:			
Unit wage cost	12	19	1
Export price of manufactures ($)	0	10	2
France:			
Unit wage cost	8	16	6
Export price of manufactures ($)	2	—2	9
Italy:			
Unit wage cost	18*	6	—5
Export price of manufactures ($)	—14	—6	—4

*1954–58.

Sources: Irish unit wage cost data based on *Census of Industrial Production* reports and *Quarterly Industrial Production Inquiry*. Irish price of manufactured exports from *Irish Statistical Bulletin*. All other data from *National Institute Economic Review*, various issues.

in manufacturing industry in Ireland and a number of other countries for the periods 1953–58, 1958–63 and 1963–68. It will readily be seen that it is not possible to establish any simple link between relative changes in unit wage cost and the improvement in competitiveness in our sense of the term. In 1963–68, when there was a substantial rise in exports due to greater competitiveness, unit wage cost in manufacturing rose more in Ireland than in any other country in the table, including the U K.[8] In the period 1958–63 unit wage cost rose more in Ireland than in the U K, though less than in Germany, Japan and France. Only from 1953–58 did Ireland's unit wage cost rise less than in the U K, but it increased more than in any other country in the table, except Italy.

One reason why the connection between relative changes in unit wage cost and in export competitiveness is bound to be vague is that the unit wage cost figures are measured in national currency units. Clearly countries can and do seek to escape the consequences of adverse movements in relative unit wage cost by devaluation. In Table 27 we also show changes in export prices of manufactures, measured in dollars for all countries except Ireland. As may be seen from the table, there is, in general, no relation whatever between movements in unit wage cost and in the dollar price of exports. One reason for this is devaluation. Thus, for example, the French devaluations of 1957 and 1958 helped to mitigate the effect on export prices of the relatively large increases in unit wage cost. Similarly, the effect of the 1967 sterling devaluation was to raise the import price in sterling of most goods exported from outside the sterling area to the U K. Thus the 34 per cent rise in import prices of manufactures for the U K includes the effect of the sterling devaluation, while the sterling price of exports from countries other than Ireland may have risen by about 15 per cent due to devaluation.

Prior to 1963–68 there was a pronounced tendency for the export price to rise less than unit wage cost even for economies such as Japan, which did not alter its exchange rate, or Germany, which revalued its currency upward against the dollar. A notable exception is the U S A, where increases in export prices exceeded changes in unit wage cost by quite a large margin. Since 1963 the tendency has been for export price changes to come close to or exceed changes in unit wage cost—Japan being an exception.

A possible reason for the divergence between changes in unit wage costs and export prices is that manufacturers engage in price discrimination, charging lower prices for exported goods than for similar goods sold on the home market. This factor would explain divergences in the *level* of domestic versus export prices. However, it would not explain divergences in the *rate of change* in these prices, unless the degree of price discrimination altered. There are very definite limits to the extent to which this could continue in the absence of special factors, such as government subsidies to exports or increased protection on the home market. In the absence of such special factors, an increasing degree of price discrimination would imply a continually diminishing contribution from exports toward reducing overheads and increasing net profits. It is possible that the greater correspondence between movements in unit wage cost and export prices between 1963 and 1968 is due to the fact that a limit was reached in the degree of discrimination between export and domestic prices for most economies.

It could, of course, be argued that unit wage cost in the production of exported goods tends to rise far less than unit wage cost in manufacturing as a whole. This is so because average earnings tend to rise at much the same rate in all manufacturing industries but productivity grows at widely different rates.[9] If the growth of output of manufactured goods entering world trade exceeds the growth of other manufactured goods, it is likely that productivity growth would tend to be greatest in the case of exports. Some support for this view as applied to Ireland is given in Table 27, where we show changes in unit wage cost in manufacturing industry, excluding the food, drink and tobacco groups. This definition of manufacturing industry corresponds closely with the definition of manufactured exports, which excludes food, drink and tobacco exports.[10] Unit wage cost in Irish manufacturing industry so defined moved much more closely in line with the export price of manufactures in 1953–58 and 1958–63 than did unit wage cost in manufacturing industry as a whole.[11] The greater divergence in 1963–68 was possibly due to increases in imported materials prices occasioned by the devaluation of November 1967.[12]

For countries generally, differences in the rate of change in materials prices compared with changes in unit wage cost is another possible reason for divergence between movements in unit wage cost and the export price of manufactures. Profits per unit of output may also change at a different rate from unit wage cost. Furthermore, special factors, such as the introduction of export subsidies or alterations in trade barriers, may also lead to a divergence between the movements of export prices and unit wage costs. Thus the tax relief for exports introduced in Ireland in 1956 might account for part of the lower rise in the export price from 1953 to 1958.[13] Given the variety of factors that may affect export prices, apart from changes in unit wage cost, it is not surprising that any connection between movements in competitiveness generally, and relative changes in unit wage cost is, to say the least, obscure.

Changes in the Irish export price relative to the U K import price or the export prices of other countries seem to fit in somewhat better with our findings on Ireland's competitive performance in the U K market. From 1963 to 1968 the Irish export price rose far less than the U K import price for manufactures—both prices measured in sterling. Moreover, in this period the Irish export price also rose less than the export price of several of the other countries in Table 27, when these prices are converted to sterling.[14] In the period 1958–63, when there was only a small improvement in Ireland's competitive performance, the Irish export price rose at about the same rate as the U K import price, though more than the export price of all other countries except West Germany. The relative price performance in the first period (1953–58) does not, however, fit in very well with the relatively substantial increases in Ireland's market shares for most commodities in the same period. The Irish export price rose by 2 per cent compared with a fall of 7 per cent in the U K import price, while of the other countries only the U S A had a higher rise in its export price. However, the Irish share of the U K market for most commodities was so small in 1953 that the factors determining variations in shares may be so specific that they cannot be linked with overall price competitiveness.

We may summarise this discussion of price competitiveness by saying that there is some indication that improvements in competitiveness in the widest sense may be partly explained by changes in the Irish export price relative to the U K import price and the export prices of other countries, though the evidence

E

we have presented is not very conclusive. We also suggested that changes in the export price of manufactures can only be related very indirectly, and with many qualifications, to changes in unit wage cost in manufacturing. This is not to say, however, that a massive and sustained disimprovement in unit wage cost relative to competing countries would not ultimately affect export competitiveness. Moreover, as the Irish share of the market in any commodity increases, exports are likely to become more sensitive to relative price movements.

The Anglo-Irish Free Trade Area Agreement

Another possible factor accounting for Ireland's increased competitiveness in the U K in the period 1963–68 is the Anglo-Irish Free Trade Area Agreement (A I F T A A), which was signed in December 1965 and became operative from 1 July 1966. However, the A I F T A A made little difference to most classes of Irish manufactured exports which already enjoyed free access to the U K market. The products which benefited from the agree-

Table 28: Irish manufactured exports to the U K as a share of U K manufactured imports in each year, 1963–68

S I T C No.		1963	1964	1965	1966	1967	1968
		%	%	%	%	%	%
5	Chemicals	0.30	0.39	0.44	0.65	0.65	0.89
6	Manufactured goods classified by material	1.78	1.88	1.89	1.88	2.06	2.00
7	Machinery and transport equipment	1.18	0.93	0.72	0.79	0.90	0.86
8	Manufactured articles n.e.s.	3.71	3.89	4.10	4.34	4.27	4.50
65	Textile yarn, fabrics, etc.	4.15	4.30	5.02	5.28	5.60	6.02
84	Clothing	6.47	6.60	8.37	8.96	8.97	9.60
85	Footwear	8.95	10.44	11.68	9.60	8.45	7.31

Sources: *Trade and Shipping Statistics, Trade Statistics of Ireland, Overseas Trade Accounts of the United Kingdom.*

ment were those containing more than 5 per cent silk or artificial fibre, to which heavy duties had previously applied. Table 28 sets out for each year from 1963 to 1968 the share of Irish manufactured exports to the U K in total U K manufactured imports for each of the four S I T C one-digit categories, and for certain subdivisions that might be expected to benefit from the A I F T A A. There has been a substantial increase in the Irish share of U K imports of textiles and clothing since the A I F T A A became operative, but the Irish share in U K footwear imports has declined considerably since 1965. However, the removal of the restrictions on the use of raw materials of artificial fibre was not expected to be of great importance for the footwear industry, the main beneficiaries being the textile and clothing industries. The fall in the Irish share of British footwear imports really reflected the displacement, at the lower-quality end of the market, of footwear formerly produced in the U K by imports from the Eastern and Far Eastern countries. It did not, therefore, reflect a major loss of competitiveness in the area of the footwear market in which Ireland was competing.

It is also apparent, however, that the Irish share in the textile and clothing classes was rising rapidly prior to the operation of the A I F T A A. The largest rise in the textile and clothing shares took place in 1965, the year *before* the A I F T A A became operative. However, in that year U K imports of these commodities fell drastically, and the increase in the Irish share reflected not an increase in the level of exports but simply the maintenance of the 1964 level. It is possible that the rise in the Irish share in 1965 was influenced by the A I F T A A, the negotiation of which took place during 1965, in that special arrangements may have been entered into between exporters and importers to maintain the level of Irish exports in anticipation of the operation of the A I F T A A. Moreover, the rise in the share is not the only measure of the benefit of the A I F T A A since the relevant comparison is with what might have happened in the absence of the A I F T A A.

However, while part of the improvement in Irish competitiveness might be accounted for by the A I F T A A, clearly it is not the only, or indeed the major, factor involved,[15] since the Irish share in many commodities, which did not at all benefit from the A I F T A A, rose markedly. Even in the case of the commodities that did benefit, the share was already rising and possibly would have gone on rising somewhat in the absence of the A I F T A A.

Exploitation of Competitive Potential

Another possible explanation of Ireland's rising market shares is that the country exploited its potential competitiveness to a greater degree. Thus, for example, Irish exports of several products (such as certain chemicals, scientific instruments, etc.) were negligible in 1963 simply because Ireland did not produce many of these items. The expansion in exports in such cases has come about mainly because of the establishment of new firms. No doubt the establishment of these new firms, and their ability to compete in export markets, was mainly due to the range of government incentives offered, notably industrial grants and export tax relief, as well as other factors, such as the availability of labour at average *levels* of earnings below those in other countries. Since the level of wage cost depends on the average earnings level relative to the level of labour productivity, presumably any deficiency in the average level of labour productivity in Ireland relative to other countries was offset by the combined effect of lower wage levels, government incentives, etc. Given that the range of government incentives did not change markedly between 1963 and 1968, it is reasonable to argue that the potential already existed in 1963 and was taken advantage of as new firms, Irish and foreign, were induced to establish factories in Ireland.

Even where a country has a price advantage in a particular product, exports do not take place automatically without a measure of entrepreneurial and marketing effort. They do not, *a fortiori*, take place automatically when a country has a potential price advantage in the production of some product which it does not at present produce. In a country that is comparatively new to industrialisation, as Ireland is, the realisation of its export potential may take some considerable time. Development of exports can, to some extent, be likened to a learning process: an initial breakthrough provides experience that facilitates further growth. Successful entry to one market provides the confidence for expansion to other markets, and the example of one firm tends to be followed by others. Nor, in this regard, ought one to neglect the cumulated efforts of Coras Tráchtála in its promotional work. These factors are reflected not only in rising shares of U K imports but even more so in the successful penetration of many new markets in recent years.

The increased export-mindedness of Irish manufacturers, as well as the introduction of suitable policy incentives, antedated the acceleration in the growth of the economy and must be regarded as a major cause of the rapid development in manufactured exports. In the early 1950s the view began to gain ground that the policy of protection had not been successful in increasing employment and reducing emigration to a degree that would stabilise population, let alone increase it. During the 1950s it was gradually recognised that, in an economy as small as Ireland, rapid growth of industry would require rapid growth of industrial exports, though, as we argue later, there was insufficient recognition of the need for a reasonable growth of home demand as well as export demand. We need do no more here than to indicate briefly the time sequence of important policy measures, since the policies for export development and their effects have already been the subject of detailed studies.[16] The first major step, taken in 1949, was the establishment of the Industrial Development Authority as a body responsible for promoting industrial development, including the attraction of foreign industry. This was followed in 1952 by the introduction of a grants scheme to cover part of the cost of buildings and equipment for new establishments. This represented a marked change in the form of incentives to industrialisation. Apart altogether from the theoretical arguments about the relative merits of subsidies *versus* protection as a means of encouraging industrial development, it is likely that the viability of new projects will be assessed more rigorously when public money is being paid out in grants than when the cost is partly concealed and diffused, as in the case of tariffs. Moreover, since existing establishments can bring strong pressure to bear against the payment of public money to a new firm which would compete with them in the home market, the grants method inevitably tended to favour new projects geared towards export markets.[17] Although the 1952 legislation was confined to the so-called undeveloped areas, the grants scheme was extended to all areas in 1956 and was given a more explicit export bias in 1959, following the emphasis in the First Programme for Economic Expansion (1958) on the development of production for export markets. The need to encourage exports had been explicitly recognised earlier in important legislation in 1956 which provided tax remissions on profits derived from increased manufactured exports. In subsequent years these measures were further developed and accompanied by other incentives such as improved credit facilities, tax concessions on depreciation of capital, etc. An important symbolic measure was the amelioration in 1958 of the restrictions imposed by the Control of Manufactures Acts, which sought to keep control of industry in the hands of Irish nationals; these restrictions were removed entirely in 1964.

An indication of the importance of these measures is given in the *Survey of Grant-Aided Industry* (1967). This shows that exports of new grant-aided projects in manufacturing industry amounted to over £29 million in 1966,[18] or 50 per cent of total manufactured exports in that year. Of this, about £26 million may be attributed to projects that commenced production in 1960 or subsequently.[19] This represented two-thirds of the rise in manufactured exports from 1960 to 1966. The exports of the grant-aided projects in manufacturing in 1966 accounted for 75 per cent of their gross output. While some of the projects might have developed without any special assistance, there can be little doubt that the government incentives and the promotional work of the Industrial Development Authority played a major part in securing their establishment.

The development of the Shannon Industrial Estate is a special case of development in a customs-free area. Although this customs-free area had been created as far back as 1947, progress in attracting industry began only with the creation in 1959 of a special authority, the Shannon Free Airport Development Company, with powers and finance to attract industry to the area. Complete exemption from taxation of profits derived from exports is provided for all industries in the area up to 1983. All goods entering the area and intended for re-export enter and leave the area without imposition of customs or excise duties and with minimal customs supervision. Exports from Shannon, which were negligible in 1960, amounted to £35 million in 1968, while imports amounted to £20 million.

CHAPTER 7

Cattle and Beef Exports

EXPORTS of beef and cattle represented one of Ireland's major exports throughout the post-war period. With the more rapid growth of other merchandise exports, cattle and beef exports declined in relative importance, falling from 37 per cent of domestic merchandise exports in 1949 to 27 per cent in 1968, but it remains a vital though highly variable component of total exports.

OUTPUT AND DOMESTIC CONSUMPTION

Chart 9 shows the volume of cattle output (including stock changes), exports, domestic consumption and stock changes from 1947 to 1968.[1] The volume figures are measured in terms of cattle numbers, and the export figures include the live cattle equivalent of dead meat exports. The most striking feature of the chart is the large degree of short-term fluctuation in all the data except those relating to domestic consumption. Stock movements vary enormously, while exports tend to fluctuate relatively more than output. Because of the size of the year-to-year fluctuations, we show in Table 29 annual average figures over each of the five-year periods 1949–53, 1954–58, 1959–63 and 1964–68.

Allowing for short-term fluctuations, the output figures show an upward trend throughout the post-war period. In 1949, output, at 951,000 cattle, was at a higher level than in any of the preceding fifteen years or more. Thereafter, apart from short-term fluctuations, there has been a fairly steady *long-term* upward trend in output, with perhaps some acceleration in the rate of increase from 1964 as a result of the calved heifer subsidy scheme, mentioned already in Chapter 5, and higher guaranteed prices for milk. Both of these factors stimulated a rise in the

CHART 9 : VOLUME OF OUTPUT OF CATTLE, 1947-1968.

A = Output (including stock changes)
B = Five-year moving average of output
C = Exports of live cattle and the live cattle equivalent of beef
D = Exports net of imports
E = Domestic consumption
F = Stock changes

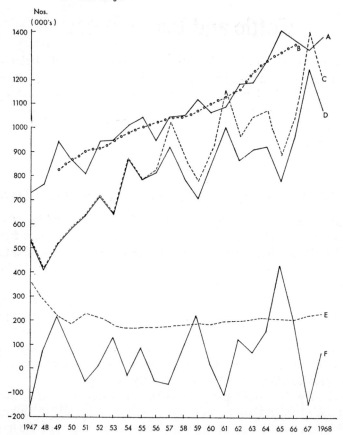

breeding stock. The longer-term trend of output can be seen more clearly in Chart 9 from the curve showing five-year moving averages of output, centred on the middle year.

Domestic consumption, which averaged about 200,000 cattle per annum in pre-war years, rose during the war and reached

Table 29: Output and exports of cattle: five-year averages, 1949–53, 1954–58, 1959–63 and 1964–68

	Annual average for each period				Percentage change between period averages		
	1949–53	1954–58	1959–63	1964–68	1949–53 to 1954–58	1954–58 to 1959–63	1959–63 to 1964–68
	Volume (Nos 000s)				%	%	%
Exports	619	882	976	1,123	42.5	10.7	15.1
Of which: Live animals	478	679	598	662	42.1	−11.9	10.7
Dead meat	141	203	378	461	44.0	86.2	22.0
Exports less imports	618	837	872	1,000	35.5	4.1	14.7
Domestic consumption	206	177	197	214	−14.3	11.5	8.3
Stock changes	80	9	63	143			
Output (including stock changes)	905	1,023	1,132	1,357	13.1	10.6	19.9
	Value (£m current prices)*				%	%	%
Exports	25.4	42.4	53.8	71.2	67.1	26.9	32.2
Output	36.5	49.9	61.4	84.5	36.7	23.0	37.6
	Unit price (£)				%	%	%
Exports	40.8	48.1	55.1	63.5	18.1	14.4	15.2
Output	40.3	48.7	54.3	62.3	20.8	11.5	14.7

*Value and unit price data are based on prices received by farmers. Thus the data here differ slightly from the external trade data, which are valued f.o.b. The differences are more fully discussed later in a footnote to the text.
Sources: *Irish Statistical Bulletin, Agricultural Statistics 1934–1956* and data supplied by the C.S.O.

a peak of 365,000 cattle in 1947. This rise appears to be due to shortages of other foodstuffs and also to the temporary large influx of tourists from the U K immediately after the war. From 1947 to 1954 domestic consumption declined almost without interruption. The fall-off in tourism, the greater availability of other foodstuffs, and the rapid rate of increase in cattle prices due to favourable export conditions probably served to reduce home consumption of beef. From 1954 there was a fairly steady upward trend in total domestic consumption. The growth rate from 1954 to 1968 was much the same as the growth rate of output, but since domestic consumption represents only a fraction of output, the absolute increase was small in relation to the increase in output.

EXPORTS

The vast bulk of the output of cattle and beef is exported—over 80 per cent in most years—and most of the output went to the U K. The conditions under which beef and cattle were exported altered several times during the post-war period. From 1940 until 1954 the U K cattle trade was controlled by the British Ministry of Food, which was the sole purchaser of fat cattle and carcase beef. The 1948 Trade Agreement with the U K was designed to restore pre-war levels of exports of store cattle and fat cattle. Irish store cattle fattened for at least two months in the U K were guaranteed purchase at a price of 5 shillings per cwt liveweight below the price of U K-bred fat cattle. As a result, the prices of fat cattle and dead meat exports tended to be linked to the price of Irish stores fattened in the U K. In 1953 the differential between U K-bred fat cattle and fattened Irish stores was reduced to $4\frac{1}{2}$ shillings with the same two-month waiting period. After 1954 the U K meat and livestock trade was decontrolled and a free market came into operation backed, however, by the U K Fatstock Guarantee Scheme which guaranteed prices for U K producers. In 1956 the waiting period for Irish store cattle was increased to three months but the differential between the guaranteed price for U K-bred and fattened Irish stores was reduced to $3\frac{1}{2}$ shillings per cwt.

In 1959 and 1960 the store cattle trade to the U K was badly affected by the restrictions imposed in Britain on the importation of cattle not tested for bovine tuberculosis. Grants towards the export of fat cattle and dead meat were introduced in Ireland to offset the serious effects of the U K regulations. The tuberculosis eradication scheme was extended rapidly and an increase in the supply of attested store cattle developed. This was aided by a 1960 agreement with the U K which abolished the $3\frac{1}{2}$ shilling per cwt differential between U K-bred fat cattle and attested Irish stores fattened in the U K for three months. By 1962 over 90 per cent of store cattle exported were of fully-attested status and in 1965 the whole country was declared fully attested. The 1965 Anglo-Irish Free Trade Area Agreement extended U K guaranteed prices to 25,000 tons of carcase beef exported annually and reduced the waiting period for Irish stores to two months.[2]

Against this background of changing marketing conditions, exports show a longer-term upward trend. The rate of increase in exports was somewhat faster than in output in the early post-war years. However, exports were well below pre-war levels in the immediate post-war years, and only in 1954 did they surpass the pre-war peak. From 1954 onwards, the rate of increase in exports over the longer run has been close to that of output: from 1954–68 the volume of exports rose by 39 per cent while output grew by 36 per cent. There has been a marked shift in the composition of cattle exports from live animals to dead meat. Up to 1950 dead meat exports formed a comparatively small share of total cattle exports. They rose to 23 per cent of the total in 1951 and, on average, maintained this share up to 1958, when a further sharp rise began, partly in response to U K restrictions on store cattle imports and a government scheme to aid fat cattle and dead meat exports in the years 1960 to 1962. Dead meat exports accounted for 39 per cent of the total in the five years 1959 to 1963 and for 41 per cent in the five years 1964 to 1968. In the two years 1967 to 1968 the proportion rose to 50 per cent of the total, an increase which was, no doubt, stimulated by the provisions of the Anglo-Irish Free Trade Area Agreement extending U K guaranteed prices for up to 25,000 tons of Irish carcase beef per annum. In addition, the Irish government offered guaranteed prices for carcase beef exports to the U K exceeding 25,000 tons per annum.

In fact, most of the rise in dead meat exports has taken place at the expense of exports of fat cattle. However, the expansion

CHART 10 : VALUE AND UNIT PRICE OF CATTLE AND BEEF EXPORTS, 1947-1968

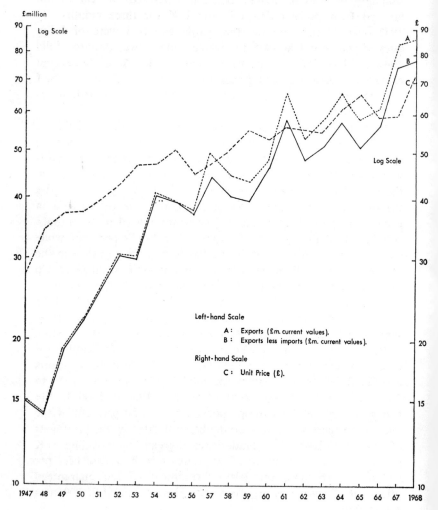

of the dead meat trade also led to the development of a significant volume of trade in imports of live cattle from Northern Ireland for slaughtering in factories. Imports of cattle to the Republic of Ireland are prohibited except for cross-border imports and imports of specialised breeding stock. Up to the mid-1950s, imports were negligible because of controls on the cattle and meat trade in the U K. With removal of controls, and the increased demand by the meat factories, a significant amount of cattle has been imported each year since 1957, so that the rate of increase in total net exports of cattle and beef (i.e. exports less imports) has been somewhat less over the whole post-war period than the rate of increase in gross exports.

The value and unit price of exports for each year from 1947 to 1968 are shown in Chart 10. It should be noted that the figures here refer to the prices received by farmers. They, therefore, differ somewhat from the data in the external trade returns, but the difference was not of major consequence.[3] The unit price is an average that may vary due to changes in the mix of cattle exported as well as changes in the prices of each of the different types of cattle. As may be seen from Chart 10, unit price rose considerably from 1947 to 1953. Major factors in the rise were the worldwide shortage of beef after the Second World War and the boom in prices due to the Korean War. Of the years 1954 to 1957, only in one year (1955) was the unit price significantly above the 1953 level. Thereafter prices moved upwards, though at a slower rate than in the early post-war years and with a considerable degree of fluctuation.

The value of exports, which is the product of volume and unit price, has risen substantially in the post-war period. The rise was exceptionally rapid up to 1954 due to rising prices and recovery in export volume to pre-war levels. There was then a long pause from 1954 to 1959, particularly in net exports, due mainly to relative stagnation in price. It was most unfortunate—and it is something that must be borne in mind in assessing economic performance in the 1950s—that this came at a time when other categories of agricultural exports were badly hit by U K agricultural policy. Since then the value of exports has risen considerably —though not steadily—due both to rising prices and rising volume.

Cattle production differed from most other Irish agricultural production in that there was comparatively free access to export markets at prices that were reasonably remunerative to the farmers. This is reflected in trends in relative output. Measuring the growth rate from the average level of the years 1947 to 1951 to the average for the years 1964 to 1968, the average annual rate of growth in volume of cattle output was 3.0 per cent compared with 2.1 per cent in the volume of total gross output in agriculture (including cattle). On average, net exports represented over 80 per cent of the volume of output sold off farms (i.e. excluding stock changes). Thus, given the comparatively small proportion consumed at home and the likely growth in domestic consumption, most of any increase in output must ultimately be for the export market. Technically speaking, increased supply of cattle depends on a range of factors such as better breeding techniques, elimination of disease, improvement of grasslands, etc., but the dominant factor is the number of milch cows. The government introduced various measures in the post-war years on all these fronts to raise the quantity and quality of output. By far the most significant attempt was the calved heifer subsidy scheme, which was introduced in January 1964, and higher support prices for dairy products—both of which tended to increase output by raising the cow population.

Apart from volume, the other factor affecting the value of cattle exports is the price at which they are sold; and, of course, higher prices may also be expected to induce a larger supply. The vast bulk of live cattle exports went to the U K, as did a significant proportion of dead meat. The other major market for dead meat was the U S A, though there were also large, though erratic, exports to Europe. But the dominant market was the U K, and the price for Irish cattle depended on market conditions there and on the trade agreements negotiated with the U K.

Fluctuations in Exports

The fluctuations in the value of cattle exports are nearly as important as the longer-term trend for the purposes of this study. This category of exports fluctuates far more than most of the remainder of domestic exports and can lead, because of its importance in the total, to sizeable fluctuations in total exports. Thus, in so far as export instability and associated balance of payments difficulties tend to retard growth by evoking measures to restrain expansion of aggregate demand, fluctuations in the price and volume of cattle and beef exports are important in any discussion of post-war economic growth.

As may be seen from Chart 10, fluctuations in cattle output and exports do not coincide. Output is equal to net exports (i.e. exports less imports) plus domestic consumption plus stock changes. The current year-to-year variations in the quantity of net exports and output of cattle are not closely correlated.[4] Given the lack of correlation between the current movements in output and exports, and the relatively small degree of variation in domestic consumption, it is to be expected that there would be a close negative relationship between changes in exports and in stock changes. The correlation for the nineteen first differences from 1949 to 1968 is, in fact, -0.91, significant at the 0.1 per cent level. Indeed, the relationship is such that changes in exports and in stock movements tend to move in the opposite direction in almost a one-for-one relationship: in other words, a rise of 1,000 in the annual change in net exports tends to be associated with a fall of approximately 1,000 in the annual change in stock-building. Thus, on the basis of experience, changes in exports and in stock movements can be looked on as being virtually alternatives to each other. Moreover, changes in exports are significant and positively correlated with changes in stock-building two years earlier ($r=0.66$), suggesting that a build-up of stocks is likely to be associated with increased exports two years later.

This is an important point in the context of the balance of payments and demand management, in view of the size and amplitude of fluctuations in cattle exports. It is one of the reasons why the balance of payments situation in Ireland must be assessed over a period of a few years rather than placing undue emphasis on the figures for one year. This is more widely appreciated in recent years but, as we shall mention later, it does not seem to have been given sufficient weight in the 1950s. In the case of cattle, experience shows that a decline in the volume of exports tends to be matched by an increase in stockbuilding which will be available for export in the next couple of years. A balance of payments deficit associated with a fall in cattle exports will therefore have a self-correcting tendency. Of course, this is not the whole story, since we have been speaking only of volume changes. Clearly it is also important in judging the balance of payments situation to try to assess the prices at which a build-up of stocks is likely to be exported later. It may be pointed out, however, that fluctuations in export prices, though not inconsiderable, have not been anything like so great as fluctuations in export volume, while the correlation between current changes in export price and volume has not been large ($r = -0.39$, significant only at the 10 per cent level). This means that fluctuations in the value of cattle exports were similar to, though slightly less extreme than, fluctuations in volume.

CONCLUSIONS

The bulk of Irish cattle output is exported, and demand conditions in export markets improved during the post-war period largely through negotiation of more satisfactory trade arrangements. The supply of Irish cattle and beef increased as a result of government policy measures and in response to better demand conditions. However, a high degree of variability in output and exports continued throughout the period leading to short-run problems in the balance of payments. Over a few years these fluctuations tend to offset each other, so that it would seem unwise to restrict aggregate demand because of a fall in cattle and beef exports in a single year. The burden could be borne by the external reserves—in the absence of an offsetting rise in the private capital inflow—since it can reasonably be argued that the major reason for holding reserves is to avoid deflationary policies in the face of temporary fluctuations in exports.

CHAPTER 8

Invisible Exports

M o s t analyses of export performance are limited to merchandise exports, and frequently only to manufactured exports. A comprehensive examination of Irish export performance, however, cannot afford to neglect invisibles, which accounted for no less than 57 per cent of exports of goods and services in 1949. Although the proportion fell considerably due to the slow growth—particularly in the 1950s—of invisible, relative to visible, exports, invisibles nevertheless still accounted for 38 per cent of total exports in 1968. Moreover, the behaviour of invisibles was quite different in the two periods we distinguished, and, as we showed in Chapter 2, the greater part of the rise in total exports from 1961–68 compared with 1949–68 can be attributed to the improved performance of invisibles.

Table 30: Main components of invisible exports at current values

| | Percentage share | | Average annual growth rate (%) | |
	1949	1961	1968	1949–61	1961–68
Investment income	24.9	27.1	24.7	4.4	6.5
Emigrants' remittances	12.7	11.5	10.3	2.8	6.2
Other factor income	7.9	7.3	9.3	3.0	11.8
Total factor income	45.5	45.8	44.3	3.7	7.4
Tourism	38.1	35.9	36.7	3.2	8.2
Other known services	8.1	12.6	14.4	7.5	9.9
Total known services	46.1	48.5	51.1	4.1	8.7
Balance not accounted for	8.3	5.6	4.6	—	—
Total invisibles	100.0	100.0	100.0	3.7	7.9
Value of total invisibles (£m)	78.7	121.3	205.2		

Source: *Irish Statistical Bulletin*, various issues.

MAJOR COMPONENTS OF INVISIBLE EXPORTS

Table 30 shows the share of the main components of invisible exports in total invisibles for each of the years 1949, 1961 and 1968, and the average annual growth rates for 1949–61 and 1961–68. The two largest items were tourism, accounting for over one-third of the total, and income on investment abroad, accounting for over one-quarter. Taken together, these two components represented over 60 per cent of total invisibles in all of the years considered. Other important components were emigrants' remittances; other factor income, made up of several items such as commission earnings of importers, pensions from abroad, etc.; and other services, the most important of which was transport receipts.

Looking at the growth rates, and taking first the overall position, it may be seen that the growth rate of total invisibles (in current values) was about twice as great in the period 1961–68 as compared with the period 1949–61. If we had used 'volume' growth rates, the contrast would have been even greater. Employing the deflating conventions adopted by the C S O, the growth rate in volume terms from 1961 to 1968 was 5.2 per cent per annum compared with 0.5 per cent per annum from 1949 to 1961. However, as the price deflators of many of the invisible items, such as investment income, emigrants' remittances, pensions, etc., are questionable inasmuch as widely different price deflators could equally validly be used, we confine our attention mainly to the current value figures.

Chart 11, which shows the annual data for invisible exports and some of the main components in the post-war period, suggests that the change in the trend of invisibles dates from about 1957. The contrast in the average annual growth rates of invisibles prior to and succeeding 1957 is considerable. The growth rate from 1949 to 1957 was only 2.0 per cent per annum, compared with 7.4 per cent per annum from 1957 to 1968. If we consider the growth of net invisibles—invisible exports less invisible imports—the contrast is even more marked. In 1949 invisible exports were almost four times greater than invisible imports. Between 1949 and 1957 invisible imports grew at an average annual rate of 5.4

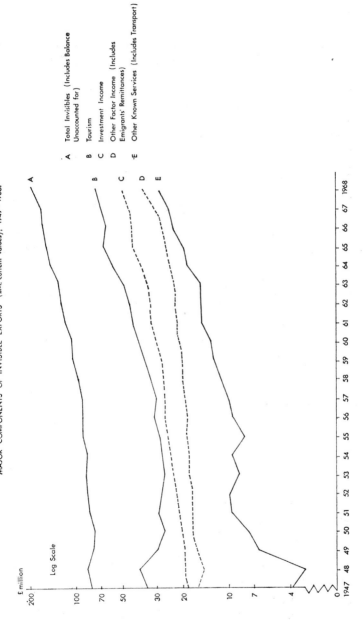

CHART 11

MAJOR COMPONENTS OF INVISIBLE EXPORTS (£M. current values), 1947 - 1968.

A Total Invisibles (Includes Balance
   Unaccounted for)
B Tourism
C Investment Income
D Other Factor Income (Includes
   Emigrants' Remittances)
E Other Known Services (Includes Transport)

per cent, so that the absolute increase in invisible imports amounted to over two-thirds of the absolute increase in invisible exports. Thus the growth rate of net invisibles was only 0.9 per cent per annum between 1949 and 1957. From 1957 to 1968 the growth rate of invisible imports (7.5 per cent per annum) was almost the same as the growth rate of invisible exports (7.4 per cent per annum), so that net invisibles grew at 7.4 per cent per annum, which meant that by 1968 net invisibles were some £74 million higher than in 1957.

Tourism accounted for over 40 per cent of the absolute increase in invisible exports between 1957 and 1968. As may be seen from Chart 11, tourist receipts fell considerably from 1948 to 1953, remained fairly static until about 1957 and from then to 1968 increased in every year except 1966. The average annual growth from 1957 to 1968 was 8.7 per cent. In 1957 the value of tourist receipts was only the same as in 1949, while the volume of tourist receipts surpassed the 1949 level only in 1963.[1] The growth in 'other known services', which was due largely to the rapid increase in transportation receipts, also contributed significantly to the rise in invisibles. This component is partly influenced by tourism in that transportation receipts depend to a considerable extent on the behaviour of tourism.

Factor income—divided in the chart into investment income and other factor income (consisting mainly of emigrants' remittances, pensions and commission earnings of import agents)—showed a steady pattern of advance up to 1963, although there was a slight quickening in the growth of investment income from about 1959. In 1964 and 1965 income from investment increased quite rapidly, but since then has reverted to the pre-1963 growth trend. Other factor income has also grown slightly faster in the post-1963 period, and although most of the items that comprise this invisible export have shared in the increase, the largest proportion of the absolute increase was due to emigrants' remittances and pensions from abroad. The bulk of the rise in these categories took place in 1967 and 1968 and was probably due to the increase in sterling terms of remittances from non-sterling areas due to the devaluation of November 1967. It may be noted that, over the whole of the post-war period, emigrants' remittances from the U K have been remarkably constant in the region of £5½ million per annum. Remittances from other countries have risen from

£3.8 million in 1949 to over £15 million in 1968, but part of this rise reflects the effects of the two post-war devaluations of sterling. It is rather surprising that the large increase in emigration in the mid-1950s appears to have had no effect on remittances from the U K. Although the magnitude of emigrants' remittances may depend on the total stock of emigrants rather than on the total flow, which may be small relative to the stock, one would have expected that remittances would tend to be greater in the first few years of an emigrant's life abroad, when the ties with relatives at home would be strongest. This would suggest that a rise in the emigration rate would be reflected in the remittances data. The large fall in emigration from about 1960 onwards does not appear to be reflected in the data either. It is, of course, possible that remittances from emigrants in the U K are not fully measured and are included in other categories of invisible exports.[2]

Given the relative importance of the two categories of invisibles, investment income and tourism, we now examine their development in greater detail.

INVESTMENT INCOME

Receipts from income on investment abroad, extern profits, etc. increased by 163 per cent between 1949 and 1968, an average annual growth rate of 5.2 per cent. Apart from the substantial increases in 1964 and 1965, the rate of increase was comparatively steady. On the debit side of the balance of payments, outgoings in respect of investment income, which were about 53 per cent of the inflow in 1949, increased by almost the same amount (164 per cent) between 1949 and 1968 and, on the whole, the outflow also rose fairly steadily. If, in order to allow for the slight decline in the outflow in 1968, we measure the changes from the average of 1948–50 to the average of 1966–68, the average rate of growth of the inflow was 5.0 per cent per annum as against 5.6 per cent for the outflow. The difference, however, is not large. Thus the observed changes in the inflow and outflow of investment income would be quite consistent with a position where the yield on Irish investment abroad and foreign investment in Ireland was similar and there was no significant change in the net external capital position.

Yet, given the very large changes in Ireland's net external

capital position in the post-war period, this equivalence in the growth of the inflow and outflow of investment income is quite remarkable. The accumulated current account deficits in the balance of payments from 1948 to 1968 inclusive amounted to £324 million, so that there necessarily has been net foreign disinvestment, in one form or another, of like amount. Estimates prepared by Whitaker (1949) in respect of the year 1947, show that in that year Irish gross external assets (private as well as official) amounted to £450 million, while external holdings in Ireland amounted to £175 million, giving a total net external asset position of about £275 million. These estimates were based on capitalised income. However, the figure for Irish gross holdings abroad corresponded very closely with an independent estimate of these holdings, so that the figures may be taken as providing reasonably reliable estimates. If we were to deduct from the stock of net external holdings in 1947 the total flow of net foreign disinvestment since then, we would find that by about 1965 Ireland's status changed from that of a net creditor to a net debtor country. The hazards of such a calculation are obvious enough and the qualifications need not be discussed in full here.[3] For example, the two sterling devaluations would have resulted in a sterling appreciation of holdings in gold or dollars which would not apply to the value (in sterling) of foreign investment in Ireland;[4] however, since only a relatively small proportion of the external holdings were in gold or dollars at the time of the two devaluations, this is not a major qualification. Another qualification that may be mentioned is the non-repayable capital grant of £6.5 million received under E C A funds. The most important qualification, however, relates to the possible appreciation (or depreciation) of capital values. Suppose, for the sake of argument, that the 1947 Irish holdings abroad and foreign holdings in Ireland had appreciated at the same rate such that the capital values in both cases had doubled between 1947 and 1968. The 1968 value of Ireland's holdings abroad in 1947 would be £900 million compared with a 1968 value of foreign holdings in Ireland in 1947 of £350 million. The capital flows since 1947, being on average of more recent origin, might be expected to have appreciated less, and in that case Ireland could still have a substantial net creditor position, though possibly smaller even in current values than in 1947. Unfortunately, data are not available that would enable us to assess the true net creditor or debtor position. But whatever the exact position, it is remarkable that, despite the very large accumulated net capital inflows in the post-war period, there has been no substantial change in the relative inflow and outflow of income on investment.

How can this be explained? Clearly, the explanation must lie either in differences in the yield or in the degree to which returns are repatriated, or some combination of these factors.[5] To understand the distinction, a word of explanation is perhaps necessary about the method used in recording the data for balance of payments purposes. The Irish balance of payments statistics record actual flows of investment income, not the yield on the investment. Thus, for example, if a subsidiary in Ireland of a foreign firm makes a profit of £1 million but reinvests all of this in Ireland, then the item does not appear in the balance of payments. From some points of view it would seem more correct to record the item as an outflow of investment income in the current account of the balance of payments, with a corresponding entry in the capital account showing a capital inflow of like amount.[6] The reinvestment in Ireland of the profits of a foreign company is equivalent to a capital inflow in that it increases foreign indebtedness. Thus, failure to count such reinvestment, as we point out below, tends towards a significant understatement of foreign investment in Ireland.

There is no substantial reason for expecting that the return per pound of Irish investment abroad is greater than the yield per pound on foreign money invested here—indeed, the contrary is more likely. A high proportion of Irish investment abroad is in gilt-edged securities, while a substantial proportion of foreign investment in Ireland is direct investment. It is true that the current yield on gilt-edged securities often exceeded that on equities, but a significant amount of Ireland's foreign assets were probably invested at a time when interest rates were quite low. Moreover, in recent years the sizeable amount of external investment in Irish government issues and the foreign borrowing by state-sponsored bodies has taken place at a time of very high interest rates.

It seems likely, therefore, that differences in the degree to which the return on investment is repatriated are responsible for the fact that outgoings of investment income have not risen any faster than the inflow. This, in turn, arises from the substantial differences in the composition of Irish holdings abroad as compared with foreign holdings in Ireland. Whitaker's estimates of Irish external assets in 1947 show that they were preponderantly in gilt-edged securities and in equities, with scarcely any direct investment holdings except in the case of the commercial banks. Although full details of the gross capital outflows since 1947 are not available, it is unlikely that much of it represented direct investment. Thus the composition of Irish investment abroad is such that most of it yields an annual inflow of investment income that appears in the balance of payments. On the other hand, a substantial amount of the external holdings in Ireland in 1947 represented direct investment in business or in property, and a large amount of the foreign capital inflow since then was of a similar nature. There has, of course, also been sizeable foreign investment that must involve an outflow of investment income; the E C A loan of £41 million bears an interest rate of $2\frac{1}{2}$ per cent; during 1961–68 foreign subscriptions to government loans and borrowing by state-sponsored bodies abroad amounted to £58 million; and there has been an inflow of £42 million during 1948–68 in respect of capital issues of companies. Income on such investment together with rising interest rates would probably account for most of the rise in the outflow of investment income since 1947.

The implication of this is that there must have been little or no outflow of income in respect of the very substantial post-war inflow of investment in business, property, etc.—amounting to well over £200 million—and the return on such investment must, therefore, have been substantially reinvested in Ireland. Since the reinvestment of such income might properly be treated as a new capital inflow, it would appear that, in this respect, the present method of calculating the capital inflow and the current balance of payments deficit significantly understates the true position.

The question arises whether foreign companies will continue to reinvest in Ireland the income from their Irish investments or whether they will at some stage wish to repatriate the income. Clearly, if our inferences above are correct, it is a matter of considerable importance, in assessing the future course of the Irish balance of payments, to secure more concrete information on the nature of foreign investment and the returns thereon, as well as on the present practice and likely future intentions of foreign investors in regard to repatriation of earnings.

TOURISM

We have already noted that the value of tourism[7] rose from 1961 to 1968 at an average annual rate more than 2½ times as great as the rate for the period 1949–61. We also saw in Chart 11 that a fairly marked change in the trend of tourist earnings took place from about 1957. The extent of the transformation can be seen in Table 31 where the annual growth rates of tourist receipts and tourist expenditures (i.e. spending by Irish visitors abroad) in value and volume terms are set out for the periods 1949–57 and 1957–68. The volume figures were derived, following the C S O convention, by using the Irish consumer price index as a deflator. The contrast in the growth of receipts before and after 1957 is due not only to the fairly high growth rate after 1957 but also to the adverse experience prior to then. The value of spending by visitors to Ireland was almost the same in 1957 as in 1949, while the volume was substantially lower. From 1957 tourist earnings have grown considerably both in value and volume terms. Since spending by Irish residents abroad grew at about 9 per cent per annum in value terms over the whole period 1949–68, the level of *net* receipts from tourism declined by 4.1 per cent in

Table 31: Average annual rates of change in tourist earnings and expenditure, 1949–57 and 1957–68

	Current values		Constant prices	
	1949 –57	1957 –68	1949 –57	1957 –68
	%	%	%	%
Earnings from visitors to Ireland	0.1	8.7	—4.0	5.2
Expenditure abroad by Irish residents	9.0	9.1	4.4	5.6
Net receipts	—4.1	8.3	—8.0	4.8

Source: *Irish Statistical Bulletin.* The published figures have been adjusted somewhat for the earlier years to make them comparable with data for more recent years.

value terms and 8.0 per cent in volume terms between 1949 and 1957. From 1957 to 1968 the growth of tourist revenue almost matched the growth of expenditure abroad by Irish residents, so that net receipts grew at an annual average of 8.3 per cent—in volume terms 4.8 per cent. However, the magnitude of the decline which took place between 1949 and 1957 may be appreciated from the fact that in 1968, despite the growth from 1957 to 1968, the volume of net tourist receipts was still about 15 per cent below the 1949 level.

Due to lack of detailed data (a reasonably comparable set of data for the major components is available only from 1953) it is difficult to analyse in detail the decline following the immediate post-war boom in tourism. However, the major reasons for the temporary boom and subsequent decline seem quite clear. The boom was largely due to the plentiful supply of unrationed food in Ireland relative to the U K, the severe currency restrictions in the immediate post-war period and the dislocation in transport and tourist facilities in Europe occasioned by the war. These factors proved to be temporary and the peak in tourist receipts was reached in 1948. From that date a decline set in and continued up to 1953 due to improved holiday amenities in Britain and continental countries, increased allowances for foreign travel, and intensive competition for tourist traffic.[8]

Given the nature of the boom in receipts, it is probable that some decline would have taken place regardless of development efforts undertaken in Ireland. But the decline might not have been so large or so prolonged had there been a more prompt response in measures to develop the tourist industry. Lynch (1969) put the matter aptly as follows:

> It would be quite wrong, of course, to use hindsight in criticism of individual policies; but especially after 1948 there was a long delay in effectively creating a satisfactory organisation for the promotion of tourism, even though that industry could be shown to be third in importance in the list of sources of external income. There seems to have been a belief that a competitive tourist industry could have established itself spontaneously.[9]

It was not until 1952 that official efforts to develop the industry began on anything like the required scale. Moreover, expansion was retarded by institutional restrictions, such as the ban on foreign coach tours, which was aimed at preserving the monopoly of the national transport authority and which was not removed until 1957. The lack of suitable car-ferry facilities was not tackled until the 1960s.

Major Components of Tourist Revenue

As mentioned above, a reasonably consistent breakdown of tourist data is available from 1953. The revenue data are broken down into three main categories: cross-channel receipts, cross-border receipts, and receipts from others coming direct to Ireland. Cross-channel receipts are those due to visitors coming direct from or via Great Britain and, therefore, include receipts from residents of countries other than Britain if such visitors travel through Britain to Ireland. Cross-border receipts are subdivided into revenue from 'excursionists' who stay less than one day and

Table 32: Shares of major components of receipts from visitors in total receipts for five selected years

	1953	1958	1961	1963	1968
	%	%	%	%	%
Cross-channel	48.9	51.1	55.9	46.2	46.2
Cross-border (excluding excursionists)	33.6	25.4	23.9	21.3	20.9
Cross-border excursionists	9.3	6.7	10.1	20.5	18.1
Overseas	8.2*	16.8*	10.1*	12.0	14.8
Total	100.0	100.0	100.0	100.0	100.0
	£m	£m	£m	£m	£m
Value of total receipts	26.8	32.3	43.5	49.8	75.7

*In 1961 the figures for revenue from overseas visitors were revised and it was noted that figures for previous years may have included some non-tourist items. Thus revenue fell from £6.8 million in 1960 to £4.4 million in 1961, although tourist arrivals only fell from 50 thousand to 46 thousand (see *Irish Statistical Bulletin*, Mar. 1962). The ratio of tourist direct revenue to total revenue shown here for 1953 and 1958 may therefore be higher than was actually the case.

Source: *Irish Statistical Bulletin*, various issues. Some revisions to the published figures for 1953 have been made for comparability with the later years.

revenue from those staying more than one day. This mode of classification means that revenue from visitors not resident in Northern Ireland or Great Britain who come via Northern Ireland is included in cross-border receipts. The category of other direct receipts is revenue from visitors coming directly to Ireland and consists mainly of receipts from U S A and continental European visitors.

In Table 32 we have set out the shares of these major components in tourist receipts for five selected years between 1953 and 1968. It is clear that cross-channel and cross-border receipts have predominated throughout. Since the vast bulk of these receipts are due to residents of the U K (i.e. Great Britain and Northern Ireland), it is clear that tourist revenue in Ireland is heavily dependent on the U K tourist market, although the rapid growth of receipts from tourists coming directly to Ireland has

CHART 12

MAJOR COMPONENTS OF RECEIPTS FROM VISITORS, 1951-1968, (at Current Market Prices)

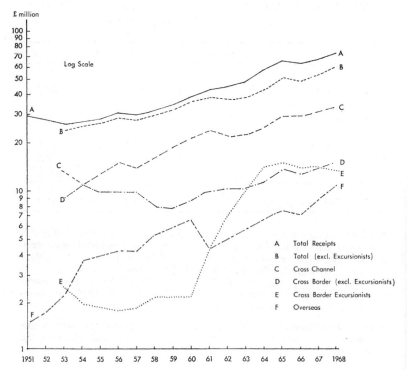

reduced that dependence somewhat. This heavy dependence on UK tourism has been an important factor in limiting the growth of tourist receipts, since expenditure abroad by UK residents has grown more slowly than in the case of most West European countries.[10]

In Chart 12 we have set out the receipts by main tourist category for the years 1951 to 1968. In spite of the unsatisfactory nature of the classification, it would, perhaps, be useful to discuss the trends in the main components of revenue over the period.

Cross-Channel Receipts. Revenue from cross-channel visitors is the largest single component of tourist receipts, accounting for between 45 and 55 per cent of the total in all years. Revenue from this source started to rise from 1954 but there was a set-back in 1957, probably due to the border conflict that commenced in December 1956. After 1957 revenue rose rapidly until 1961. Between 1953 and 1961 revenue from cross-channel visitors accounted for two-thirds of the rise of £16.7 million in total receipts. Between 1961 and 1968 receipts grew at a slower pace and accounted for only one-third of the rise of £32.2 million in total receipts over the period. The growth rate of receipts from 1953 to 1961 was 8.0 per cent per annum while from 1961 to 1968 it was 5.4 per cent per annum. The decline in the growth rate was due in large measure to a fall in the average length of stay of cross-channel visitors, which declined by 2.7 per cent per annum in the period 1961–68. A further reason for the fall in the growth rate was a marked decline in the receipts from those coming to visit relatives: revenue from this source fell by 1.2 per cent per annum for 1961–68 compared with a growth rate of 7.2 per cent per annum between 1953 and 1961. One explanation for this might be the considerable reduction in emigration that took place in the later period.[11] In contrast, the growth of receipts from cross-channel visitors classified as tourists only fell from 10.5 per cent per annum for 1953–61 to 9.2 per cent per annum for 1961–68.

Cross-Border Visitors. In 1953 revenue from cross-border visitors (excluding excursionists) was an important source of tourist revenue as it accounted for about one-third of total receipts. It was undoubtedly affected by the IRA border campaign and declined from 1954 to 1959. It was not until 1962 that revenue had recovered to the 1954 level. From then until 1968 revenue rose by nearly 50 per cent.

The rise was mainly due to increased expenditure per visitor, since numbers grew slowly in the 1960s and in 1968 the number of such visitors was only two-thirds of the number in 1956. The rise in average spending was probably due to a shift from the visitor to the excursionist category of those wishing to make a short visit. With improved transport facilities, especially increased car ownership and less document formalities at the border, short-term visitors, who previously stayed overnight in the Republic, probably tended to return the same day. Thus the cross-border visitors probably now include a higher proportion of those making longer trips, thereby raising average expenditure per visitor.

Cross-Border Excursionists. While one must treat the data on cross-border excursionists with considerable scepticism, we assume that the figures present the rough orders of magnitude and that we can, at least, draw some broad-based conclusions from them. From 1953 to 1960 revenue from cross-border excursionists never exceeded £3 million in any year. Annual revenue rose rapidly from £2.2 million in 1960 to £15.5 million in 1965 and subsequently declined to £13.7 million in 1968. What was the cause of such a rapid expansion in the 1960s of this category of tourist receipts? One reason, suggested above, is the shift in numbers from the visitor to excursionist category, but this would account for only a small proportion of the vast rise in excursionist numbers. The more important factors were associated with two major legislative changes that took place in 1959 and 1960. The first of these was the abolition in 1959 of the triptych requirement for south-bound cars. In 1959 the number of visitors increased considerably over 1958 and previous levels. Expenditure by visitors did not rise along with the increased numbers. However, in 1960 revenue began to expand. And it was in that year that the other legislative change took place—the reform of the licensing laws for the sale of drink which extended evening opening hours and Sunday opening. This meant that public houses in the South were open for some considerable time after they had closed in the North, and led to a very considerable increase in cross-border trips to adjacent public houses in the South. The fall-off in revenue from 1965 could plausibly be explained by the relatively sharper rise in the prices of drink and tobacco in the South.

Direct Receipts. Revenue from visitors coming direct to Ireland from places other than the U K grew at a fairly rapid rate throughout the period under review. The major part of this category is receipts from visitors from the U S A. Most of the decline shown by the figures in 1961 is purely notional since the method of estimating direct receipts changed in that year. Overall, this category of revenue has shown the strongest and steadiest advance since 1951.

Irish Share of U K and U S A Tourist Market

We have noted that the method of classification in the official tourist statistics does not allow us to distinguish receipts by place of residence of tourists. Thus cross-channel and cross-border receipts include expenditures by residents of the U S A and else-where who come via Northern Ireland or Great Britain. However, the balance of payments statistics include an estimate of aggregate earnings from U K visitors to Ireland. Relating this figure to the estimate of total spending abroad by U K visitors, taken from the U K official statistics, it is possible to get some idea of changes in the Irish share of the overall U K tourist market. In Table 33 we have set out the Irish share of total spending abroad by U K residents in each year from 1949 to 1968.

Between 1949 and 1957 expenditure abroad by U K residents nearly doubled, whereas their spending in Ireland was less in 1957 than in 1949. Thus, as may be seen from Table 33, Ireland's share, which fell in almost all years from 1949 to 1957, was more than halved in this period. Thereafter the downward trend was arrested. From 1957 to 1968 total spending by U K visitors rose by 72 per cent, whereas their spending in Ireland rose by 146 per cent. Ireland's share thus rose substantially in this period. How-ever, the greater part of the rise in the share was due to the big increase in spending by cross-border excursionists. Table 33 also shows the share of Irish receipts from U K visitors excluding cross-border excursionists. As may be seen from these figures, there was no rise in the Irish share except in 1967–68. The rise in these years may have been due to the U K restrictions on travel allow-ances for visits to non-sterling countries. These restrictions were imposed in July 1966 and were not relaxed until January 1970. The devaluation of November 1967 may also have helped to raise the Irish share in 1968.

Most of the non-U K visitors to Ireland were residents of the U S A, and though their numbers were small in comparison with U K visitors, their average expenditure was nearly three times as

Table 33: Share of Irish receipts from U K visitors in total spending abroad by U K residents, 1949–68

Year	Irish Receipts	Share in U K total	Irish receipts (excl. cross-border excursionists)*	Share in U K total (excl. cross-border excursionists)*
	£m	%	£m	%
1949	27	24.5		
1950	24	19.8		
1951	26.6	16.7		
1952	25.0	16.3		
1953	23.3	15.0	20.8	13.7
1954	22.6	12.8	20.6	11.8
1955	23.5	12.2	21.6	11.4
1956	25.5	12.3	23.7	11.6
1957	24.5	11.3	22.6	10.6
1958	25.3	11.4	23.1	10.5
1959	27.7	11.8	25.5	11.0
1960	31.2	12.0	29.0	11.3
1961	37.4	13.6	33.0	12.1
1962	38.6	13.2	31.4	11.0
1963	41.2	12.6	31.0	9.8
1964	49.5	13.8	34.9	10.1
1965	57.2	14.7	41.7	11.1
1966	55.3	13.5	40.9	10.3
1967	56.2	14.9	41.6	11.5
1968	60.3	16.3	46.6	13.1

*Figures for cross-border excursionists are not available prior to 1953.

Sources: Irish data from the balance of payments statistics in *Irish Statistical Bulletin*, various issues. The figures relate to spending by visitors who are residents of the U K and exclude spending by non-U K visitors who travel via the U K. Figures for 1949 and 1950 are approximations. U K data from *Annual Abstract of Statistics*, various issues.

high. To analyse the Irish share of the U S A tourist market (or, more precisely, the Irish share of U S A tourist expenditures in Europe and the Mediterranean) we have had to rely on data from U S A sources. Information on the numbers and expenditure of U S A residents visiting Ireland is available in the U S A *Survey of Current Business* for most years. The data cover those coming via the U K as well as those travelling directly to Ireland. In Table 34 we have set out the figures for every available year from 1950 to 1968, together with Ireland's share in the numbers and expenditure of U S A residents visiting Europe and the Medi-

Table 34: Numbers and expenditure of U S A visitors, 1950–68

Year	Expenditure in Ireland	Expenditure in Ireland as % of expenditure in Europe and the Mediterranean	Numbers of visitors to Ireland	Numbers of visitors to Ireland as % of numbers of visitors to Europe and the Mediterranean	Average expenditure per visitor in Ireland relative to the European average*
	$m	%	000s	%	%
1950	6	2.7	26	8.6	32.6
1951	4	2.1	18	7.2	28.7
1952	4	1.8	24	7.2	24.0
1953	6	2.0	33	8.8	22.5
1954	n.a.	n.a.	38	9.1	n.a.
1955	8	1.9	43	8.9	21.7
1956	11	2.3	51	9.8	23.6
1957	12	2.5	55	9.9	23.2
1958	13	2.3	61	9.6	24.0
1959	n.a.	n.a.	n.a.	n.a.	n.a.
1960	12	1.7	n.a.	n.a.	n.a.
1961	12	1.9	n.a.	n.a.	n.a.
1962	15	2.3	75	8.1	30.4
1963	16	2.1	80	7.3	29.4
1964	20	2.5	114	9.1	27.5
1965	20	2.3	105	7.5	20.3
1966	24	2.6	132	8.4	32.8
1967	28	2.8	154	8.6	32.9
1968	32	3.2	180	9.3	34.6

n.a. 'not available'.

*This is average expenditure per U S A visitor to Ireland as a percentage of average expenditure per U S A visitor to Europe and the Mediterranean. The tendency for U S A tourists to visit several countries accounts for the small size of the ratio.

Source: U S A Department of Commerce, *Survey of Current Business*, various issues. It may be noted that the figures in column (5) are calculated directly from the actual figures on average expenditure per visitor given in the survey. In principle, the figures should be equal to column (2) divided by column (4) but, because of rounding, slight discrepancies emerge.

F

terranean. It should be emphasised that the fact that Ireland's share in total revenue is less than its share in numbers does not imply that Ireland has a relatively low expenditure per person from U S A visitors. The reason is that U S A tourists tend to visit several countries, so that their expenditure in any one country is only a part of their total spending in Europe. Thus, for every individual European country, the revenue share is considerably less than the share in number of visitors. The true position as regards average expenditure per U S A visitor in Ireland, compared with other European countries, is that in recent years it has been relatively high. In 1968, for example, of the sixteen countries separately listed in Europe and the Mediterranean, average expenditure per U S A visitor was higher than in Ireland in only five countries (the U K, Italy, Spain, Greece and Israel).

The numbers of U S A residents visiting Europe have increased enormously in the post-war period. In the eight years 1952–60 numbers rose by 150 per cent from 332,000 to 832,000. In the succeeding eight years, 1960–68, the absolute increase was greater (to 1,937,000 in 1968), though the percentage increase (130 per cent) was slightly lower. However, there was a marked difference in the revenue figures. From 1952 to 1960 average expenditure per visitor (in dollars) rose by 8 per cent, whereas it fell by nearly 40 per cent from 1960 to 1968—the fall began, in fact, after 1956. Thus, whereas total revenue increased by 170 per cent from 1952 to 1960, it rose by only 43 per cent from 1960 to 1968.

Broadly speaking, the Irish position corresponds roughly to the general European pattern in regard to numbers of U S A visitors. The Irish share of total U S A residents visiting Europe and the Mediterranean remained roughly in the region of 9 per cent, though with a fair degree of short-term fluctuation. Average expenditure per U S A visitor in Ireland, however, behaved rather differently from the overall pattern. It tended to fall up to the mid-1950s when it was rising in Europe. It then remained comparatively stable in Ireland for several years when it was falling in Europe. In the 1960s, although average expenditure in Ireland has fallen, the fall was not nearly so great as in Europe as a whole. We show in Table 34 the ratio of average expenditure per U S A visitor in Ireland to the overall average for Europe. The ratio dropped from 32.6 per cent in 1950 to 21.7 per cent in 1955, but then began to recover and rose to 34.6 per cent in 1968. The result of maintaining the share in numbers and increasing the average expenditure per visitor relative to the overall average was that in the 1960s Ireland's share in total European receipts from U S A visitors has tended to rise and reached a record figure of 3.2 per cent in 1968. The *relative* improvement in average expenditure per U S A visitor in Ireland from about the mid-1950s may be chiefly due to the greatly improved quality of hotel accommodation in Ireland, which we discuss below.

Tourist Development Measures

We noted earlier that it was not until 1952 that a major government effort was undertaken to develop the tourist industry and arrest the post-war decline. The Tourist Traffic Act of 1952 established Bord Fáilte and Fógra Fáilte, the former with responsibility for developing tourist facilities, the latter for promotion campaigns, marketing, etc. In 1955 Fógra Fáilte was dissolved and its functions transferred to Bord Fáilte, renamed Bord Fáilte Éireann, which since then has had overall responsibility for all aspects of tourist development.

The setting-up of these bodies represented the beginning of a conscious policy for tourist development. Their initial efforts, however, did not make a sizeable impact, partly because of inadequate funding and partly because it is often necessary to acquire experience in order to develop the most satisfactory schemes. The 1952 act provided for government guaranteed loans for improvement of hotels and guesthouses, with Bord Fáilte grants to cover the interest charges for the first three years (later extended to five years). A limit of £3 million was placed on the total of loans to be guaranteed. The scheme involved so much administrative red tape (with applications for grants being examined by officials from Bord Fáilte, the Department of Industry and Commerce and the Department of Finance) and complicated legal arrangements that few loans were guaranteed. By 1958, guarantees to the value of £236,000 had been given with little impact on the hotel industry. From 1952 to 1957 the number of bedrooms in hotels and guesthouses declined from just over 17,000 to 16,000.

It is obvious now that such a scheme was too cumbersome to provide much of an incentive to hoteliers, though this may not have been so clear when the scheme was launched. Frequently,

one idea has to fail before a better one can replace it. The Tourist
Traffic Act of 1957, which took effect at the end of 1957, allowed
Bord Fáilte Èireann to pay grants to cover the interest costs of
loans not guaranteed by the state. This eliminated many of the
administrative complexities inherent in the previous scheme. In
mid-1958, grants to cover 20 per cent of the construction costs
of new bedrooms and one-third of the cost of central heating in
these were introduced. Subsequently a depreciation allowance
amounting to 10 per cent per annum of the capital cost incurred
on or after 1 January 1960 was granted for tax purposes.
Improvement grants, relating to the installation of private bath-
rooms and central heating in existing accommodation, were also
available, covering 20 per cent of the capital cost. The consequence of these measures was an impressive expansion in the
quantity and quality of hotel accommodation. The number of
bedrooms in hotels and guesthouses rose from 16,000 in 1957 to
26,000 in 1968 and the number of rooms with private bathroom
increased from 800 in 1957 (330 in 1952) to 8,400 in 1968.

Of course, the rise in the supply of new and improved accommodation was also stimulated by the growth in tourist revenue
from abroad which, as we have seen, began about 1957. Furthermore, the relatively rapid growth of real personal income *per
capita* in Ireland from 1958 onward probably stimulated the
growth of domestic tourism. Official development measures were
not, therefore, the only factors at work. These measures
undoubtedly raised the attractiveness of investment in the tourist
industry but would hardly have been so successful without the
growth in domestic and foreign tourism. At the same time the
growth of revenue from foreign tourists may have been induced,
in part, by the improved level of accommodation. It is likely that
the two trends in tourist revenue and investment in accommodation reinforced each other. The increased incentives for accommodation and the large-scale expansion in other programmes of
tourist promotion (e.g. publicity abroad, resort development, etc.)
has involved a considerable increase in the amount of official
funds devoted to tourist development. In 1952 the combined
annual grant of Bord Fáilte and Fógra Fáilte was set at £250,000.
By 1958, the grant for Bord Fáilte Éireann had risen to £500,000.
In the next ten years, 1958–68, expenditure increased ninefold to
£4.64 million in 1968.

Conclusions

Tourism was an important factor in the more rapid growth of the recent period. The decline and stagnation in earnings up to the mid-1950s was arrested, and was followed by fairly rapid growth thereafter which both stimulated demand and aided the balance of payments. Institutional changes, along with a reorganisation of public bodies dealing with tourism, aided the growth in revenue. There can be little doubt that improvement in the scope and administration of incentive schemes for tourist development played a significant role in the expansion of the industry.

CHAPTER 9

Conclusions on Exports

IRISH exports of goods and services posed various structural problems in the early post-war years. Further expansion of industry depended, in an important way, on the development of industrial exports, which then amounted to only a tiny proportion of either industrial output or total exports. Tariff protection was already operative on a broad scale and only marginal advances could be expected from further tariff protection. The maintenance of a high rate of growth of domestic demand would undoubtedly stimulate further expansion of the industrial sector. However, no conceivable increase in the home market could provide sufficient outlet for the efficient development of many individual industries. Moreover, domestic demand could not continue indefinitely to grow at a rapid rate unless exports as a whole expanded at a satisfactory rate.

In addition, important categories of exports were in a state of decline and it was necessary to switch toward exports that would provide a firmer basis for growth. This was true of various classes of food which were curtailed by changes in British agricultural policy. It was true also of the type of tourist boom experienced just after the war: a sustained expansion in tourism depended on factors other than food rationing or currency restrictions in the UK, which were bound to be temporary. The heavy dependence on livestock exports, which were subject to large fluctuations in price and volume, involved considerable instability in export receipts, thereby causing difficult problems for short-term demand management.

The 1950s may be seen, therefore, as a transitional phase for exports during which it was necessary to achieve a more export-oriented industrial development and to secure a more balanced range of exports. The popular view that official and unofficial attempts to achieve the transition were not initiated until the end of the decade is not in accordance with the facts, though it is true that only in 1958, with the publication of *Economic Development* (Whitaker (1958)), were the measures elaborated fully in a coherent and unified policy programme. We have shown that manufactured exports were expanding rapidly in the 1950s even before the fiscal incentives for such exports in 1956. The establishment of the Industrial Development Authority as the body responsible for industrial development, including foreign enterprise, and the setting-up of Coras Tráchtála to develop exports were important steps taken around the beginning of the decade. Measures to reverse the decline in tourism were initiated in 1952, although they were not very successful until some years later.

It might be said that the efforts of the various development agencies and the measures taken achieved little success and that the scale of effort was too small and diffuse. While not denying that much more could have been done, a more understanding view would also take into account that, even with the maximum energy and the most appropriate measures, some time was bound to elapse before the efforts yielded fruit. Moreover, it demands a good deal to expect that the most suitable measures could be selected in the first instance without any basis of practical experience in Irish conditions. Furthermore, given the international conditions prevailing in the first half of the 1950s, some of the measures that were later successful would scarcely have operated so well earlier, even if they had been introduced then and vigorously pursued. For example, total direct foreign investment abroad by some of the countries (notably Germany) that established a significant amount of new manufacturing capacity in Ireland in the 1960s was minimal in the 1950s.

The fact of the matter is that, by the end of the 1950s, exports were already placed on a much sounder footing for growth. Manufactured exports in 1960 accounted for 17 per cent of domestic exports as against only 6 per cent in 1950. Tourist revenue was rising relatively rapidly. Steps to eradicate bovine tuberculosis—a necessary step to safeguard cattle exports—were well under way. The scale of development incentives had been greatly expanded, and their administration smoothed, in a way that could not confidently be done without experience of what was likely to work.

The greater impact of exports on economic growth in the second period was due chiefly to the faster growth of invisible exports and the higher ratio of exports to output. The latter factor was due not only to the growth of exports in the second period, but also to the rapid increase in exports relative to output in the first period. Even though visible exports grew as rapidly in the first period as in the second, their impact was relatively less, since they represented a much smaller share of output. The greatest contrast in the growth of exports between the two periods was in invisibles, particularly tourism. This had important implications for economic growth apart from its effect on the balance of payments. Tourism has a relatively low import content compared with many other categories of demand.[1] Moreover, the benefits tend to be widely spread regionally and to generate income and employment in areas where development of other industries would present serious problems. The greater stability of expansion in exports generally in the second period, which was also favourable to growth, was mainly due to steadier demand conditions abroad and reduced dependence on the categories of exports most subject to fluctuation. The latter is again something that was partly achieved as a result of development in the 1950s.

If, as we argue, the 1950s can be regarded as a transitional phase between the autarkic policies that preceded it and the much greater reliance on trade in the 1960s, then the attainment of a high rate of growth of output during this phase would require a high rate of growth of domestic demand—indeed a higher rate of growth of domestic demand than after the transition was achieved. This would still be so even if more vigorous and more successful efforts at export expansion had been made earlier. For example, even had the rate of increase in manufactured exports in the 1950s been much greater than was actually achieved, the contribution to total manufacturing output would still be comparatively small until the export base expanded. The evidence we examined does not suggest that a more rapid rate of growth of home demand would have retarded the expansion of exports, nor would this seem likely on *a priori* grounds in Irish conditions. It is highly implausible that such major export categories as agricultural exports, tourism and other classes of invisible receipts would be affected by any considerable change in the pressure of home demand. Manufactured exports might be more sensitive to pressure of home demand. But even here it seems likely that any adverse effect would be small. Throughout the 1950s there was a high level of unemployment and substantial emigration, much of it, no doubt, due to the shortage of jobs at home. Many of the new manufacturing industries that were established produced almost exclusively for the export market, and were encouraged to do so by official incentives: any diversion of their output to the home market, as a result of greater home demand, was unlikely to be of much significance. Indeed, it is possible that a faster rate of growth of home demand in the 1950s might have benefited manufactured exports by its effects on investment, productivity and profits.

Even assuming that a higher rate of growth of home demand in the 1950s did not retard export expansion, it might, nevertheless, very well have involved greater strain on the balance of payments through its effects on imports. Whether such a possible larger balance of payments deficit could and should have been tolerated in the interests of growth seems, in retrospect, the key policy issue of the 1950s. How the authorities viewed the balance of payments constraint, and how the tension between this constraint and development needs was resolved in their management of domestic demand, is discussed in Part IV.

PART III

SAVINGS AND INVESTMENT

CHAPTER 10

The Rise in the Savings Ratio

I N an open economy the counterpart of a current balance of payments deficit is an excess of investment over savings. Maintenance of a high rate of investment generally requires a high rate of saving. While current deficits in the balance of payments can be financed by foreign disinvestment—either by running down external assets or securing capital inflows from abroad—this process is not unlimited. It may be limited by reluctance of the country concerned to reduce external reserves or engage in substantial foreign borrowing, a factor that undoubtedly influenced policy in Ireland in the 1950s, as we show later in Part IV. However, even if a country was prepared to tolerate unlimited foreign disinvestment, funds would not be forthcoming indefinitely. Thus the rise in the savings ratio from an average of 12.8 per cent of G N P in the years 1949 to 1960 to an average of 17.6 per cent in the years 1961 to 1968 was crucial in permitting an expansion in investment without excessive balance of payments difficulties. Furthermore, the greater stability in the savings ratio in the second period reduced the need for measures that would tend to restrain investment and interrupt the rate of growth of output.

SAVINGS AND THE TERMS OF TRADE

While the average savings ratio in current values rose between the two periods from 12.8 per cent to 17.6 per cent, the rise in the savings ratio in constant prices was shown in Chapter 2 to be considerably less. Since the volume of savings was measured as the difference between the volume of G N P and the volume of total consumption, this discrepancy implies that the share of real output devoted to real consumption declined less than the current value share of output devoted to consumption. The explanation of this phenomenon, which lies mainly in the behaviour of the terms of trade, is of interest in itself and also throws light on the improvement in the savings ratio.

A divergence between the current and constant value shares of consumption in G N P is associated with differences in the movements of the price of consumption and the price of G N P. Since the volume share fell by less than the value share in the 1961–68 period, the implied price of total consumption must have risen less than the implied price of G N P. This was, indeed, the case. However, since consumption accounted for 80 to 85 per cent of G N P, the G N P price would not normally deviate much from the price of total consumption if the other items (viz. investment and the balance of payments) were directly deflated by appropriate price indices. In fact, the balance of payments is not deflated directly in arriving at the volume of G N P. Instead, the balance of payments in real terms is estimated by deflating separately the current values of exports and imports. Given the magnitude of exports and imports, a comparatively small change in their relative prices can, on this basis, yield an estimate of the real balance of payments substantially different from, and even of opposite sign to, that derived by deflating the balance of payments directly by either the import or export price index. For this reason the implied G N P price that emerges when imports and exports are separately deflated may move in a substantially different manner from the price of total consumption.[1]

The difference between the real balance of payments arrived at by *separately* deflating exports and imports and the real balance of payments arrived at by *directly* deflating the current balance of payments by some appropriate price deflator (such as the export price index or the import price index) is known as the external trading gain (loss). When the terms of trade improve (i.e. when the export price rises more than the import price), there is a trading gain; when the terms of trade disimprove, there is a trading loss. It must be emphasised that the external trading gain (loss) is not simply a statistical peculiarity: it has substantive economic content and implications. Moreover, both methods of arriving at the real balance of payments are meaningful; and neither can be said to be superior to the other, since both have important implications in different contexts. This can be shown by a simple example. Suppose that between year 1 and 2 there is no change whatever in any price or volume component of G N P, except that the export price rises by 5 per cent. Assuming no deficit or surplus in the current balance of payments in year 1, and that the value of exports in that year was £400 million, there would then be a current balance of payments surplus in year 2 of £20 million. Since, by assumption, there has been no change in the volume of any component of G N P, then it is perfectly correct to say that the volume of G N P is unchanged, and this is the result that emerges when real G N P is measured by deflating exports and imports separately.

However, that is only one side of the story. In fact, in the circumstances mentioned, the nation in year 2 has available, by reason of the improvement in the terms of trade, an extra £20 million of purchasing power. This can be spent on additional consumption (either by increasing imports or reducing exports) without reducing savings or causing a deterioration in the balance of payments. Alternatively, it can be used for greater physical capital formation (again, either by increasing imports or reducing exports) or for increasing external reserves, and in either of these circumstances there will be a rise in savings without any greater abstinence from real consumption than in the previous year. Whichever way it is used, the external trading gain is a benefit to the nation.[2] If one regards the gain as being available for spending on imports, then in the present example it can be measured in year 1 prices by deflating the balance of payments surplus by the import price index, in which case the gain would be £20 million. On the other hand, if the gain is regarded as being available for spending on goods that would otherwise be exported, the real gain in the present example is equal to the balance of payments surplus deflated by the export price index, i.e. £19 million.[3]

We have thought it worth while giving the foregoing simplified discussion of the concept of the external trading gain[4] because, as we shall show, improvements in the terms of trade facilitated the rise in the savings ratio since 1961. Taking the two periods 1949–61 and 1961–68, the position was that in both 1949 and 1961 the external trading gain (measured at 1958 prices) amounted to 0.4 per cent of real G N P in those years, whereas in 1968 the external trading gain amounted to 2.5 per cent of real G N P. Thus in 1968 as compared with 1961 an additional 2.1 per cent of G N P could have been saved without reducing the share of real

consumption in real G N P. This is not to say that the external
trading gain is automatically saved: rather, what we are saying
is that a favourable movement in the terms of trade makes it
possible to raise the savings ratio in current money values without
reducing the share in the volume of G N P devoted to real consumption. Thus, the gain from the terms of trade[5] can permit
an effective rise in the savings ratio without as much sacrifice of
consumption as would otherwise be necessary.

Turning to the experience within each of the two periods, we
find that in the first period the export price index was substantially
lower than the import price index (both to base 1958=100) in
several years, so that there were trading losses in these years,
whereas in all years in the second period the export price index
was above the import price index, so that there were trading
gains in all years (by reference to 1958).[6] For the twelve years
1949 to 1960, there was an average annual trading *loss* (at 1958
prices) amounting to 0.3 per cent of G N P, whereas in the eight
years 1961 to 1968 the average annual trading *gain* was 1.7 per cent
of G N P. Thus, on average, as between the two periods, approximately 2 per cent more of G N P could have been devoted to
saving each year without lowering the volume share of consumption in G N P. This was undoubtedly an important factor in
easing the strain of raising the average savings ratio.

The foregoing point can be illustrated in another way, by
relating the volume of consumption to the volume of G N P
including the external trading gain (loss). The average shares on
this basis are set out in Table 35. The decline between the two
periods in the average share of total consumption is now 5.1
percentage points, which is close to the decline of 4.8 percentage
points in the share in current values, as shown earlier in Table
9. Correspondingly, the rise in the average share of real savings
in Table 35 is very close to the rise in current values. The average
savings ratio of 17.8 per cent in the second period in Table 35
now effectively includes the average annual trading gain of 1.7
per cent, while the average savings ratio of 12.7 in the first period
effectively includes the *negative* trading gain of 0.3 per cent per
annum on average. Thus we may say that about 2 per cent of the
rise in the average savings ratio can be accounted for by the
more favourable terms of trade. This is, of course, in the sense
that, if there had been no difference in the terms of trade effect

Table 35: Average of annual shares of consumption and savings in G N P including the external trading gain (at constant 1958 prices), 1949–61 and 1961–68*

	1949–61	1961–68
	%	%
Total consumption	87.3	82.2
Private	75.6	71.6
Government	11.7	10.6
Savings	12.7	17.8
Total G N P including external trading gain	100.0	100.0

*See note to Table 9.

Source: *National Income and Expenditure 1969.*

between the two periods, then an extra sacrifice of real consumption, amounting, on average, to about 2 per cent of G N P per annum, would have been required to raise the savings ratio by the amount it did actually rise.[7] The same factor largely accounts for the greater rise in the share of domestic investment in G N P in volume terms than in value terms and the more favourable position in the balance of payments in current prices than in constant prices, both of which facts were pointed out in Chapter 2.

The effect of the terms of trade on saving might be said to be a permissive factor rather than a causal factor. An improvement in the terms of trade, all other things being unchanged, allows the savings ratio to rise in current values without sacrifice of existing real consumption standards. However, the benefit might also be taken in the form of higher real consumption, and we have not yet shown a mechanism by which it might *cause* a rise in savings. Moreover, improved terms of trade can account for only part of the rise in the savings ratio. Hence, we must examine further the factors underlying changes in the savings ratio. Before doing so it is helpful to look at the major components into which total savings can be divided.

MAJOR COMPONENTS OF SAVINGS

Total savings are divided in the national accounts into two major categories: depreciation, which is the estimated provision for fixed capital consumption during the year, and the balance, which may be called net savings. Net savings is divided in turn into three main components: personal savings, company savings and public authorities' savings. This is a sectoral classification: the personal sector includes all households and unincorporated businesses such as farms, shops, professional partnerships, etc.; the company sector includes all public and private limited companies and certain semi-state bodies; the public authorities' sector includes central and local government. Company savings is the undistributed income of companies net of taxes, and public authorities' savings represents the difference between current revenue and current expenditure.[8] Public authorities' savings assumed negative values (i.e. dissaving) in some years, whereas the other two sectors have always had positive savings since the war.

Chart 13 shows the value of total savings and various components for each year from 1947 to 1968. Personal savings is the largest component, generally accounting for about two-thirds of total net savings. It is clear from the chart that fluctuations in total savings are dominated by fluctuations in personal savings. This is true for gross as well as net savings, since the trend of depreciation is almost a straight line for the post-war period, indicating a near constant rate of growth throughout. The very steady rise in depreciation also implies that the *relative* degree of variability has been greater in net savings than in total savings. Personal savings fluctuated a great deal up to about 1960 but their growth since then has been markedly more stable. This has tended to stabilise the growth of total savings.

Company savings rose little during the 1950s: they were below the 1950 level in every year except 1954 and did not rise much above that level until 1960. Since then there has been a moderate rise. Public authorities' savings generally represented a small component of total net savings. Over the post-war period as a whole they accounted for only $3\frac{1}{2}$ per cent of total net savings, though in the three years 1966 to 1968 they amounted to $11\frac{1}{4}$ per cent on average of the total. Although such savings have been small on the average, they are of considerable importance from the short-term viewpoint. Variations in public authorities' savings have in a few years been far greater than in the other two classes of

CHART 13

MAJOR COMPONENTS OF SAVINGS (£M CURRENT VALUES), 1947-1968

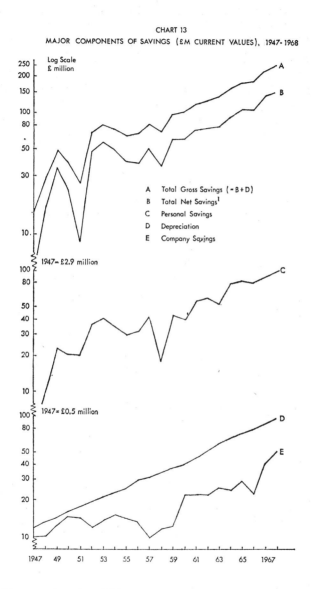

A   Total Gross Savings (= B + D)
B   Total Net Savings[1]
C   Personal Savings
D   Depreciation
E   Company Savings

[1].This comprises, in addition to C and E shown here, the savings or dissavings of public authorities and a correction for appreciation in value of non-agricultural stocks due to price changes.

net savings combined. The large fall in savings in 1951, for example, was almost entirely due to a swing of £8 million in public authorities' savings, involving a dissaving by public authorities of £7½ million in that year. Again in 1966 there was a small rise in total savings despite sizeable falls in personal and company savings due to a rise of £12 million in public authorities' savings. Variations in public authorities' savings are considered further in Part IV as an aspect of fiscal policy. In the next two sections of this chapter we examine more closely the other two components of net savings—personal savings and company savings.

PERSONAL SAVINGS

In an earlier paper we have already published the results of an extensive analysis of the determinants of personal savings in Ireland.[9] Here we need only summarise the main findings and mention their implications for the present study. The analysis referred to sought to explain variations in the annual time series of the personal savings ratio. This is the ratio of personal savings to personal disposable income. Personal disposable income represents the incomes and government transfer payments received by households and unincorporated bodies less direct tax deductions (i.e. income tax, surtax and social insurance contributions). It is, in effect, the income out of which persons are free to make decisions as between personal consumption and personal savings.

The personal savings ratio is plotted on Chart 14 from 1947 to 1968 and, as may be seen, it exhibits considerable variation. We felt that the extremely low levels in 1947 and 1948, probably due to exceptional factors associated with the termination of war-time restrictions, might distort the analysis; accordingly, we used in the regression analysis only the data for the twenty years 1949 to 1968 inclusive. In 1949 the ratio was 7.1 per cent, and during the 1950s it ranged from as high as 9.7 per cent in 1953 to as low as 3.8 per cent in 1958. After 1960 the ratio fell below 9 per cent in only one year (1963). The average level for the eight years 1961 to 1968 was 9.9 per cent as against 7.4 per cent for the twelve years 1949 to 1960.

A wide range of possible explanatory variables was tested, many of them being alternatives for each other. What seemed to

CHART 14: RATIO OF PERSONAL SAVINGS TO PERSONAL DISPOSABLE INCOME, 1947 - 1968

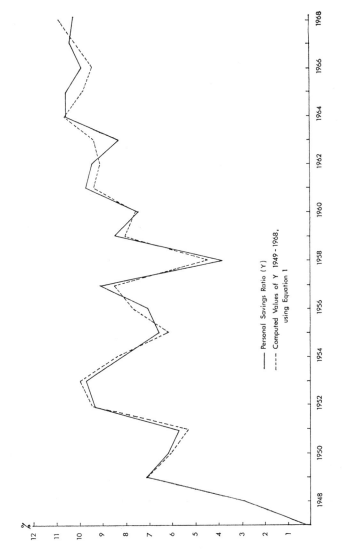

—— Personal Savings Ratio (Y)

---- Computed Values of Y 1949 - 1968,
using Equation 1

us the most satisfactory explanatory equation, from an extensive number of trials,[10] is as follows:

$$Y = 14.52 + \underset{(4.49)}{0.118X_1} + \underset{(4.75)}{0.551X_2} - \underset{(4.93)}{1.945X_3} + \underset{(4.46)}{1.055X_4}$$

$$ 1.8556 \quad 0.8646 \quad 1.509 \quad 1.991$$

$$-\underset{(4.15)}{29.707X_5} + \underset{(4.45)}{2.231X_6} - \underset{(2.16)}{0.067X_7} + \underset{(1.55)}{0.105X_8} \qquad (1)$$

$$ 1.7047 \quad 0.5798 \quad 0.2327 \quad 0.1326$$

$$R^2 = 0.939; \text{ s.e.} = 0.608; \; F = 21.08; \; \tau = 11$$

where Y = ratio of personal savings to personal disposable income.

X_1 = total real personal disposable income *per capita*.

X_2 = ratio of farmers' income (excluding agricultural stock changes) to personal disposable income.

X_3 = ratio of taxes on personal income to non-agricultural personal income.

X_4 = ratio of indirect taxes, less food subsidies, to personal consumption.

X_5 = employment dependency ratio (i.e. ratio of total population less total employment to total employment).

X_6 = annual percentage change in population.

X_7 = annual percentage change in private net credit.

X_8 = real interest rate (i.e. nominal interest rate less percentage change in price).

The figures in brackets are the t-ratios for the significance of the individual coefficients; the figures underneath the t-ratios are the *beta* coefficients, which illustrate the relative importance of the different explanatory variables in accounting for the variance of the dependent variable; R is the multiple correlation coefficient; s.e. is the standard error of estimate; F is the usual F-value for testing the significance of the equation; τ is Geary's statistic of the number of sign changes in the residuals for testing for auto-correlation. The computed values of the savings ratio are plotted in Chart 14, along with the actual values. As may be seen, the fit is remarkably good. The value of the τ-statistic indicates that there is no evidence of autocorrelation.

The dominant variable in explaining variations in the personal savings ratio in Ireland is the level of real income *per capita* when changes in the share of farmers' income in the total personal income are taken into account. An alternative formulation of the income variables, distinguishing farmers' income from non-agricultural income, suggested that farmers' income was a powerful explanatory variable and that farmers have a higher propensity to save than the non-agricultural community. There are several plausible economic reasons for the higher saving propensity of farmers. One is that farmers do not, in effect, pay income tax on their agricultural income. More important, perhaps, is the fact that farmers' income is subject to very considerable fluctuation, so that farmers probably save a high proportion of income increases in good years to provide a cushion for the bad years.

An increase in the ratio of direct taxes to personal income was found to have a strong negative influence on the savings ratio. On the other hand, a rise in the ratio of indirect taxes to personal expenditure tended to raise the savings ratio. These findings may be rationalised as follows. Direct taxes apply with equal force to saving and consumption decisions since the taxes are levied on total income. Indirect taxes, on the other hand, discriminate in favour of saving, though they would also reduce the real value of income. Also direct taxes, being in the main progressive, fall relatively more heavily on the wealthy who are likely to have a comparatively high propensity to save.[11]

A rise in the number of dependants per worker was found to reduce the savings ratio. Dependants here include, as well as those usually classified as dependent on an age basis (i.e. 14 years and under and 65 years and over), married women not in the labour force, students, the unemployed, etc. Such persons contribute to current consumption but not to current production (in the national accounts sense), and it is to be expected that a rise in their share in population would tend to reduce the savings ratio.[12] This dependency ratio rose substantially in the post-war period, particularly in the years 1951 to 1959 when it increased by 0.25 from 1.43 to 1.68. Since our regression results suggest that a rise of 0.1 in the dependency ratio causes a fall of almost 3 percentage points in the savings ratio, it will be appreciated that this factor exercised a substantial drag on the savings ratio in the 1950s. In contrast, the dependency ratio rose by only 0.05 from 1959 to 1968, so that the negative effect on savings was greatly reduced. The rise in the dependency ratio has been due to the interaction between the size and pattern of emigration and the reasonably high birth rate maintained through high fertility rates.

A rise in the rate of growth of population (or, what amounted to the same thing in Ireland, a fall in the emigration rate) was found to increase the savings ratio. This effect seemed to be independent of the effect of the dependency ratio. The high emigration rate of the 1950s may have adversely affected saving through its depressing effects on confidence. Moreover, the emigration rate may be a proxy for a number of other factors influencing saving, such as changes in the composition of persons in receipt of non-agricultural income, and variations in consumption in Ireland in response to consumption standards in the U K.

The influence of the two monetary variables (the rate of change in credit and the real interest rate) was comparatively weak, though the signs of the regression coefficients are in line with what might be expected on *a priori* grounds.

How does our earlier analysis of the influence of the terms of trade relate to the results we have obtained? With an improvement in the terms of trade, the gains accrue in the form of higher incomes for exporters. For the personal sector this could mean higher real income, which would tend to raise the savings ratio. In particular, it may be noted that an important source of improvement in the terms of trade is higher prices of agricultural exports. In that case, the gain accrues to farmers[13] who, according to our model, have a relatively high propensity to save.

COMPANY SAVINGS

There are considerable difficulties attached to attempting an analysis of company savings on the lines of our study of personal savings. Most of these difficulties arise from the lack of adequate data. The company savings data in the national accounts represent the earnings retained by companies after tax, dividends and interest have been paid. This gives a rough measure of company savings. However, data on company income, from which tax and distributions are paid, are not available in the national accounts. The company profits data there relate only to profits arising from domestic activity and are calculated without adjustment for interest received from, or payable to, other sectors. The profits figures also exclude income on investments held abroad by domestic companies. The matter is further complicated by the tax situation. The company tax data in the national accounts relate only to that portion of total tax paid by companies attributable to retained earnings (viz. savings plus company taxes). This is because the tax paid on distributed earnings is considered a tax on the personal sector, and separate figures are not given in the national accounts. If a company were to make no dividend payments, it would have to pay taxes on all profits and the company tax figure derived from national accounts data would rise. What we would wish to have is an estimate of the total earnings, less total tax liabilities, available to companies for distribution or retention, since companies presumably base savings decisions on this figure.

In order to attempt any sort of analysis we were forced to make certain arbitrary assumptions. The first was that the national accounts company profits data represented the total income of companies before tax. This is almost certainly an understatement of the appropriate income figure. Secondly, in order to calculate the total tax liability, the average rate paid on retained income (before tax) was applied to the total income figure. Given these assumptions, an estimate of company income after tax was derived which can be divided into company savings and the balance which approximates to distributed income after tax.

In Chart 15 we set out total company profits (before tax) in each year from 1947 to 1968, together with our estimates of profits after tax and the share of company savings in after-tax profits. There was comparative stagnation in company profits from 1949 to 1957 followed by a strong and relatively steady upward trend from 1957 to 1968. The relative stagnation of company profits in the first decade of the post-war period involved a substantial decline in its share of national income from 10.6 per cent in 1947 to 7.6 per cent in 1957. From 1957 the trend in the share of company profits in national income was upward, reaching 10.3 per cent in 1963. Although the share fell back in 1964 and in 1966, it had risen to 10.8 per cent in 1968. Thus, even if the share of savings in company profits were constant throughout, company savings as a proportion of national income would have fallen up to 1957 and risen thereafter. In fact, this pattern was reinforced

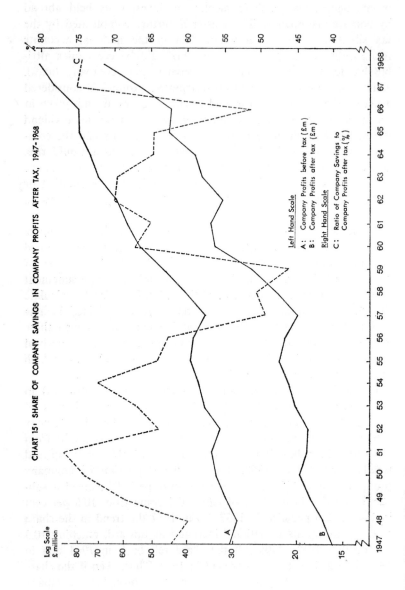

CHART 15: SHARE OF COMPANY SAVINGS IN COMPANY PROFITS AFTER TAX, 1947–1968

Left Hand Scale

A: Company Profits before tax (£m)
B: Company Profits after tax (£m)

Right Hand Scale

C: Ratio of Company Savings to
     Company Profits after tax (%)

Log Scale
£ million

by the fact that company savings as a proportion of company profits fell during the 1950s. Thus the ratio of company savings to national income fell from 4.3 per cent in 1950 to 2.1 per cent in 1957. In 1960 the ratio rose sharply to 4.1 per cent and stood at 4.9 per cent in 1968.

Company profits after tax moved in a similar fashion to profits before tax. Although there were changes in tax rates during the period, these were not sufficiently large to alter the broad picture of comparative stagnation up to 1957 followed by a strong rise thereafter. The share of savings in after-tax profits rose up to 1951, but then fell substantially, reaching a low point of 46 per cent in 1959. Following a sharp rise to 67 per cent in 1960, the share remained at about this level for most years in the 1960s, apart from the recession year 1966 when it fell to 51 per cent.

The behaviour of company savings in the 1950s bears a remarkable resemblance to that of manufacturing investment. One would expect to find a relationship between the saving and investment behaviour of companies since, on the one hand, investment is partly financed by retained earnings, while, on the other hand, the availability of profitable investment opportunities helps to determine the savings policy of companies. We do not have data on company investment, but a large number of the companies were engaged in manufacturing and it might reasonably be argued that manufacturing investment could be used as a rough proxy for company investment. Up to about 1960 there was a close relationship between movements in manufacturing investment and in company savings *in the preceding year*. The correlation for the thirteen first differences from 1947–48 to 1959–60 is 0.72, significant at the 1 per cent level.[14]

It might be argued that this relationship reflected primarily the influence of savings on investment: thus when company savings were low, firms did not have sufficient funds to undertake investment in the following year. This view, however, does not accord with experience. From 1947 to 1951 (a time when aggregate demand was expanding relatively rapidly and investment opportunities were reasonably buoyant) the ratio of company savings to profits after tax rose from 62.5 per cent to 77.2 per cent. The slow rise in demand in the 1950s severely limited opportunities for manufacturing investment. Even though profits after tax were nearly 50 per cent higher in 1959 than in 1951, savings were lower in 1959 (and in every intervening year except 1954) than in 1951. On the other hand, distributed profits (after tax) rose throughout the period from £4.3 million in 1951 to £14.3 million in 1959. Thus the ratio of company savings to after-tax profits fell from 77 per cent in 1951 to 46 per cent in 1959. If profitable manufacturing investment were limited by lack of finance, companies would scarcely have allowed the proportion of profits retained to decline so much.

CONCLUSIONS

The picture that emerges for company savings is not unlike that for personal savings. The stagnation of aggregate demand in the 1950s was a major cause of the stagnation in both categories of savings. As we shall discuss more fully in Part IV, the growth of domestic demand on the 1950s was very slow, principally due to the absence of fiscal stimuli. The non-expansionary fiscal policy itself was founded on the belief that current domestic savings would be inadequate to finance increases in the Public Capital Programme, and that expansion of public investment would, therefore, cause intolerable strain on the balance of payments. But the failure to expand demand led to self-fulfilling prophecies about the level of savings. With exports in a transitional state, the absence of sufficient stimuli to domestic demand resulted in a slow growth of output and real income *per capita*, falling population, a rising dependency ratio, near-stagnation in profits and decreasing opportunities for profitable investment. These factors tended to lower the level of personal and company savings.

Whether increased savings generated by higher incomes in response to stronger pressure of home demand would have been sufficient to avoid balance of payments difficulties depends on a number of factors. These include the adequacy of external reserves and the degree of confidence regarding the satisfactory development of exports, factors which we will consider in more detail in Chapters 13 to 15 dealing with short-term policy. But at the risk of anticipating our conclusions, it does seem that the policy-makers of the 1950s were unaware of, or discounted heavily, the dynamic relationship between income, savings and investment and failed to adopt bolder measures that might have pushed the economy onto a faster growth path.

CHAPTER 11

The Role of Investment

I N Chapter 2 it was shown that the growth rate of investment was much higher from 1961 to 1968 than from 1949 to 1961, and that the investment ratio also rose somewhat. In this chapter we examine the relation between investment[1] and the growth of output.

The trend of total fixed investment broadly mirrors that of total output. This can be seen by comparing Chart 16, showing the volume of gross fixed investment for each year from 1947 to 1968, with Chart 1, which gives the data for real G N P. There was a strong rise in investment in the early post-war years, comparative stagnation during the 1950s with a large decline during the 1956–58 depression, and then a strong upward trend from about 1960, with the exception of the recession year 1966. Recovery in the economy following the 1956–58 depression tended to lead recovery in total investment rather than *vice versa*. The decline in investment during the 1956–58 period was so great that the 1955 level was only reached again in 1961, whereas real G N P was 13 per cent above the 1955 level. Thus the ratio of fixed investment to G N P in 1961 was below the 1955 ratio.

MAJOR COMPONENTS OF FIXED INVESTMENT

Different types of investment have widely different effects on such variables as capacity, aggregate demand and productivity. Some investments yield a relatively large and immediate rise in capacity, whereas others contribute to output relatively slowly over a long period. Even if the present value of the output streams of both types of asset (i.e. the output streams discounted at some appropriate interest rate) is the same, the former type of investment will

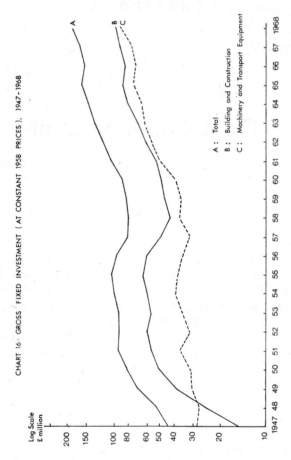

CHART 16: GROSS FIXED INVESTMENT (AT CONSTANT 1958 PRICES), 1947-1968

A: Total
B: Building and Construction
C: Machinery and Transport Equipment

yield a faster output growth in the short run, provided, of course, that adequate demand is maintained. This distinction between the relative size and time pattern of output streams of different types of investment dominated public policy towards investment in the second half of the 1950s. It was linked to a large extent to the merits of investment in building and construction, particularly for social purposes (such as hospitals, schools and houses), as against investment in more immediately productive assets like machinery. The volume of investment in building and construction in post-war Ireland was predominantly determined by the Public Capital Programme, which financed a substantial part of such investment and influenced much of the remainder through incentive grants, etc. In the mid-1950s the view gained ground that a good deal of this investment contributed little to productive capacity and that, even where it did, it did so only slowly. Hence the basis of the view that it was essential to shift to more immediately productive investment.

However, the importance of such investment in maintaining aggregate demand was not adequately taken into account. The creation of immediately productive capacity would not raise output unless adequate demand were maintained. In so far as domestic demand was concerned, public investment was one of the most important autonomous stimuli. The stimulative effect of investment on domestic demand and employment depends on the import content of the investment itself and, in relation to the income it induces, on the marginal propensities to save and import and the marginal tax rate. There is no reason to suppose that, in the case of induced income, the marginal saving, import and tax rates would be significantly different for different types of investment. However, building and construction, because of its low import content, has a far greater impact on demand in Ireland than investment in machinery, the bulk of which is imported. The direct and indirect import content of building investment is only about 25 per cent, as against an import content of 73 per cent for the remainder of total fixed investment.[2]

When the economy was operating well below capacity, investment designed to increase capacity (but with little impact on domestic demand) might do little to raise output growth. Indeed, in the face of inadequate demand, it might prove impossible to encourage increased investment of a more immediately productive type in the private sector since, with existing capacity not fully utilised, the incentive to add new capacity would be greatly weakened. On the other hand, investment providing a strong stimulus to demand, although it only raised short-run capacity by a small amount, would lead to increased output as existing capacity was more fully utilised.[3] However, if the economy were operating at full capacity, further stimulation of demand, without markedly increasing capacity, would lead to inflationary pressures. In that case, investment with a low degree of domestic stimulation, which increased short-run capacity substantially, would be preferable. This, then, is one of the trade-offs between different categories of investment that must be borne in mind when examining the role of investment in relation to output.

Investment by Type of Capital Good

Chart 16 shows the annual data for investment divided into building and construction and machinery (including transport equipment). The rapid rise in total investment from 1947 to 1951 reflected chiefly building investment, which rose nearly fourfold. The 30 per cent increase in investment in machinery and transport equipment, although by no means small, was dwarfed by the massive rise in building investment. In 1947 building and construction accounted for 34½ per cent of the relatively small volume of investment in that year, the balance of 65½ per cent being devoted to machinery and transport equipment. The share of building rose to a record figure of 65.3 per cent in 1951. The stabilisation of the level of building investment from 1951 to 1956 at about £60 million (at 1958 prices) was not compensated for by any substantial rise in investment in machinery etc. Thus the share of building remained high because of the failure of other investment to expand. A large decline in building investment took place in the years 1956 to 1958, due mainly to cut-backs in public investment in housing. At that time there was near stagnation in the volume of investment in machinery etc., which declined from 1954 to 1957 and recovered to the 1954 level only in 1960. Thus, while there was a significant shift in the share of building in total investment (involving a reduction from an average of 62 per cent in the first half of the 1950s to 53½ per cent in 1958), this took place in the context of a falling level of total investment and an even greater fall in the ratio of investment to G N P. From 1958 to 1968 total investment rose rapidly. The share of building investment remained at about the 1958 level, implying that in this period the growth of building investment was about the same as investment in machinery etc.

As already mentioned, the cut-back in building investment, particularly housing, in the mid-1950s was due to a deliberate policy designed to achieve a shift in total investment to assets that would yield a larger immediate increase in output. Reading policy statements of the time, it appears as if the authorities regarded the total volume of investment as fixed, and that only by reducing one category would it be possible to increase another. Such a view paid inadequate attention to the possibilities that demand was insufficient to maintain output growth, that rising investment was important in maintaining demand, and that rising investment might be impossible to achieve in the context of a reduction in social and infrastructural investment. We have already suggested that in the conditions of the 1950s, given the small proportion of manufacturing output exported and the decline in tourism, domestic demand was crucial in maintaining a satisfactory growth of output in the manufacturing and services sectors until such time as the attempts to raise exports bore fruit. Building investment, because of its high labour content and the relative ease with which it could be influenced by the authorities, was one of the most crucial policy instruments for this purpose. It was undoubtedly important also to channel resources into other types of investment, particularly for exports. But this did not necessarily call for a cut-back in building investment, and the evidence suggests that the effect of this policy was to reduce, rather than increase, the volume of other investment.

When the volume of building was stabilised from the early 1950s, investment in machinery etc. also remained virtually stagnant. Thus the volume of total investment was stagnant for most of the 1950s and, undoubtedly, this contributed to the slow growth of output and was, in turn, reinforced by the slow growth of output. Although the cut-back in building after the mid-1950s did raise the *share* of investment in machinery in the total, there was a fall in the *level* of such investment, as well as in total investment. At the end of the decade greater government incentives to investment and exports were available. In addition, manufactured exports, as a result of their rapid growth since the early 1950s, now represented a more important component of demand for increased manufacturing output, thereby providing greater inducement for investment in machinery, etc. Moreover, tourist receipts were rising relatively rapidly. However, the sustained rise in total investment began only in 1959, when the level of building activity rose again, and both classes of investment expanded at much the same rate thereafter. Thus the outstanding difference between the growth of investment from 1961 to 1968 and earlier was not that building investment grew more slowly, which it did not, but rather that other investment grew more rapidly. Comparing 1949–61 with 1961–68, we find

G

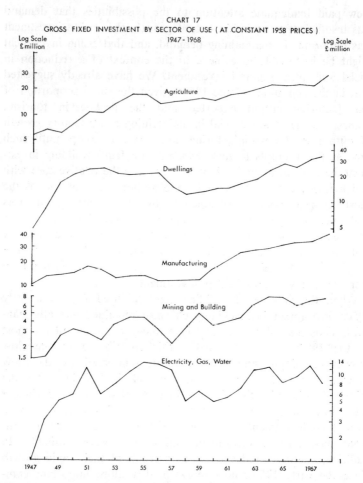

CHART 17
GROSS FIXED INVESTMENT BY SECTOR OF USE (AT CONSTANT 1958 PRICES)
1947 - 1968

that the rate of growth of total investment rose from 3.4 per cent per annum to 8.9 per cent per annum, the growth rate of investment in machinery, etc. rose from 4.0 per cent to 8.9 per cent, while the growth rate of building nearly trebled from 3.1 per cent to 8.8 per cent.[4] Thus, even in the period 1961–68, building activity was an important element in raising the growth of investment and demand.

Investment by Sector of Use

It could be argued that the sub-categories of total investment

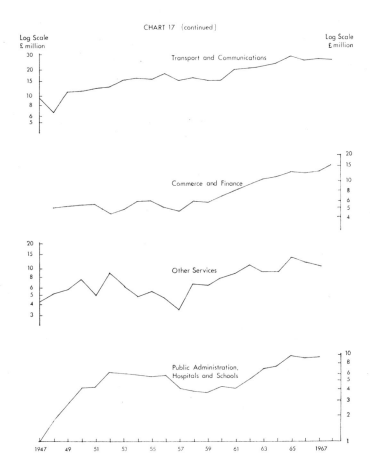

CHART 17 (continued)

we have used are too broad in that not all building and construction increases output capacity slowly and that not all investment in machinery, etc. increases output capacity relatively quickly. It is of interest, from this and other viewpoints, to examine the components of investment in greater detail. For this purpose, we have divided total fixed investment by sector of use, and the volume of investment in the main sectors is plotted in Chart 17 for the years 1947 to 1968.

Given that the stress on shifting investment from 'social' to 'productive' sectors focused particularly on channeling investment away from housing towards manufacturing, it is of special interest to compare trends in those two sectors. The volume of investment in dwellings (at 1958 prices) rose almost fivefold between 1947 and 1951, from £4.9 million to £23.6 million. It increased only slightly in 1952 and was cut back somewhat in 1953 and 1954, remaining at about £21 million until 1956. The cuts imposed in 1957 and 1958 reduced the volume of investment in dwellings to just over half the 1956 level of £21.6 million. Thereafter housing investment expanded fairly rapidly (10.7 per cent per annum from 1958 to 1968), though the 1952 level was only reached again in 1965. It is not without significance to our earlier discussion that investment in manufacturing has shared a similar, though less extreme, pattern. It rose relatively rapidly by 62.1 per cent (or 12.8 per cent per annum) between 1947 and 1951 (from £10.8 million to £17.5 million). It declined in 1952 and 1953 and for the rest of the 1950s remained at about the 1953 level of £13 million, the lowest point being £12.0 million in 1957. Since 1959, investment in manufacturing has shown a strong rise at an average annual rate of 13.9 per cent, even greater than that experienced between 1947 and 1951. However, the 1951 volume of investment in manufacturing was not exceeded until 1961, and the 1951 share of manufacturing investment in total GNP was not exceeded until 1962. Thus there is no strong evidence of a rise in the level of manufacturing investment, or its share in GNP, prior to the increase in the growth rate of GNP. Neither does it emerge that cutting back housing investment in any way helped to raise the level of manufacturing investment: indeed, the contrary is indicated.

The average of the annual shares of major sectors in total fixed investment (at constant 1958 prices) are given in Table 36 for the years 1949 to 1960 inclusive and 1961 to 1968 inclusive. Looking at the three major sectors of the economy (agriculture, industry and services), it is clear that the shifts in shares between these sectors have been comparatively small. Agriculture's share remained virtually unchanged, while industry gained slightly at the expense of services. Shifts in the components within these sectors were rather greater. Thus the share of manufacturing in total investment rose by over 5 percentage points but was partly offset by a fall in the share of electricity, gas and water. The decline in the housing share was nearly 5 percentage points.

Table 36: Average annual shares of components (classified by sector of use) in total fixed investment, 1949–60 and 1961–68 inclusive*

	1949–60	1961–68
	%	%
Agriculture	14.7	14.9
Industry	29.6	32.3
Mining, building and construction	4.0	4.5
Manufacturing	16.1	21.2
Electricity, gas and water	9.5	6.6
Services	55.7	52.8
Transport and communications	16.2	16.0
Commerce and finance	6.2	7.7
Dwellings	20.8	16.0
Public administration, schools and hospitals**	5.4	5.3
Other services	7.0	7.7
Total	100.0	100.0

*The calculations are based on the data in constant (1958) prices.
**The figures for schools and hospitals refer to building activity only. Investment in school and hospital equipment is included in 'other services'.

Source: The data on which the above calculations are based are prepared by the C S O for the United Nations and published in the U N *Yearbook of National Accounts Statistics.* The figures for all years at 1958 prices used here were kindly supplied direct by the C S O. The figures for school and hospital building do not appear separately in the U N data, but were also supplied by the C S O.

However, as we have already argued, these changes in shares seem to us of far less consequence for growth in the period 1961–68 than the relatively rapid growth of all categories of investment.

INVESTMENT, OUTPUT AND LABOUR PRODUCTIVITY

The ratio between the volume of investment in a given period and the change in the volume of output in the same period is known as the incremental capital-output ratio (I C O R). It may conveniently be calculated by dividing the average investment ratio (i.e. the average of the annual ratios of investment to output) by the average annual growth rate of output.[5] The I C O R, if regarded as a means of organising data for further analysis, rather than as an end in itself, can be a helpful tool in comparing the relation between investment and increased output in two different periods or in two different countries. The concept has been subject to considerable criticism, but much of this applies to misuses of the concept. A low I C O R in a given period indicates that a relatively low rate of investment was associated with a relatively high rate of growth of output, but it does not indicate the reasons why this was so. Neither can it be presumed that the I C O R will continue at the same level unless the factors influencing it are likely to remain unchanged. Since the I C O R is simply a measure of the relation between investment and a change in output, the inference should not be drawn that investment, or investment alone, is responsible for the rise in output.[6]

Ideally the I C O R should be measured in terms of net investment and net output. However, in the absence of satisfactory data on the net magnitudes, the analysis must often be conducted, as here, in terms of the relation between gross investment and changes in gross output (G I C O R).

Economy-wide G I C O R

Table 37 sets out the average annual investment ratio, the

Table 37: Average annual investment ratio, average annual growth rate of output, and G I C O R, 1949–61 and 1961–68*

	1949–61	1961–68
Average gross fixed investment ratio (%)	14.8	18.3
Average growth rate of G N P (%)	1.9	4.1
G I C O R	7.8	4.5

*All the figures are derived from data in constant (1958) market prices. The investment ratio is calculated by taking the ratio of gross fixed investment to G N P each year and averaging over the period. For 1949–61 the average of the twelve years 1949 to 1960 inclusive was used, and for 1961–68 the average of the seven years 1961 to 1967 inclusive. Average annual growth rates of G N P were based on the beginning and end year of each period. The G I C O R is derived by dividing the investment ratio by the growth rate of output. The figures have been rounded to one decimal place for simplicity.

Source: *National Income and Expenditure 1969.*

average annual growth rate of output, and the derived G I C O R for the economy as a whole for the periods 1949–61 and 1961–68. The fall in the G I C O R between the two periods (from 7.8 to 4.5) was considerable.[7] If we make the assumption that the G I C O R is unaffected by a rise in the investment ratio—though, as we point out below, this may be an incorrect assumption—then it follows that the faster growth of output from 1961 to 1968 was due much more to the rise in the productivity of investment in relation to output (as indicated by the fall in the G I C O R) than to the rise in the investment ratio. This may be illustrated as follows. The average annual growth rate rose from 1.89 per cent from 1949 to 1961 to 4.08 per cent from 1961 to 1968—a rise of 2.19 per cent. If the G I C O R had remained unchanged while the investment ratio rose as shown, then the growth rate for 1961–68 would be 2.34 per cent—a rise of 0.45 per cent compared with the earlier period. If, on the other hand, the investment ratio had not changed but the G I C O R had fallen as shown, the growth rate would be 3.30 per cent, or a rise of 1.41 per cent[8]—more than $2\frac{1}{2}$ times as large as the effect of the higher investment ratio. Putting the matter another way, if the G I C O R had remained unchanged, the growth rate achieved from 1961 to 1968 would have required an average annual investment ratio of 31.9 per cent.

These calculations are based on the assumption that a rise in the investment ratio would not alter the G I C O R. However, if, as may plausibly be argued, a rise in the investment ratio were in itself likely to lower the G I C O R, then clearly the calculations may underrate the contribution of the rise in the investment ratio. The argument is as follows.[9] We are here relating gross investment to the change in gross product whereas ideally, given suitable data, we would wish to relate net investment to the change in net product. The relevant concept of net investment in this context is gross investment less replacement of retired assets. The reason for deducting the cost of replacing assets actually retired is that assets are assumed to retain their capacity to produce output throughout their active life. The fact that the efficiency of some assets declines with age would modify this, but the presumption here is that assets are retired before their current capacity to produce output has declined substantially. The replacement cost of retired assets is not the same as depreciation in the national accounts, since the depreciated value of an asset for national accounts purposes generally has little relation to its annual capacity to produce output *while still in use.*[10]

When the ratio of gross investment to output rises, the proportion of new assets to old assets tends to rise, unless the effect is completely offset by a reduction of the length of life of assets. The rise in the proportion of new assets to old will lower the ratio of replacement to gross investment, so that the net investment ratio, as defined above, will rise relatively more than the gross investment ratio.[11] Given an unchanged *net* I C O R, the rise in the net investment ratio will involve an equi-proportionate rise in the growth rate of output. Since the gross investment ratio has risen relatively less than the net investment ratio, the G I C O R must, therefore, fall even though there has been no change in the net I C O R.[12] It is possible that at least some of the decline in the G I C O R during 1961–68 compared with 1949–61 can be accounted for in this way, but it is worth considering other factors that might explain the substantial fall.

G I C O R by Sector

It is possible, for instance, that the fall in the G I C O R can be explained by shifts in the sectoral shares of investment. A shift in the share of investment from a sector with a high G I C O R towards a sector with a low G I C O R would tend to lower the economy-wide G I C O R, although the sectoral G I C O Rs remained unchanged. In view of the fact, already mentioned, that changes in sectoral shares of investment were not large, it is unlikely that this factor would account for much of the fall in the overall G I C O R. However, the sectoral G I C O Rs are of interest in themselves and are shown in Table 38 for each of the three major sectors of the economy (agriculture, industry and services) and for certain components of the industrial and services sectors. In calculating the G I C O Rs here, the concept of output used is the volume of gross domestic product at factor cost. Hence the level of the G I C O R for the whole economy differs from that in Table 37, where output is measured in terms of G N P at constant market prices. However, the rate of fall in the overall G I C O R between the two periods is much the same.

It may be seen from Table 38 that in both periods the G I C O R for agriculture and services was large compared with that for

Table 38: GICORs for major sectors of the economy, 1949–61 and 1961–68*

	Average ratio of investment to GDP (%)		Average annual growth rate of GDP (%)		GICOR	
	1949–61	1961–68	1949–61	1961–68	1949–61	1961–68
Agriculture	9.9	14.2	0.9	1.2	11.1	12.2
Industry	18.7	21.3	3.6	6.5	5.2	3.3
Mining and building	8.3	11.7	1.5	5.7	5.6	2.1
Manufacturing	16.5	21.1	4.4	6.5	3.8	3.3
Electricity, gas and water	81.5	50.1	6.3	8.8	13.0	5.7
Services	23.1	28.2	1.6	3.3	14.3	8.5
Dwellings	n.a.	96.7	n.a.	2.1	n.a.	46.0
Rest of services	n.a.	21.6	n.a.	3.4	n.a.	6.3
Total	18.2	22.5	2.0	3.9	9.2	5.8

*The GICOR estimates are derived as explained in the note to Table 37 except that here the concept of output used is gross domestic product (GDP) at constant factor cost, whereas in Table 37 it is GNP at constant market prices. This table is based on data published in *National Income and Expenditure 1968* which has been since revised. No account was taken of these revisions in calculating the GICOR but the magnitude of the revisions was not such as to significantly alter the figures presented here.

Sources: *Investment*: Data supplied by CSO. The data are prepared for the UN *Yearbook of National Accounts Statistics*. *Output*: The estimates of GDP at constant (1958) factor cost for the whole economy and for agriculture, industry and services for the years 1949 to 1957 were derived as explained in Table 4. For the years 1958 to 1968, data taken from *National Income and Expenditure 1968*. Real product each year in manufacturing was derived by multiplying the 1958 GDP in manufacturing by the index of volume of output in manufacturing (to base 1958 = 100), taken from the *Census of Industrial Production* (CIP). The real product of electricity, gas and water was similarly estimated. In both cases the GDP at factor cost was estimated from the CIP using ratios derived from comparison of the 1964 Input-Output Table with the 1964 CIP. GDP in dwellings represents the value of rent (actual and imputed) plus depreciation, for which figures in value and volume have been prepared by the CSO for the UN *Yearbook of National Accounts Statistics*, covering the years 1958 to 1968. It was not possible to derive estimates in volume terms for years preceding 1958.

industry. Thus the shift in the share of investment from services to industry would tend to lower the overall G I C O R, although the sectoral G I C O Rs were unchanged. The effect, however, would be small, given the small change in investment shares. Clearly changes in the G I C O R within the sectors were of much greater consequence. The G I C O R for services, which accounted for more than half of total investment, fell from 14.3 to 8.5, proportionately greater than the fall in the economy-wide G I C O R, while the industry G I C O R fell by the same proportion as for the economy as a whole. In agriculture there was a slight rise in the G I C O R, but agriculture accounted for only 15 per cent of total investment. To some extent, the reduction in the G I C O R for the industrial and services sectors also represented a shift from investment with a high G I C O R to investment with a low G I C O R. In the industrial sector in the period 1949–61 the G I C O R in manufacturing was 3.6, against 13.0 for electricity, gas and water. The shift in the share of investment from electricity to manufacturing would tend to reduce the G I C O R for the industrial sector if there was no change in the G I C O R of the components. The effect would be small, however: the shift in investment shares alone would lower the industrial G I C O R from 5.2 to 4.7, whereas it actually fell to 3.3. Of greater significance in lowering the G I C O R for the industrial sector was the fall in the G I C O R for the components. The large fall in the G I C O R for electricity—from 13.0 to 5.7—suggests another factor accounting for the fall in the overall G I C O R in the more recent period, namely greater utilisation of capacity that had been provided in the earlier period.[13] There can be little doubt that the large-scale investment in electricity, particularly in the transmission network, in the first period involved the provision of capacity that could become more fully utilised only with a considerable time-lag as demand expanded.

The large fall in the G I C O R for services might be attributed partly to the shift away from investment in dwellings which had an enormous G I C O R for the period 1961–68—46.0 compared with 6.3 for the rest of services.[14] Unfortunately, there are no figures for the volume of gross product of dwellings prior to 1958 so that it is not possible to estimate the G I C O R for dwellings in the earlier period. However, there are no compelling reasons to suppose that the G I C O R in dwellings would have altered much in the two periods, and by assuming the same G I C O R for dwellings in the period 1949–61 as in the period 1961–68, we can then estimate the G I C O R for the rest of services for 1949–61. The figure arrived at on this basis for the G I C O R in the rest of services (i.e. excluding dwellings) was 10.1 for 1949–61 compared to 6.3 for 1961–68, representing a fall of 38 per cent. The G I C O R for total services (i.e. including dwellings) fell from 14.3 to 8.5, a decrease of 40 per cent. Thus it would seem that only a small proportion of the fall in the services G I C O R was due to the shift in investment away from dwellings.[15]

How then can we explain the bulk of the fall in the services G I C O R? The chief explanation, we would suggest, is the same as that put forward in the case of electricity: the capacity provided by investment in services in the first period was much more fully utilised in the second period. Because of the indivisibilities involved, it is in the nature of infrastructural investment (in activities such as roads, harbours, airports, etc.) that capacity has to be provided well in excess of existing demand, and that subsequently, as demand grows, output can expand with relatively lower investment.

It is important to recognise this link between the two post-war periods. Faster growth in the second period depended in no small way on the social overhead capital provided in the first period, the fruits of which were only fully reaped later. The large-scale provision of such capacity in the first period allowed growth to proceed more rapidly in the second period without a correspondingly large increase in investment. It is, of course, true that the larger investment in the second period in sectors with a low G I C O R was necessary to make possible the greater utilisation of the social overhead capital provided in the first period. But it does not necessarily follow from this that a faster long-term growth rate would have been achieved in the post-war period as a whole by devoting a smaller share of the *actual* amount of investment undertaken in the first period to social overhead capital. A certain minimum of infrastructural facilities is a necessary prerequisite to successful investment in a sector like manufacturing. Investment in a factory is unlikely to succeed unless the employees are housed and there are adequate facilities to transport raw materials and output. Because of the indivisible nature of much social overhead capital, it cannot, in general, be provided in small doses. We do not deny, of course, that a better balance might have been maintained between social overhead investment and other categories of investment. But on the whole it seems to us that the weakness in the first period was not that an excessive amount was invested in infrastructural facilities, but rather that not enough was invested in sectors which would have yielded a relatively early growth of output—in other words, faster growth would have required more rapid expansion of total investment. This weakness, as we discuss more fully in Part IV, hinged both on the smaller scope and scale of government incentives to industrial investment and on the view taken of the balance of payments.

Investment and Changes in Labour Productivity

Consideration of the very high G I C O R in agriculture suggests another possibility that might account for the lower aggregate G I C O R in the more recent period, namely that investment in a given industry (or over a given time period) may be devoted relatively more to raising labour productivity than to raising capacity compared with other industries (or other time periods). This is the well-known distinction between capital deepening and capital widening. Of course, much new investment is designed to increase both labour productivity and capacity, but the balance may differ from one industry to another or from one period to another.

The I C O R measures the relation between investment and the increase in output, but it gives no information about the relation between investment and the increase in labour productivity. It is possible that the relatively high G I C O R in agriculture is due to the fact that investment in agriculture has been primarily directed towards raising labour productivity rather than output. Productivity gains in agriculture are sometimes viewed as an automatic response to rural migration. Workers in that sector are regarded as so underemployed that a large decline in the numbers can occur without reducing total output. Although there may be some degree of 'disguised unemployment' in agriculture, it is unlikely that, in the face of the large decline in numbers engaged, the level of output could be maintained without considerable technical progress, much of which would be incorporated in new machines. Moreover, the investment in certain agricultural construction works, such as water supply, was also undoubtedly designed to increase labour productivity.

A measure of the relation between investment and the change in labour productivity, analogous to the G I C O R as a measure of the relation of investment to changes in output, has been suggested by Lamfalussy (1963). This is the ratio of investment per worker to the change in output per worker, which can be conveniently calculated by dividing the investment ratio (i.e. the ratio of gross investment to output) by the growth rate of labour productivity.[16] This may be called the gross investment-productivity ratio, and in Table 39 we set out this ratio for various sectors of the economy in the periods 1949–61 and 1961–68.

Table 39: Gross investment-productivity ratios for major sectors of the economy, 1949–61 and 1961–68*

	1949–61	1961–68
Agriculture	2.7	3.6
Industry	4.9	5.3
Manufacturing	6.2	4.8
Services	11.4	12.9
Services (excluding dwellings)**	8.0	9.4
Total	5.5	6.1
Total (excluding dwellings)**	4.5	5.2

*The gross investment-productivity ratio is measured by dividing the average annual ratio of gross fixed investment to G D P by the growth rate of G D P per worker, all variables measured at constant (1958) prices. **The calculation of the figure for services (excluding dwellings) was done by assuming that the G I C O R for dwellings in the first period was 46, the same as in the second period: this assumption permitted estimation of an output figure for dwellings, for which no data were available prior to 1958. In calculating the productivity change for services (excluding dwellings) the same employment figures were used as for total services. A similar procedure was followed for the total (excluding dwellings).

Sources: Investment and output data estimated as described in Table 38. For employment sources see Table 4.

While the agricultural sector has a very high G I C O R, it has by far the lowest gross investment-productivity ratio. This result is quite consistent with the view that investment in agriculture was directed substantially towards replacing labour. It does not necessarily imply, of course, that investment was the cause of the displacement of labour. Rather, investment may replace labour that was already moving out in response to factors such as the low income per head in agriculture. Comparing the two periods 1949–61 and 1961–68, the gross investment-productivity ratio in agriculture was significantly lower in the first period. Since the GICOR was also lower, it appears that the productivity of investment in relation to both output and labour productivity in agriculture was somewhat greater in the first period. This is not an implausible finding and might be accounted for on several grounds. It is possible, for instance, that the capital intensity of production was considerably lower in 1949 than in 1961, so that additional injections of capital yielded rather more in the way of expansion of output and labour productivity in the earlier period. There was also probably a greater degree of disguised unemployment in the first period.

In the industrial sector the gross investment-productivity ratio was also slightly lower in the first period. However, in manufacturing the ratio was markedly lower in the second period and, since the GICOR was also somewhat lower in the second period, it would seem that the productivity of investment both in capital widening and in capital deepening was greater for manufacturing in the second period. This may be due to a faster rate of technical progress in the second period resulting from the faster growth of output and also from the establishment of many branches of technologically advanced foreign companies catering primarily for the export market.

In services the gross investment-productivity ratio was somewhat lower in the first period. Thus, while the productivity of investment in capital widening was far greater in the second period, its productivity in capital deepening appears to have been slightly greater in the first period. This result is not inconsistent with our argument that the substantial fall in the services GICOR in the second period was due mainly to greater utilisation of infrastructural capacity provided in the first period. The exploitation of this capacity, while allowing a rapid rate of growth of output relative to the investment ratio, might require a greater rise in the growth of labour input.

Looking at the position for the economy as a whole, the gross investment-productivity ratio was slightly lower in the first period than in the second. Thus there is some suggestion that, while investment was markedly more productive in relation to output in the second period, it was slightly more productive in relation to labour productivity in the first period.[17] In order to assess the combined productivity of investment in relation to output *and* labour productivity, we would need to know the elasticity of substitution between labour and capital.[18] However, given that the rise in the aggregate gross investment-productivity ratio was so slight, it is probably safe to conclude that the far lower G I C O R in the second period was not due in any large measure to greater concentration in the first period on investment designed to raise labour productivity.

CONCLUSIONS

The large fall in the G I C O R in the period 1961–68 as compared with the period 1949–61 was important in permitting a faster rate of growth of output in the more recent period, without a substantial rise in the investment ratio and the probable resulting pressure on the balance of payments. We considered various factors that might account for the fall in the G I C O R. Among these, the rise in the ratio of investment to output and the shift in the share of total investment toward assets yielding a larger immediate increase in output may be of some consequence. But a key factor appears to us to be the greater utilisation of infrastructural capacity provided in the earlier period. If this is correct, it establishes a major connecting link between the two periods, which makes it misleading to treat them as completely dissociated from each other.

We also suggested that the marked curtailment of building activity, especially housing, for most of the 1950s (in particular the severe cut-back in 1957–58) retarded the growth of domestic demand. In turn, the slow growth of domestic demand adversely affected demand for investment in manufacturing. In the 1950s manufactured exports, though expanding rapidly, were a relatively small proportion of output; substantial government incentives to encourage manufacturing investment were developed fully only towards the end of the decade; and tourism, a further source of demand for output of manufacturing, was declining or stagnant in the first half of the decade. In these circumstances, expansion of manufacturing output and investment depended to a considerable degree on expansion of domestic demand. While it would undoubtedly have been desirable to maintain a better balance in the first period between social overhead capital and more immediately productive investment, it appears to us that this balance could only have been achieved through a greater overall growth of investment and not, as was thought at the time, by cutting back on social overhead capital formation.[19] Such infrastructural capacity was in any event a necessary prerequisite to economic development and, as we mentioned, its provision in the 1950s greatly facilitated growth in the 1960s.

In the 1960s substantial incentives were available for investment in manufacturing, including foreign investment. Manufactured exports represented a considerably larger share of output at the end of the 1950s, compared with the beginning, and their continued expansion was further encouraged by the tax relief measures of 1956. Moreover, tourism was at this stage growing rapidly. Nevertheless, it is important to note that building activity (including housing) began to expand again in 1959, and thereafter its expansion kept pace with the rapid growth of other forms of investment. Had this not been so, then, despite all the other incentives to more immediately productive activities, it is unlikely that a satisfactory growth rate of output would have been achieved in the 1960s.

PART IV

DEMAND MANAGEMENT

CHAPTER 12

Introduction

S o far we have concentrated mainly on longer-term trends and have given only passing attention to the course of the economy through time. In this part of the study we discuss short-term fluctuations in the economy and the policy responses to these fluctuations. In addition, we will be concerned with how demand management operated in relation to longer-term economic growth.

In the management of the post-war Irish economy, fiscal policy played a crucial role in relation both to the short-term and the longer-term situation. As is well known, an increase in public expenditure, even if matched by an increase in public revenue, generates increased demand in the economy. In Irish circumstances, the stimulating effects were likely to be relatively large compared with other autonomous components of demand. The volume of total public spending was substantial relative to G N P,[1] while its import content was relatively low.[2] From the longer-term viewpoint, a significant proportion of public expenditure was directed towards raising the growth potential of the economy. This was true in particular of the Public Capital Programme, which was initially designed largely to establish the infrastructure for development but subsequently also provided substantial finance for capital formation in agriculture, industry and tourism. Current expenditure also contributed in part to raising the growth potential through expenditure under such headings as education, retraining of workers, etc.

On the other hand, there was not much in the way of an independent monetary policy for most of the post-war period. The Central Bank exercised little or no control over the reserves of the commercial banks or the level of interest rates, both of which are generally regarded as crucial for effective monetary policy. No control was maintained by the monetary authorities on the volume of bank credit until towards the end of our period, and even then the Central Bank guidelines were not closely adhered to. Monetary factors arose, of course, in relation to the amount and character of borrowing by the government for financing the overall fiscal deficit. On the whole, however, the basic decisions were made by the fiscal authorities—influenced, no doubt, by monetary considerations—and monetary policy represented chiefly a passive accommodation to these decisions.

In discussing fiscal policy, we have used the data on expenditure and receipts of public authorities as classified for national accounts purposes. This classification differs in several respects from the traditional accounting basis used by the authorities, and the major differences are explained in an appendix to this chapter. The public authorities include both central and local government. While conscious decisions on the use of fiscal policy for demand management are taken only by the central government, it is, nevertheless, appropriate to include the local authorities' figures, since much of their spending is decided on and financed by the central authority.

In Chart 18 we set out figures for the current and capital expenditure of the public authorities, and the balance (i.e. surplus or deficit of expenditure over receipts) on the current account and overall for each year from 1947 to 1968. Current expenditure includes both direct spending on goods and services by the public sector and transfers (e.g. social welfare benefits, subsidies, national debt interest) to the private sector. In considering the effect of public spending on demand, there is an argument for separating public expenditure on goods and services from transfer payments. An increase in the former will, at the first round, raise the level of demand by the full amount of the increase in public spending. A rise in this category of expenditure will therefore tend to raise demand even if matched by an equal rise in tax revenue, since the increase in revenue is likely to be partly at the expense of saving. This is the basis of the concept of the balanced budget multiplier. On the other hand, an increase in transfer payments does not affect the level of demand until it is spent by the recipients, at which stage they may save part of the transfer payments. If the marginal propensity to save was the same for transfer recipients and tax-payers, then there would be no stimulation of demand arising from equal increases in transfer payments

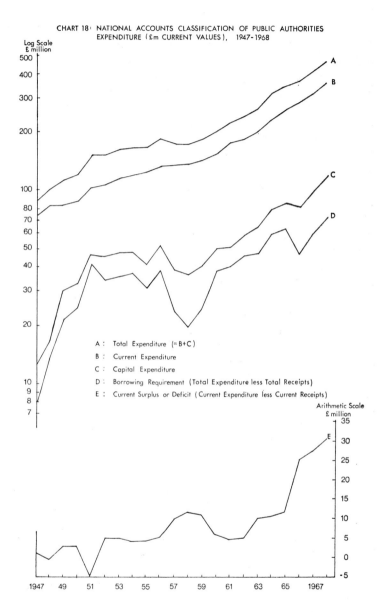

CHART 18: NATIONAL ACCOUNTS CLASSIFICATION OF PUBLIC AUTHORITIES EXPENDITURE (£m CURRENT VALUES), 1947-1968

A : Total Expenditure (= B+C)

B : Current Expenditure

C : Capital Expenditure

D : Borrowing Requirement (Total Expenditure less Total Receipts)

E : Current Surplus or Deficit (Current Expenditure less Current Receipts) and tax revenue, and the balanced budget multiplier would not apply. However, in Ireland many, though not all, forms of transfer payments are made to persons who have probably a negligible marginal propensity to save, so that there is likely to be some balanced budget multiplier effect arising from increases in such payments even when matched by a rise in tax revenue.

The balance on the public authorities' current account represents the surplus (deficit) of current expenditure over current revenue.[3] In Ireland up to very recently the authorities aimed at balance on the current account, as judged by the traditional accounting method. Whenever a current deficit emerged, this was regarded as an adverse development to be corrected as soon as possible. As explained in the appendix to this chapter, balance on the current account in the traditional accounting framework generally implied a surplus on the national accounts basis, so that the use of the former accounting framework probably led to more deflationary fiscal policy than if the latter accounting method had been employed. However, the division of government spending into current and capital items, while of undeniable advantage for certain forms of economic and financial analysis, is of less consequence in assessing the impact of fiscal policy on demand. More relevant in this context are changes in the total of current and capital expenditure, the overall deficit (surplus) of total expenditure over total receipts, and how the overall deficit is financed. The overall deficit, or the amount which the government must finance by borrowing of one form or another, is equal to the sum of the balance on current account and the amount of public capital expenditure, less capital receipts (e.g. taxes on capital).[4]

Changes in the size of the overall deficit give a broad indication of the direction of fiscal policy. An increase in the deficit[5] compared with the previous year suggests that fiscal policy is expansionary, while a reduction in the deficit suggests that policy is deflationary. However, the overall deficit is an *ex post* magnitude, so that the interpretation of changes in the deficit must be treated with caution since fiscal policy affects the state of the economy, and the latter, in turn, affects the size of the actual deficit. With the same tax and expenditure policies, the overall deficit will tend to differ depending on the state of the economy. The size of the deficit is likely to be greater the more depressed is the state of the economy, since tax revenue will be lower due to reduced incomes and consumption, while certain categories of public expenditure (e.g. unemployment benefit) will tend to rise automatically. Thus the public authorities' deficit may change from one year to the next as a result of 'automatic' effects (i.e. those taking place in the context of unchanged fiscal policies) as well as 'discretionary' effects (i.e. deliberate changes in tax rates or expenditure programmes). Moreover, changes in fiscal policy can themselves affect the state of the economy in a way that will react back on the size of the deficit. Analytically, it is possible to construct a measure of the fiscal balance that is free from these influences by considering changes in the full employment outcome (i.e. the deficit or surplus that would emerge from different fiscal policies if the economy were fully employed) and by segregating automatic and discretionary effects. To do so, however, would require a sophisticated empirical model of the economy—a major undertaking beyond the scope of the present study. We therefore use the movements in the overall deficit, or borrowing requirement, as an indicator of the ease or tightness of fiscal policy, although we draw attention qualitatively to the points mentioned above.

It can also be argued that the total borrowing requirement of the public authorities is not a good measure of the direction of fiscal policy since only part of this borrowing is financed by the banking system. It has been claimed[6] that funds raised by the government from the non-bank public (e.g. in the form of National Loans or Post Office Savings Bank deposits) lead to offsetting reductions in private expenditures. If so, then an increase in government spending financed by borrowing from the non-bank public leaves total expenditure by the public and private sectors unchanged, and attention should properly be focused only on 'residual' borrowing (i.e. borrowing from the banking system and abroad). However, this appears to us to ignore the dynamic inter-relationship between public expenditure, income and savings. Without the increased public expenditure, income (and hence savings) might well have been lower, and the savings/investment identity would then be established at a lower level of aggregate demand. It is hard to believe that increases in public investment displace an equivalent amount of private investment when it is realised that a significant amount of public capital spending is in the form of grants linked to private investment. There is a further problem attached to the notion of residual borrowing in that it may be affected by changes in portfolio preferences of the non-bank public. Thus investment in national loans and deposits in government savings institutions may become less attractive than deposits in the banking system. If this change in portfolio behaviour occurred, the residual borrowing requirement would rise without any change in government revenue and expenditure. While it is probably true that a deficit financed by increasing bank reserves is, on the whole, more expansionary than a similar deficit financed by long-term debt from the domestic non-bank sector,[7] the latter method of financing a deficit does not seem to us to have, except under exceptional circumstances, a neutral impact on aggregate demand.

The figures in Chart 18 suggest that the period 1947–68 can be divided into three distinct phases.[8] From 1947 to 1951 total public expenditure expanded rapidly due in large measure to an almost fourfold increase in public capital spending, though current expenditure also increased considerably in this period. The overall borrowing requirement rose substantially. From 1952 to 1958 there was virtual stagnation in the overall level of public expenditure, with current expenditure tending to rise over the period while capital expenditure tended to decline. There was a current account surplus throughout the period, and the overall borrowing requirement had fallen considerably by 1958. From 1959 onwards both current and capital expenditure rose strongly. Current revenue grew slightly faster than current expenditure, particularly at the end of the 1958–68 period, and the current surplus increased. However, the overall borrowing requirement rose nearly fivefold between 1958 and 1968.

In the next three chapters we explore the short-run behaviour of the economy in these three periods, and the extent to which it was influenced by fiscal policy.

APPENDIX TO CHAPTER 12

THE CLASSIFICATION OF PUBLIC AUTHORITIES' EXPENDITURE AND RECEIPTS

I N discussing the effects of fiscal policy, we have used the national accounts tables of public expenditure and receipts rather than the traditional accounting basis used in the budget. There are significant differences of classification and coverage between the two accounting systems, the more important of which are summarised in this appendix.[9]

The national accounts classification was first published in the *Irish Statistical Survey 1958* and the reasons for its introduction were summarised as follows in Broderick (1960):

> This reclassification is necessary because it is difficult to obtain a complete picture of government transactions from the existing accounts even when all transactions between different parts of the government sector have been eliminated. This difficulty arises because the accounts have been prepared on an accounting basis and are primarily designed for facility in tracing the expenditure of the moneys allocated for specific purposes and are not specifically designed for economic analysis. The summaries presented in the Finance and Appropriation Accounts tend to be based on administrative units rather than on an economic classification of the expenditure, which is the relevant type of classification for national income purposes. The reclassification may be looked upon as a form of processing of the existing accounts in order to derive from them information in a form suitable for economic analysis.

Little use appears to have been made of this classification in formulating fiscal policy. Up to 1971 the data became available on the national accounts classification only retrospectively—about one year after the year to which they related—while the traditional accounting basis was the only one employed at the time budgetary policy was formulated each year.[10]

Although the traditional accounting system is probably convenient from a financial point of view, it is not as useful in evaluating the effects of fiscal policy as the national accounts classification, since the latter is more compatible with other national income and expenditure components. Thus repayment of public debt, which is treated partly as current expenditure in the traditional finance accounts, is properly treated as capital payments in the national accounts classification. Likewise, road improvement works are rightly treated as capital expenditure in the national accounts but as current expenditure in the finance accounts. During the post-war period, the current budget outturn often showed a deficit on the basis of the traditional classification whereas, on the national accounts classification, there was a surplus in all years subsequent to 1951. Moreover, the year-to-year changes in the current balance were often of significantly different amounts.

The fact that the traditional accounting basis tended to show a larger deficit (or a smaller surplus) on the current account may have led to a deflationary bias in fiscal policy. Up to recently[11] the authorities were opposed to the idea of a planned current surplus and even more so to the idea of a planned current deficit. Whenever a deficit emerged *ex post*, this was regarded as a major problem and something to be set right immediately. Because of this, sole reliance on an accounting framework that put the current account position in a more unfavourable light—as the authorities viewed it—may have led to a more deflationary approach than would have occurred had the national accounts classification been used.[12] Instances of this will be cited later in the appropriate places.

The national accounts classification gives details of expenditure and receipts, both current and capital, of the central government and local authorities. In the traditional accounting system, the budget for current revenue and expenditure relates only to the expenditure and revenue of the central government (including, of course, transfers to and from the local authorities).[13] We have decided to take into account the data for local authorities, since they are as much a part of the public domain as the central government and their expenditure and revenue is strongly determined by central government policy.

In regard to capital expenditure, the traditional accounting system is more comprehensive in coverage than the national accounts basis. This is so because the former gives details of a comprehensive Public Capital Programme, which includes not only the central government and local authorities but also the state-sponsored bodies. On the other hand, the national accounts classification covers the capital expenditure of state-sponsored bodies only to the extent that it is financed by the central government. This generally represented the bulk of the capital expenditure of these bodies, but in some years changes in the method of financing used by them could distort the picture. Thus, if a state-sponsored body changed in a particular year from borrowing from the government to direct borrowing from the public, this would lead to a fall in total capital expenditure and in the overall deficit on the national accounts classification. In view of the role of capital spending by the state-sponsored bodies in fiscal policy formation in Ireland, this could scarcely be considered deflationary. Attention will be drawn to such discrepancies when to ignore them might give rise to misleading conclusions about the direction of fiscal policy.

A difficulty that applies to both bases of classification is that the data relate to the financial year (i.e. 1 April to 31 March) rather than the calendar year. Neither are quarterly data available to adjust the figures to a calendar year basis. All that we can do in this respect is to pay due regard in the text to the timing of important budgetary changes. A further difficulty in relating the public authorities' data to the level of economic activity is that some payments are made in respect of activity undertaken in the previous year. This could arise, for example, in the case of capital grants to enterprises. On the other hand, some capital goods (e.g. aeroplanes) require advance payments to be made some years prior to delivery. In a more refined analysis of fiscal policy it would be desirable to obtain systematic data on these matters.

CHAPTER 13

1947-51:
The Post-War Expansionary Phase

THE Irish economy at the start of the post-war period contained many structural weaknesses. The ratio of fixed investment to GNP was low—only 9 per cent in 1947. There were major deficiencies in social and infrastructural facilities. Savings, which were relatively high during the war because of the shortage of consumer goods, had declined considerably; in 1947 total savings amounted to only 4½ per cent of GNP and personal savings in that year were virtually zero. Manufacturing industry accounted for less than one-fifth of total employment, and a high proportion of it owed its existence to the protectionist policies of the 1930s and had not yet launched into export markets. There was comparatively little tradition of enterprise, and considerable difficulties faced the prospective entrepreneur in raising capital. Invisible exports accounted for more than two-thirds of total exports of goods and services, and the temporary boom in tourism, the largest component of invisibles, was soon to end. Visible exports were dominated by agricultural products, which were subject to considerable fluctuations. The unemployment rate stood at 9.3 per cent in 1947, and the rate in building and construction was 15.7 per cent.[1]

On the positive side, Ireland had important assets from a development viewpoint, notably a plentiful supply of labour and a large accumulation of external reserves built up during the war. In these circumstances, there was a strong case for an expansionary fiscal policy and direct state intervention to raise the investment rate.

THE LAUNCHING OF THE PUBLIC CAPITAL PROGRAMME

In fact, the government launched a large and increasing programme of public investment, financed mainly by borrowing.[2] In doing so, the authorities wished both to expand domestic demand and provide capacity for output growth. Much of the Public Capital Programme was devoted to building and construction; this was sensible, given the need for infrastructural facilities and the high unemployment rate in the building industry. Moreover, the inevitably large outflow of unskilled workers from agriculture could often be absorbed most readily in building activities in the first instance. It would, however, be wrong to think of public capital spending as being entirely 'social': while there was substantial expenditure on houses, hospitals and schools, there was, as we saw in Chapter 11, a significant volume of investment in power, transport and communications.

In the first few years of the post-war period the policy had considerable success. The share of fixed investment in G N P (both at 1958 prices) rose from 8.6 per cent in 1947 to 12.6 per cent in 1949. At the same time total savings as a proportion of G N P rose from 4.6 per cent to 12.8 per cent, while personal savings, which were virtually non-existent in 1947, represented 7.1 per cent of personal disposable income in 1949. Moreover, the balance of payments position improved considerably at first. The large current account deficit of £30 million in 1947, which was substantially due to post-war re-stocking, fell to £19.6 million in 1948 and £9.7 million in 1949. Due to a substantial net inflow of private capital, aided by £17 million of Marshall Aid funds in 1949, the external reserves rose and stood at £256 million at end-1949. This was equivalent to twenty months' purchases of imports of goods and services. Some progress was made in lowering the unemployment rate, which in the fourth quarter of 1949 was down to 8.3 per cent (seasonally corrected) compared with 9.6 per cent in the first quarter of 1947.

In retrospect, however, this policy, in many ways admirable, could be held to have been deficient in two respects. It did not provide any direct stimulus to the expansion of manufacturing output and investment, nor did it provide any direct encouragement to exports. The first was, perhaps, a less serious weakness. As we pointed out in Chapter 11, so long as demand in general expanded, led by increasing public investment and expansionary fiscal policy, manufacturing investment also tended to grow rapidly. This growth reflected the direct demand of the construction industries for manufacturing products (such as cement, furniture and fixtures, etc.), and the induced demand for manufacturing output due to the increased income generated. It also reflected post-war replacement of outworn or outmoded equipment and the establishment of some new tariff-protected industries.

The absence of direct encouragement to exports could be considered a more fundamental limitation. An expansionist fiscal policy was ultimately limited by balance of payments considerations: unless exports could keep pace with imports, or continuing large inflows of capital were assured, a decline in reserves would *eventually* call for corrective policy measures. The range of instruments that might normally be considered available for this purpose was, however, limited, partly by the situation of the economy and partly by the attitude of the authorities. The scope for further tariff and quota restrictions to defend the balance of payments was small. Finished consumer goods represented a relatively small proportion of total imports. Trade restrictions on materials for further processing or on capital goods, while reducing imports, would also adversely affect output and employment in industries dependent on them. Devaluation would probably have only limited effect, given the structure of exports and imports. In any event, the authorities did not apparently consider this measure seriously and had clearly set their face against changing the parity with sterling. The scope for higher interest rates to attract capital flows was limited by the close financial and banking ties between Ireland and the U K. Moreover, higher interest rates might have adversely affected domestic capital formation. Thus, if balance of payments problems arose, the major instrument left to the authorities was deflation of home demand, which would, of course, interrupt growth.

To forestall the need for deflationary measures, therefore, it would have been desirable, if at all possible, to adopt measures for the encouragement of exports. It must be conceded, however, that the climate for such measures at that time was less favourable than later on. Manufactured exports in the early post-war years were negligible, so that, even had there been more active measures to develop such exports, it would take some considerable time before they could make a decisive contribution. Moreover, the measures later used to attract foreign investment in export production could scarcely have been so successful at this time, since the degree of such investment generally was then much more limited. Agricultural exports were sensitive to changing economic conditions and policies in the U K. Expansion of the potential for greater agricultural exports depended a good deal on trade negotiations, which evidently were pursued as forcefully as possible. Perhaps the area in which the authorities can most justly be blamed for failure to act decisively was tourism. This was a substantial export category which, with suitable developmental and promotional measures, might have provided both a considerable stimulus to aggregate demand and a valuable foreign exchange contribution.

However, it would remain true that, if progress were to be made in dealing with development and employment problems, there would still be a need for strong growth of domestic demand with consequent risks to the balance of payments. Moreover, the timing and extent of any cut-back in demand should properly depend, not only on the current balance of payments position but also on the level of reserves. As already mentioned, external reserves were high, so that a considerable reduction in their level could be tolerated in the interests of providing the infrastructural basis for future development.

THE BALANCE OF PAYMENTS CRISIS OF 1950–51

There was a deterioration in the current balance of payments in 1950, which intensified in 1951. A current account deficit of £30 million in 1950 was followed by a deficit of £61.6 million in 1951 which represented 14.7 per cent of G N P and which was, relatively, the largest ever recorded in Ireland. Despite these large current account deficits, the external reserves were not seriously affected. In 1950, due to Marshall Aid funds of £21 million and the private net capital inflow, the reserves actually rose by £4 million. In 1951, despite a continuance of the large private capital inflow, the reserves fell by £39 million or about 15 per cent, but the remaining level was still high.

The reasons for the deterioration in the current balance of payments and the resulting decline in external reserves in 1951, must be considered in evaluating the authorities' response to the situation. Chart 19 shows quarterly, seasonally corrected, figures[3] for total merchandise exports and imports (at current prices) from

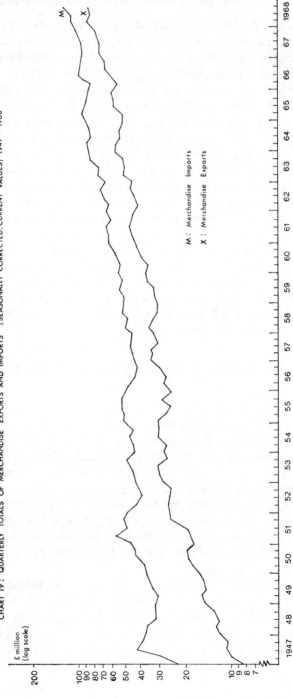

CHART 19 : QUARTERLY TOTALS OF MERCHANDISE EXPORTS AND IMPORTS (SEASONALLY CORRECTED, CURRENT VALUES) 1947 – 1968

£ million
(log scale)

M : Merchandise Imports

X : Merchandise Exports

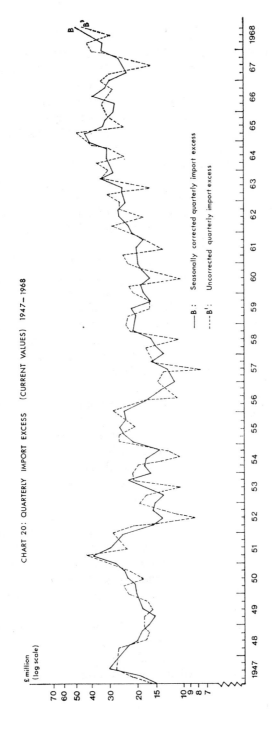

CHART 20: QUARTERLY IMPORT EXCESS (CURRENT VALUES) 1947–1968

£ million (log scale)

——B : Seasonally corrected quarterly import excess

----B¹: Uncorrected quarterly import excess

H

1947 to 1968, and Chart 20 gives the current balance of trade deficit, both uncorrected and seasonally corrected, for the same period. As may be seen from Chart 19, merchandise exports rose strongly and fairly steadily from the first quarter of 1947 to the third quarter of 1953. There are dips in the curve but the main impression is one of strong upward trend. Merchandise imports, on the other hand, fell fairly steadily from the third quarter of 1947 to the second quarter of 1949. A small part of this fall was due to a decrease in import prices, but the greater part was associated with a reduction in the rate of non-agricultural stock-building following the large build-up of such stocks in 1947: the value of non-agricultural stock-building fell by £13 million in 1948 and by £6.5 million in 1949.

Imports rose sharply in the third quarter of 1949 and continued rising steeply until the second quarter of 1951. In the two years from the second quarter of 1949 to the second quarter of 1951 the quarterly value of imports, seasonally corrected, rose from £30.5 million to £57 million. In the same period the quarterly, seasonally corrected, deficit on merchandise trade more than doubled—from £15 million to £39 million. The major factor underlying the rise in the trade deficit was the enormous rise in import prices. Import prices began to rise in the fourth quarter of 1949; the rate of increase accelerated sharply in the third quarter of 1950; and the rise continued until the third quarter of 1951, after which import prices turned downwards. In the year 1951 as a whole, import prices were $33\frac{1}{2}$ per cent above the 1949 level. Export prices did not rise until the third quarter of 1950 but thereafter rose rapidly. In 1951 export prices were, on average, 21 per cent above the 1949 level.

It is important to realise that, given the structure of Irish trade, these large price increases would tend to affect the balance of trade adversely even had merchandise import and export prices risen at the same rate. The reason is that merchandise imports were much larger than merchandise exports—in 1949 the ratio was more than 2:1. Thus the same rise in prices of merchandise imports and exports would, *ceteris paribus,* mean a larger absolute increase in the value of imports than in the value of exports.[4] Hence, the trade gap tended to widen as import and export prices rose. Added to this was the fact that the increase in import prices exceeded the increase in export prices. The total rise of £53.8 million in the balance of trade deficit between the years 1949 and 1951 can be broken down as follows: £30.6 million was due to price increases, £16.8 million was due to a faster rise in volume of imports than in volume of exports, and the residual component of £6.4 million may be attributed to the joint effects of price and volume. Thus the major cause of the massive deterioration in the balance of trade was the rise in merchandise trade prices.

Two factors were chiefly responsible for the enormous rise in import prices, and both were largely beyond domestic control. The first was the devaluation of sterling in September 1949, which Ireland followed immediately and by the same amount. This devaluation almost certainly had an adverse effect on the Irish economy. Since most Irish exports, both of goods and services, were to the sterling area, any benefit to exports in such markets applied only to competition with non-devaluing countries—not to competition with the sterling area markets themselves. But, in fact, the volume of some of the major components of Irish exports, such as cattle, were not, in the main, determined by international price competitiveness and so received little or no benefit. No doubt, potential opportunities were created for exporting to non-devaluing countries, but, since such exports were relatively small, it would take time before they could be built up to significant proportions. On the other hand, a sizeable share of imports came from non-devaluing countries and, given the limited possibilities of substituting similar goods from devaluing countries or from the home market, these tended to bear the full impact of the import price rise. Hence the losses were certain and immediate, while the gains were speculative and remote.[5]

The rise in import prices might have tapered off about the middle of 1950 but for the renewed spurt caused by the Korean War, which the U S A entered at the end of June 1950. Prices of basic raw materials were particularly affected by precautionary stock-piling by the U S A government and also by speculative demand generally resulting from fears of rising prices and shortages. In addition, the record rise in world industrial output in 1950 put pressure on raw materials prices.[6] Apart from the effect of prices, imports in 1950 and 1951 were also affected by stock-piling due to fears of shortages. In 1950 the volume of non-agricultural stock-building rose by £7 million and in 1951 by £9 million. There was also substantial personal stock-piling of basic foodstuffs, which would be classified under consumption in the national accounts and for which we do not have separate figures.

Thus the greater part of the very substantial deterioration in the balance of trade deficit—and hence in the current balance of payments, since net invisibles changed little—can be explained by price increases and stock-building occasioned by factors largely outside the country's control. In such circumstances, the question of applying corrective measures on balance of payments grounds should properly be influenced by whether or not the circumstances occasioning the deficit were thought to be permanent. If the factors making for the deficit were seen to be due to extraneous and temporary factors, then, given a reasonable level of reserves, there was clearly not a strong case for altering course in domestic policy. In the event, no significant restrictive action was taken by the government in 1950 or in 1951. Fiscal policy was moderately expansionary in 1950 and highly expansionary in 1951, while in both years there were large increases in credit. The value of total expenditure of public authorities rose by 6 per cent in 1950 and by over 23 per cent in 1951, representing volume increases of about 3 per cent and 14 per cent respectively. The balance on the public authorities' current account changed from a surplus of £3.0 million in 1950 to a deficit of £4.7 million in 1951, a swing of £7.7 million. The overall borrowing requirement (excluding redemption of securities) rose from £20.2 million in 1949 to £22.9 million in 1950 and to £35.5 million in 1951. Indeed, the rise in the borrowing requirement between 1950 and 1951 was probably more expansionary than in a normal year because of the small proportion financed by domestic savings: roughly £34 million was raised by use of Marshall Aid funds and sales of foreign reserves held in departmental funds. Bank credit also expanded rapidly. The data for total bank credit in each year from 1947 to 1968 are given in Chart 21.[7] The rise in 1950 was 15.2 per cent and in 1951 12.4 per cent. However, the rise in credit can scarcely be regarded as a conscious decision of the authorities since, as already explained, for most of the post-war period, the Central Bank was passive in regard to the control of credit creation or the liquidity of the banking system.

Despite criticisms that were subsequently made, it seems to us that a strong case existed for the continuation of expansionist

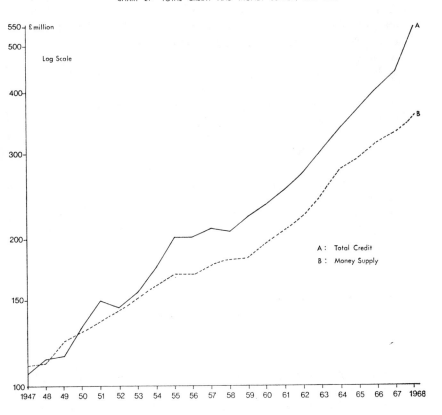

CHART 21: TOTAL CREDIT AND MONEY SUPPLY. 1947-1968

A : Total Credit
B : Money Supply

policies. The domestic economy was by no means overheated in 1950 and 1951—quite the reverse. Admittedly, the personal savings ratio fell in both years. However, the rise in volume of personal consumption was modest—2½ per cent in 1950 and no increase in 1951. The volume of net output in agriculture fell substantially in 1950, due to the effects of exceptionally bad weather on crop production, and remained depressed in 1951. Real income *per capita* in agriculture fell by 9 per cent in 1950 and, though there was some recovery in 1951, it was still 5 per cent below the 1949 level. Real personal disposable income *per capita* outside of agriculture fell by 1 per cent in 1951. The non-agricultural unemployment rate (seasonally corrected), which had been progressively reduced to 6.6 per cent in the second quarter of 1951, began to move upwards again in the third quarter of that year. The volume of output in transportable goods industry turned down in the third quarter of 1951 (see Chart 22). This decline was partly due to difficulties experienced by the textile and clothing industries. These difficulties were not confined to Irish manufacturers. In the latter half of 1950 and the first half of 1951 large stocks of raw materials were built up by the textile industries at exceptionally high prices in anticipation of future shortages and continued increases in textile prices. But prices began to decline in the second half of 1951, and the textile and clothing manufacturers were unable to dispose of highly-priced stocks as consumers postponed purchases in anticipation of further price declines.

Fiscal policy undoubtedly served to arrest a more serious depression. It may be argued that it did so only by tolerating a large current balance of payments deficit and a significant loss of reserves. However, because of the factors already mentioned, the deficit would probably have been large anyway in 1950 and 1951 even if deflationary measures had been taken. Had the current balance of payments deficit disimproved further, or even continued, criticism of the policy followed might have more force. But the remarkable fact is that before the deflationary budget of 1952 (described in the next chapter) could have affected the situation significantly, the balance of payments position was improving. As may be seen from Chart 19, imports began to fall rapidly in the second half of 1951. This was partly due to falling import prices which reached a peak in the third quarter of 1951.

CHART 22

QUARTERLY, SEASONALLY CORRECTED, INDEX OF VOLUME OF OUTPUT IN TRANSPORTABLE GOODS INDUSTRIES,
1947 - 1968

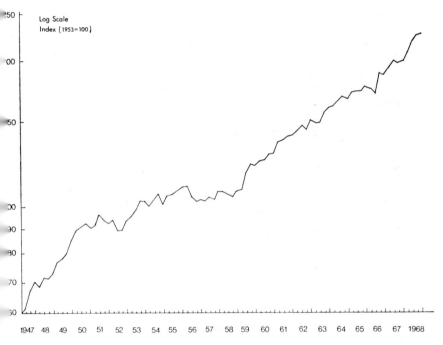

There was also, however, a substantial fall in volume of imports. Thus in the second quarter of 1952 the balance of trade deficit (seasonally corrected) was down to £16.4 million compared with £38.8 million in the second quarter of 1951.[8] The deficit of £16.4 million in the second quarter of 1952 was only £1 million above the previous low point in the second quarter of 1949 before the crisis started. This would seem to confirm the wisdom of the government's action in 1951 in holding back on deflationary measures.

ACHIEVEMENTS OF THE PERIOD 1947–51

In summing up the post-war years up to 1951, it can be described as a period of very considerable progress in the face of substantial external difficulties. A greatly enlarged Public Capital Programme and an expansionary fiscal policy helped to maintain a high growth of demand when the immediate post-war buoyancy would otherwise probably have tapered off. The ratio of fixed investment to GNP (both at 1958 prices) rose from 8.6 per cent in 1947 to 16.6 per cent in 1951. True, much of public investment was devoted to social and infrastructural projects that would not produce an early rate of return. Yet it is an astonishing fact that in this period the ratio of fixed investment to gross domestic product (both at 1958 prices) in *industry* rose from 15.4 per cent in 1947 to 24.9 per cent in 1951, and the latter ratio has never since been surpassed, at least up to 1970, the latest year for which figures are available. In *manufacturing* the fixed investment ratio rose from 19.5 per cent in 1947 to 21.9 per cent in 1951 and the latter figure was surpassed again only in 1967.

The volume of industrial output in the four-year period 1947–51 rose by 44 per cent (9.5 per cent per annum) in transportable goods,[9] and by 50 per cent (10.7 per cent per annum) in all CIP industry—despite a slowing-down in 1951. The rapid growth of transportable goods output depended to some degree on the fact that, in addition to re-imposing pre-war tariffs that were in abeyance during the war, some new tariffs were added. However, expansion of output was diffused among all the main manufacturing groups and the additional tariffs must be regarded as a less important factor than the overall buoyancy of demand.

The total non-agricultural unemployment rate fell from 9.3 per cent in 1947 to 7.3 per cent in 1951. In the same period the unemployment rate in the construction industry declined from 15.7 per cent to 11.4 per cent, the latter being the lowest level ever attained in any year in the post-war period. The rise in non-agricultural employment almost kept pace with the fall in agricultural employment, so that there was only a small fall in overall employment. If this does not seem to be a particularly good performance, it was, at least, far better that that achieved from 1951 to 1958 and compares favourably with that from 1958 to 1968, as the figures in Table 40 show.

Table 40: Changes in employment, various periods

Period	Agriculture	Non-Agriculture	Total
	Average numbers per annum		
1946–51	—14,200	+12,500	—1,700
1951–58	—12,700	—8,600	—21,300
1958–68	—9,400	+9,100	—300

Sources: *Review of 1969 and Outlook for 1970, Economic Statistics 1964*, and *Census of Population* data for 1946, adjusted for comparability with later years.

It might be argued that the progress made was achieved at the cost of a very serious deterioration in the current balance of payments. But we have already shown that a substantial part of the deterioration was due to factors beyond domestic control, that these factors proved to be temporary and that the deficit was falling well before any official restrictive action was taken. Moreover, because of the availability of Marshall Aid funds and the private net capital inflow, the accumulated current balance of payments deficits of £150 million in the five years 1947 to 1951 involved a fall in reserves of no more than £30 million. The reserves at the end of 1951 stood at £221.5 million, which was equivalent to almost a year's imports—a high level by any standard.

CHAPTER 14

1952-58:
Withdrawal from Expansion

As indicated in the last chapter, the balance of trade position was improving considerably by the time the 1952 budget was introduced in April of that year. On the other hand, output in transportable goods industry was falling and the unemployment rate (seasonally corrected), which started to rise in the third quarter of 1951, stood at 8.6 per cent in the first quarter of 1952, compared to 6.6 per cent in the second quarter of 1951. In these circumstances, it would appear that there was little need for deflationary policy, but, in fact, a deflationary budget was introduced in 1952. However, there were other considerations that could provide some justification for this action. At the time the budget was introduced, the latest available trade figures related to February 1952. Although the trade deficit was then falling, it was still high and there was no assurance that it would continue to fall. The absence of seasonally corrected trade figures also made it much harder to recognise the decline in the trade deficit.[1] Moreover, there was considerable official concern at the time with the dollar deficit, which was large in 1951, as well as with the overall deficit. It was considered necessary, as part of the obligations of sterling area membership, to make efforts to reduce the dollar deficit. Concern with the size of the dollar deficit was accentuated by the fact that the Marshall Aid funds were now almost exhausted. Given that the official attitude of the time was strongly opposed to reliance on foreign borrowing,[2] the termination of Marshall Aid meant that future current account deficits in excess of the normal net capital inflow (averaging about £15 million) would involve a fall in reserves. It was several years later before the use of foreign capital for domestic development became more generally accepted.

THE 1952 BUDGET AND ITS AFTERMATH

The main deflationary measures of the 1952 budget were directed towards current expenditure and revenue. Subsidies on tea, butter and sugar were removed, there were substantial increases in indirect taxes, and the standard rate of income tax was raised by one shilling. Current expenditure rose only slightly, while current revenue increased considerably. In national accounts terms, the outturn for the year shows that the balance on the public authorities' current account swung from a deficit of £4.7 million in 1951 to a surplus of £5.3 million in 1952. The value of capital expenditure (excluding debt redemptions and payments abroad) increased at a much lower rate than in the preceding years, rising to £42.9 million compared with £40.2 million in 1951, while the public authorities' borrowing requirement fell from £35.5 million in 1951 to £32.3 million in 1952. It should be noted that the figures for the outturn, being *ex post* data, almost certainly understate the deflationary nature of the 1952 budget for reasons discussed in Chapter 12. The economy was already in recession at the time the budget was introduced and budgetary policy itself exacerbated the position. Hence, if data were available on the full employment balance of the public authorities' account in these years, the deflationary swing in policy in 1952 would probably appear rather greater.

Budgetary policy was aimed primarily at reducing the current balance of payments deficit. This aim was certainly achieved, though not solely due to fiscal policy. We suggested earlier that the balance of payments was already improving before the 1952 budget took effect. Moreover, for reasons unconnected with the budget, merchandise exports rose strongly (by nearly £20 million or 25 per cent), led by a substantial rise in the volume and price of live cattle and beef. Manufactured exports fell, but this was largely because of conditions in the U K and the difficulties in the clothing and textile industries. Merchandise imports declined by £33 million or 16 per cent in current values and by 17 per cent in volume terms. A great deal of the fall was associated with a reduction in non-agricultural stock-building, which declined by £20 million. Increased exports and reduced imports both therefore contributed to the large reduction of over £50 million in the trade balance. Although net invisibles remained stagnant, the current balance of payments deficit fell from £62 million in 1951 to £9 million in 1952, and the external reserves rose by £5 million.

It may seem surprising that the growth rate of GNP in 1952 (2¾ per cent) was greater than in 1950 or 1951. However, this was due almost entirely to agricultural output, which fell substantially in 1950 due to abnormal weather conditions and remained depressed in 1951: on the other hand, the volume of net output in agriculture rose by 11 per cent in 1952. Thus all of the rise in GNP in 1952 was due to recovery in agricultural production, there being virtually no increase in non-agricultural output. The volume of output in transportable goods industry was 2½ per cent below the 1951 level, but it began to rise again in the fourth quarter of 1952, partly as a result of direct government action to limit imports of clothing and textiles. The level of non-agricultural employment fell, and both emigration and the unemployment rate rose.

Although the 1952 budget was inappropriate in the prevailing economic condition, the check to economic expansion would not have been serious were it not for the excessively cautious fiscal policy that persisted in the following years. By the time the 1953 budget was introduced, the balance of payments situation was fully under control and the economy was ripe for renewed growth. However, there was to be no return until after 1958 to the expansionary fiscal policy that characterised the first five years or so of the post-war period. In the three years following 1952, as may be seen in Table 41, public capital expenditure and the borrowing requirement, in current values, were maintained around the 1952 level and in 1957 and 1958 were cut back significantly. While the pause in 1952 might be excused in the light of some of the considerations mentioned earlier, the failure to resume expansionary fiscal policy in the next few years is more difficult to justify. The current balance of payments deficit was only £7 million in 1953 and £5.5 million in 1954. Both of these deficits were more than covered by capital inflows, so that the external reserves rose by £14 million in 1953 and by £4 million in 1954.

Without the stimulus of an expanding public capital programme, the volume of total fixed investment advanced only slowly. In housing, the volume of investment fell by 10 per cent in 1953

Table 41: Expenditure by public authorities and borrowing
requirement, 1952–58 (current values)

Year	Capital	Expenditure Current	Total	Borrowing Requirement
	£m	£m	£m	£m
1952	42.9	108.0	150.9	32.3
1953	44.5	115.4	159.9	33.3
1954	40.6	120.3	160.9	30.6
1955	36.0 (46.0)*	125.8	161.8 (171.8)*	25.7 (35.7)*
1956	46.0	133.5	179.5	33.8
1957	33.2	134.8	168.0	17.9
1958	31.3 (36.3)*	136.3	167.6 (172.6)*	13.9 (18.9)*

*Figures in parentheses include borrowing by the Electricity Supply
Board (E S B) directly from the public to finance capital expenditure. In
the other years such borrowing was financed through the central government
and, as explained in the Appendix to Chapter 12, its exclusion from the
national accounts classification of public authorities would tend to give
a misleading impression of the direction of fiscal policy.

Source: *National Income and Expenditure,* various issues. Figures for years
before 1953 kindly supplied by C S O. See text of Chapter 12 and Appendix thereto for explanation of the figures. It may be noted that figures in
Table 41 differ a little from those in Chart 18 due to the exclusion in
Table 41 of redemption of securities.

to £20.6 million and remained at this level until 1957, when it was
cut back further. This fall could be tolerated if other categories
of investment had increased to maintain expansion, but the
importance of an expanding investment programme does not
appear to have been well appreciated then. In fact, in the 1953
budget speech the Minister for Finance expressed doubt about
'whether a programme of the present size can be continuously
sustained'.[3]

Reasons for Withdrawal from Expansion
One can only speculate about the reasons for the retraction
from the expansionary policy pursued earlier.[4] The shock of the
1951 balance of payments deficit was evidently not easily shaken
off. The emergence of this very large deficit appears to have
been taken as discrediting a policy of expanding home demand,
whereas the deficit was, in fact, largely due to highly exceptional
—and mainly external—factors. It would appear that concern
with maintaining external reserves took precedence over concern

about employment and development. Thus the fact that total exports were static or falling in the years 1953 to 1956 (due to a considerable extent to difficulties created by changes in British agricultural policy) was given as justification for ruling out expansion of home demand. Had there been greater concern with employment, these export difficulties would, in fact, have represented an argument for greater expansion of home demand to maintain the growth of overall demand until the work of bodies such as Coras Tráchtála and Bord Fáilte began to bear fruit. Moreover, fiscal policy was more restrictive in its implementation than in its intentions in that there was a remarkable inability to carry out in full the programmes authorised in the budget. In 1953 the capital budget (on the traditional accounting basis) provided for expenditure of £39.3 million, but only £34.6 million was spent; and in 1954 £39.5 million was provided for, but only £32.9 million was spent.

A more expansionary fiscal policy might have involved greater risks with the balance of payments and external reserves. But in retrospect it now appears that a bolder approach could have been pursued without undue risk. Moreover, it is not clear that a greater expansion of demand through public investment would have had a substantial net adverse effect on the balance of payments. A more rapid growth of manufacturing output could have induced a more rapid rate of productivity growth. Given the plentiful supply of labour available, it is doubtful if average earnings would have risen much more than they did, so that unit wage costs might well have risen less. Moreover, as already shown, manufacturing investment, which had risen rapidly up to 1951, declined substantially in 1952 and 1953 and remained depressed until 1960. The rise in emigration and the fall in population, together with the accompanying rise in the dependency ratio—all following from the policy pursued—had depressing effects generally and made development efforts more difficult and more costly *per capita*. We showed earlier their adverse effects on the savings ratio. Thus, while the policy undertaken, by limiting expansion of demand, may have aided the balance of payments in the short run, it tended to weaken it in the long run.

THE BALANCE OF PAYMENTS CRISIS OF 1955

A relatively large deficit of £35 million emerged in the current account of the balance of payments in 1955. The deficit was associated largely with a rise of £27 million (or 15½ per cent) in merchandise imports, but there was also a decline of £5 million in merchandise exports. In addition, there was a net outflow of capital, and the external reserves declined by £47 million. This was taken as further evidence that expansionary programmes of public investment could not be sustained. If such a deficit could arise in the absence of strong fiscal stimuli to demand, so the argument went, would not the strain on the balance of payments be intolerable with a strongly expansionary policy?

The main source of expansion of home demand in 1955 was a rise of 5.1 per cent in volume of personal consumption, involving a *per capita* rise of 5.8 per cent—one of the largest experienced in the post-war period. The reasons for this large increase are not clear.

Fiscal policy was only moderately expansionary in 1955.[5] Bank credit was allowed to expand considerably in 1954 and 1955:[6] there were successive increases in credit creation in 1954 and 1955 of 12.1 per cent and 15.7 per cent respectively. However, one would expect this to be a permissive factor rather than a prime cause. The chief reason was probably that following an increase in incomes in that year[7] consumers spent heavily on consumer durables. Evidence for other years suggests a similar bunching of purchases of consumer durables in response to an incomes increase, especially when the increase is back-dated (thereby providing consumers with the means for a sizeable initial deposit) and credit is freely available. Whether or not this was so, it is not inconsistent on our part to favour a rapid and *steady* expansion of domestic demand while at the same time admitting that an excessive and erratic increase in consumer demand may have been permitted in 1955. We would add, however, that such large, erratic increases in consumption tend to be partly self-correcting in that the rise in consumption is unlikely to be maintained, and, indeed, consumption may even fall back. Since consumers are involved for the next year or two in repaying debt, they are not, therefore, able to sustain the same level of acquisition of durable goods.

The increase in consumption of 1955 was undoubtedly a major factor contributing to the large rise in imports. The volume of fixed investment rose by only 3¾ per cent, and the level of imported capital goods did not rise at all. There was, however, a considerable rise in non-agricultural stock-building.[8] The fall in merchandise exports was chiefly due to a decline of nearly £7 million in cattle and beef exports, which was more than matched by a rise in agricultural stock-building of £8½ million. Manufactured exports continued to rise relatively rapidly. Although the increase in the trade deficit for the year as a whole was large, the seasonally corrected figures show that there was no significant upward trend in merchandise imports *during* 1955, while the trade deficit fell in the fourth quarter (Charts 19 and 20). Moreover, the increase in the current account deficit in 1955, though large, would not have seriously depleted reserves were it not for the adverse change on the capital account of the balance of payments. The current deficit of £35½ million would in most post-war years up to then have been offset by a private net capital inflow of about £15 million, so that the loss in external reserves would then be no more than £20 million. In fact, the loss in external reserves in 1955 was £47 million, due to a net outflow of capital in addition to the current deficit. We discuss movements in the capital account below, where we suggest that a major reason for the fall in the net capital inflow was the relative stagnation in economic activity and the resulting lack of real investment opportunities.

FISCAL POLICY 1956–58

Action was taken to curb the trade deficit in March 1956. By that time, as shown in Chart 20, the trade deficit had already come down from the peak reached in the third quarter of 1955. However, there was at that time no assurance that, in the absence of corrective action, the deficit would not rise again. In March 1956 special import levies of 37½ per cent full rate, and 25 per cent preferential rate,[9] were imposed on a wide range of consumer goods. Restrictions were placed on hire-purchase credit. The action taken was designed to cut back consumer demand and consumer imports directly and with as little dislocation as possible. Since many consumer imports were semi-finished goods which received further processing in Ireland, it was inevitable that employment in many industries would be badly hit. However, given that consumer demand had been allowed to get out of hand and that corrective action was felt to be necessary, the measures taken seem even now to have been reasonable. Reduction of the adverse trade balance could be achieved at less cost to domestic output and employment by limiting imports directly rather than by general deflationary policy. In fact, fiscal policy in 1956 was only moderately deflationary. Public capital expenditure was maintained at the 1955 level in value terms, though this involved a fall of over 5 per cent in volume terms. The total borrowing requirement declined slightly to £33.8 million from the 1955 level of £35.7 million (Table 41).

The balance of trade deficit was already substantially reduced by the time the second round of corrective measures was introduced in July 1956. The seasonally corrected trade deficit had fallen to £19.4 million in the second quarter of 1956, compared with the peak of £26.9 million in the third quarter of 1955. It is difficult to justify the second round of levies so soon after the first round and before the adequacy of the first-round measures could be properly evaluated. In the event, however, most of the levies imposed in March 1956 were raised in July to 60 per cent (40 per cent preferential) and a new range of goods was made subject to the levy.

By the time the 1957 budget was introduced in May of that year, the economy was already in a depressed condition. This was due not only to the corrective measures but also to other disturbing factors such as the Suez crisis and the fall in manufactured exports arising from conditions in the U K. The volume of output in transportable goods industry in 1956 was 2 per cent below the 1955 level, while the volume of building activity, as covered by the C I P, decreased by 11 per cent. The balance of trade position, however, was fully under control. Our seasonally corrected figures show that in the first quarter of 1957 the quarterly trade deficit had been reduced to £11.4 million, by far the lowest figure ever attained in the post-war period. Although seasonally corrected figures were not then available, the uncorrected figure of £15.1 million for the first quarter of 1957 was also the lowest first-quarter figure attained since 1947. These conditions clearly provided a strong argument for reflationary policy. Indeed, the argument was in some respects stronger on the basis of the figures available at the time. The depression in industrial output in 1956 appeared far greater in the preliminary figures then available than in the figures as subsequently revised: the data available in the first quarter of 1957 showed a fall in transportable goods output of 5.1 per cent in 1956, whereas later revised figures revealed a fall of only 2.0 per cent.

Instead of reflating, however, policy became more deflationary. The special import levies were maintained in 1957 and 1958, though progressively relaxed. The value of current expenditure of public authorities rose little in current values in 1957 and 1958, implying that in both years the volume was below the 1956 level. Public authorities' capital expenditure fell from £46.0 million in 1956 to £33.2 million in 1957 and recovered only to £36.3 million in 1958. The chief target of these cuts was housing. The overall borrowing requirement fell from £33.8 million in 1956 to £17.9 million in 1957, and remained at much the same level in 1958 (allowing for direct borrowing from the public by the E S B—see Table 41).

These policies were successful in achieving a substantial improvement in the current balance of payments. The deficit on current account of £35.5 million in 1955 was reduced to £14.4 million in 1956 and was converted to a surplus of £9.2 million in 1957. In 1958 there was a deficit of £1 million, but the deterioration in that year compared with 1957 was partly due to a fall in cattle exports which was fully offset by a rise in cattle stocks. However, the measures taken, combined with a large fall in agricultural production in 1958 due to adverse weather conditions—the volume of net output fell by almost 12 per cent—intensified and prolonged the depression, with particularly adverse effects on employment. The overall unemployment rate, which was 6.8 per cent in 1955, rose to 7.7 per cent in 1956 and to 9.2 per cent in 1957 and remained high at 8.6 per cent in 1958. In building, the unemployment rate rose from 13.9 per cent in 1955 to 15.7 per cent in 1956, to 19.5 per cent in 1957 and stood at 19.0 per cent in 1958. Emigration reached a post-war peak of 58,000 in the twelve months from June 1957 to June 1958.[10]

The obvious question arises as to why deflationary policy was pursued for so long when it was so at variance with the developmental needs of the economy and was far more restrictive than was necessary in the light of the current balance of payments situation. There appear to us to be two major reasons (leaving aside such factors as errors of judgment, excessive caution or wrong priorities): first, the behaviour of the capital account of the balance of payments at this time, and second, the desire to effect a shift in the Public Capital Programme from what was considered unproductive to productive projects.[11]

The Fall in the Capital Inflow

As already mentioned, a significant net outflow in the capital account of the balance of payments contributed to the considerable loss of reserves in 1955. Although the position improved in the following year, there was still a small net capital outflow in 1956 and in 1957. Thus in 1956 there was a further loss of reserves of £15 million, and in 1957, even with a current account surplus of £9 million, the reserves only rose by £7 million. In 1958 the capital account returned to a more normal state, with a net inflow of £17 million. The behaviour of external capital movements may have inhibited the authorities from taking reflationary action earlier, following the large improvement in the current account in 1956. The drying-up of the net capital inflow of earlier post-war years removed the 'cushion' which would allow a moderate current deficit without loss of reserves— reserves which had already been considerably depleted in 1955. The authorities may have feared also that, if a significant deficit on current account re-emerged at this time, it would reduce confidence further and lead to a larger net capital outflow.

What caused the change in the capital account of the balance of payments? It should first be noted that the deterioration seems to have begun in 1954, as may be seen from Table 42, which gives figures (based on C S O data) for the gross inflow and outflow of capital (excluding official and Associated Banks' movements) for the years 1953 to 1958. There are a number of factors that might explain the deterioration on capital account. Firstly, the period was one of considerable pressure on sterling. The U K gold and dollar reserves began to decline in the third quarter of 1954 after rising steadily for two years. Foreign confidence in sterling diminished and over the next few years there were recurrent and severe speculative attacks on sterling. These

Table 42: Private external capital flows, 1953–58

Year	Inflow	Outflow	Net inflow (+) Net outflow (−)
	£m	£m	£m
1953	25.7	6.5	+19.2
1954	19.1	10.3	+8.8
1955	13.3	20.9	—7.6
1956	16.5	15.0	+1.5
1957	17.6	16.5	+1.1
1958	33.1	15.4	+17.7

Sources: *Irish Statistical Bulletin.* The data are the totals of all capital flows excluding government transactions and changes in the net external assets of the Central Bank and the Associated Banks. It may be noted that the total private net inflow (outflow) based on these figures differs slightly from that obtained in Table 15 by adding the change in external reserves, as then defined, to the current balance of payments deficit. The latter method, which excludes non-reserve government transactions, gives the following figures for 1953–58:

	1953	1954	1955	1956	1957	1958
£m	20.9	9.7	—11.8	—0.3	—2.3	16.9

attacks were associated with a variety of factors such as the heavily adverse U K trade balance in the autumn of 1955, the fear that the re-introduction of sterling convertibility would be accompanied by devaluation of sterling, the Suez crisis of 1956, and rumours of revaluation of the deutschmark in the summer of 1957. These factors may also have caused a flight from Irish currency by encouraging the belief that any devaluation of sterling would also involve a corresponding devaluation of the Irish pound. Moreover, the general restrictions on credit in the U K may have limited U K investment in Ireland.[12]

Secondly, in March 1955, for the first time Irish interest rates on overdrafts and deposits were not adjusted upwards in line with the rise in British bank rate. The lower overdraft rate was intended to encourage domestic capital formation, but it is possible that the lower deposit rate may also have encouraged a net outflow of funds. Thirdly, the large current deficit in 1955 may have caused a weakening of confidence about the ability to maintain the value of the Irish currency in terms of sterling. Fourthly, the decline in manufacturing investment from the early

1950s indicated a lack of profitable investment opportunities. This would have reduced the incentive for direct foreign investment and made Irish producers less willing to seek external finance for capital expansion.[13]

It is impossible for us to say which of these factors is the more important or whether, taken together, they provide a satisfactory explanation of the change in external capital flows. The available data are poor and there has been little by way of systematic inquiry into the causes of fluctuations in capital flows. In so far as capital flows are influenced by the situation in the Irish economy rather than by external forces, it is likely that the factors affecting the gross inflow differ from those affecting the gross outflow. The former may be more influenced by the availability of investment opportunities in Ireland, since a good deal of incoming capital represents either direct investment or direct borrowing for investment purposes; while the latter may be more influenced by financial confidence, since it comprises mainly investment in stocks and shares. If so, then it is significant that the net capital inflow began to fall in 1954 before there was any reason for a decline in financial confidence as a result of the balance of payments situation, and that the larger part of the fall in 1954 was a decline in the gross inflow. This suggests that failure to renew expansionary policies in 1953, and thereby create investment opportunities, may have initiated the fall in the net capital inflow. Financial factors (e.g. interest rates, degree of confidence about the stability of the currency, etc.) may have played a bigger role in 1955, when the larger part of the decline in the net capital inflow was due to a rise in the gross outflow. The revival in the net capital inflow in 1958—entirely due to a rise in the gross inflow—might be attributed chiefly to the response of foreign firms to the more favourable climate for foreign investment geared to export markets created by the new incentives in the form of grants, tax reliefs on exports, etc., as well as to the easier credit conditions in the U K.

The Shift in Public Capital Expenditure

The main reason for prolonging and intensifying the deflationary measures in 1957 and 1958, however, was the desire to alter the structure of the Public Capital Programme in order to achieve faster growth. It would be difficult to explain otherwise why demand was so severely deflated at a time when the priorities of the authorities were changing towards greater emphasis on economic development and reduced concern about external reserves. The increased concern for development is evidenced by the scheme of tax concessions and grants to encourage industrial investment and exports, and by the publication of Dr Whitaker's blueprint, *Economic Development*.[14] Indeed, it is our contention that the desire to lay a basis for long-term growth—in particular by changing the composition of the Public Capital Programme—involved an excessive emphasis on supply aspects at the expense of demand considerations, with adverse effects on employment and growth.

The case for shifting the balance of the Public Capital Programme away from 'social' or 'redistributive', and towards 'productive', investment had long been pressed by the Central Bank. It was also advocated in Whitaker (1956), the majority reports of the Capital Investment Advisory Committee and in *Economic Development*. The crucial question arises, however, whether the shift was to be achieved within the context of an expanding Public Capital Programme, or within a fixed volume of public investment. In the former case, the shift could be effected by keeping social investment constant or growing slowly, while encouraging the more immediately productive investment to expand more rapidly. In the latter case, only by securing a sizeable cut-back in social investment, could the balance be significantly altered. In fact, at that time the latter was how the shift was envisaged by most of the government's advisors. It was certainly the view that informed government policy in 1957 and 1958, and was incorporated in the projections in the First Programme for Economic Expansion. The results of attempting to effect the shift in this way had severe deflationary effects in 1957 and 1958, which retarded the development of the economy; and there can be little doubt that, had the attempt been maintained after 1958, it would have been impossible to achieve the rapid growth that was attained.

In practice, the cut-back in social investment in 1957 and 1958 involved a fall in the total Public Capital Programme, as well as a fall in almost every category of investment in the economy, whether productive or not. The total volume of fixed investment in the economy fell from £97 million in 1956 to £82 million in

1957 and to £80 million in 1958. The reasons for this are not hard to find. It would have been virtually impossible to raise productive investment quickly enough to compensate for the cut in social investment. In the case of government grants to private investment, for instance, it would obviously take time to publicise them and to prepare and evaluate new projects. Besides, many elements of productive investment depended on the level of aggregate demand, which was depressed by the precipitate cuts in social investment, especially housing. Even had the Public Capital Programme been maintained at the 1955 level, the cut-back in the building and construction components would still have been, on balance, deflationary. This would be so, as has been fully argued in Chapter 11, because of the far greater impact on demand of building and construction compared with other components of investment.

Table 43: Projected and actual Public Capital Programme, 1958–63

	Projected			Actual		
Year	Social	Other	Total	Social	Other	Total
	£m	£m	£m	£m	£m	£m
1958	14.8	26.4	41.2	10.2	27.7	37.9
1959	15.2	26.5	41.7	11.6	32.5	44.1
1960	15.0	29.5	44.5	12.9	37.4	50.3
1961	14.0	31.8	45.8	14.2	41.4	55.6
1962	13.1	30.9	44.0	15.7	44.7	60.4
1963	12.5	32.0	44.5	18.9	51.7	70.6

Notes and Sources: Projected figures for 1959–63 are taken from the *First Programme for Economic Expansion*, and for 1958 from *Economic Development*. Actual figures are taken from the annual publication *Capital Budget* and are converted to constant (1958) prices for comparison with the projected data. All data relate to the government accounting year (e.g. 1958 refers to the period from 1 April 1958 to 31 March 1959). 'Social' refers to housing, sanitary services, education, health. and certain other building and construction. 'Other' comprises all of the remainder of the Public Capital Programme, defined on the government basis of accounting, and includes ports, harbours and airports; transport and communications equipment; fuel and power; loans and grants to industry, agriculture and tourism; etc.

It does not appear, therefore, that the desired shift could have been effected without depressing consequences unless the overall level of investment were raised. Moreover, it is unlikely that the overall level of investment could have been raised other than in buoyant demand conditions, for which a rising level of social investment provided an important stimulus. This is confirmed by experience after 1958. In Table 43 we show the Public Capital Programme projected for 1958–63 and the actual outturn. A distinction is drawn between investment in housing, health and education ('social') and other investment ('productive'). It was envisaged at the time that the volume of public capital spending would remain fairly stable, with social investment declining and the other components rising.[15] Had this occurred, it is probable that the economy would have achieved a poor growth rate. In fact, what happened was that social, as well as productive, investment rose substantially. Of course, the share of productive investment in the total Public Capital Programme was greater in the years 1959 to 1963 than in 1956 as a result of the cut-back in the volume of social investment in 1957 and 1958. But this shift in share seems to us of far less consequence for growth than the fact that there was a much greater volume of productive investment within the context of a rapidly rising *total* Public Capital Programme.

At the time, the only advocates of the view advanced here were the authors of the Minority Report of the Second Report by the Capital Investment Advisory Committee. The Second Report, which was completed in November 1957, dealt with housing. The majority advocated a new housing policy involving, *inter alia,* a cut-back in state investment in housing, the resources freed thereby to be devoted to 'the promotion of productive projects'. The minority felt, however, that the circumstances of the time called for an increase, rather than a decrease, in total public investment, and that such an increase would be impossible if state investment in housing were reduced. Contrary to the view of the majority that such investment must be deferred until economic growth had accelerated, the minority argued that it should be 'considerably expanded at times such as the present and diminished when its continuance would put a strain upon the resources of the [building] industry'. They drew attention to the role of the building industry in generating economic growth, the damaging consequences to that industry of cutting back housing before other forms of investment had been developed, and the difficulty of stimulating these other investments in the conditions of depressed demand likely to follow from the reduction in housing. They also stressed the importance of housing for workers as a precondition to industrial and agricultural development and diversification.

Although the arguments of the Minority Report had little influence at the time, in retrospect they appear to have been well founded. It would be unfair, however, to place all the blame for the severity of the housing cut-back on the Majority Report, which envisaged a more gradual approach than actually took place. In fact, even before their report was completed, state expenditure on housing had been reduced substantially. The report, therefore, served to endorse rather than initiate a policy that was already in train.

The Majority Report was also influenced by the belief, evidently based on submissions from government departments, that the demand for housing was going to fall anyway because housing needs were largely met. This belief was contested in the Minority Report. As Finola Kennedy (1970) has pointed out, subsequent knowledge and events were to show that it was not well based, and that even at the time there was considerable evidence to the contrary:

> In relation to housing, the notion that a 'virtual satisfaction of needs' had been achieved proved to be illusory. The belief may be understood in light of the then declining population and the vacancies which existed in certain housing estates, notably those of Dublin Corporation. Nevertheless, in other areas there was an awareness of persistent housing needs. 'In some areas it was found that a large proportion of persons in need of re-housing were of the poorest sectors of the community and unable to pay the rents for the normal types of houses being built by local authorities.' A review of needs by the local authorities indicated that about 11,000 working-class families were awaiting re-housing by them at 31 March 1958. Further, evidence was then available which suggested that the housing situation in Ireland was unsatisfactory by international standards.

Moreover, the fact that a surplus of houses developed in some areas cannot be divorced from the fact that workers were emigrating due to the depression caused partly by the cut-back in social investment. Otherwise, it is difficult to reconcile the existence of a *surplus* of houses in Dublin in 1957 and 1958 with the existence of housing *shortages* indicated by the Minister for Finance in the 1956 budget speech, when he stated that 'It is recognised that a grave problem exists in our two principal cities.'[16]

The Third Report of the Capital Investment Advisory Committee, signed by all the members, introduced a distinction between 'productive' and 'redistributive' investment, an investment being productive only if it produced goods or services capable of being sold in a competitive market at a price sufficient to cover all costs, including interest on capital and depreciation. It would take us too far afield to enter into a detailed critique of this report, which in any event appeared only in June 1958 when all the cuts had already been made. It may be pointed out, however, that the report paid no regard to the long-standing distinction in economic theory—emphasised in particular by Pigou—between private and social costs and benefits. Thus, for example, when resources are unemployed, market costs and prices do not necessarily provide a correct basis for evaluating the economic merits of an investment from the national viewpoint. Although the individual employer must treat the market wage as the cost to him of hiring an unemployed worker, the cost from the national viewpoint may be far less, perhaps even approaching zero. Similarly, the benefits from any given investment must not be viewed in absolute terms but with regard to the alternatives available—if there are no better alternatives, it might even be sensible to put people to work digging holes and filling them in again. There were, however, far better alternatives at that time. It must be emphasised that this criterion does not provide a licence for any and all forms of investment, and that it need not ignore limitations in capital or in foreign exchange. If these are relatively scarce, their 'shadow' price could be higher than the market price, and investment projects involving a heavy draw on them would consequently emerge as relatively less desirable. The essential point is that analysis on the basis of this approach would probably have led to rather different, and more sensible, recommendations in regard to the scope and composition of public investment at a time of large-scale unemployment and few specific ideas about alternative investment choices.[17] Moreover, a more dynamic view of the relationships between investment, income and savings would have reinforced the conclusions based on such an approach.

CHAPTER 15

1959-68:
Fiscal Policy for Sustained Growth

I T is not necessary for us to discuss short-term trends from 1959 to 1968 in the same detailed manner in which we treated them in the earlier post-war phases, because (except in 1965–66) both economic policy and the economy itself maintained a more even course. Besides, these short-term trends have been much more extensively analysed already than in the earlier years of the post-war period.[1]

One of the outstanding features of the period was the strongly expansionary fiscal policy. Recovery from the 1956–58 depression was greatly aided by renewed expansion of the Public Capital Programme and by the large increase in the borrowing requirement in 1959 and 1960. Subsequently, public current and capital expenditure, and the overall deficit, rose relatively rapidly in most years (Chart 18). This expansionary fiscal policy, which was accompanied by a high rate of increase in total credit (see Chart 21), helped maintain a fairly high growth of domestic demand which was important for the attainment of a high rate of growth of output. The increased domestic stimulation to demand proceeded alongside a strong rise in exports. Rising exports both generated increased domestic activity and allowed fiscal policy to remain expansionary with less risk to the balance of payments.

RECOVERY FROM THE DEPRESSION
1956–58

The initial stages of recovery after the depression were aided by a number of fortuitous factors. The terms of trade improved substantially in 1958 (by 7.1 per cent) and in 1959 (by 4.8 per cent). Following the bad harvest in 1958 which severely depressed agricultural production, the volume of net output in agriculture rose by 8 per cent in 1959 and by a further 4 per cent in 1960. Manufactured exports jumped by 62 per cent from 1958 to 1960, aided by a rise of 56 per cent in U K manufactured imports as well as by the tax and other policy incentives. Initially, however, domestic expenditure provided the main impetus to recovery. Despite the large rise in manufactured exports, the volume of total merchandise exports fell slightly in 1959 due to a fall in the volume of cattle exports. Even with a relatively large rise in invisibles, total exports rose little. The re-building of stocks, severely depleted in the depression, was the chief expansionary factor in demand: the rise in non-agricultural stock-building between 1958 and 1959 was £22 million, equal to $3\frac{3}{4}$ per cent of total G N P. Recovery in industrial production was well under way by the second quarter of 1959 and, for the year as a whole, the volume of output was $10\frac{1}{2}$ per cent above the 1958 level.[2]

After 1959 both exports and domestic expenditure contributed to a rapid rise in aggregate demand. The period 1959–68 in general exemplifies a much bolder approach to demand management and a greater willingness to take risks with the balance of payments in the determination to maintain a high rate of growth of aggregate demand. Thus an expansionary fiscal policy was initiated and maintained though the external reserves did not reach the pre-1955 level until March 1964, by which time, of course, they were *relatively* much smaller in terms of, for example, the number of months' imports they would cover. In 1962, when there was no growth in total exports, expansion of aggregate demand was fairly well maintained by the rise in public investment and in the borrowing requirement. Not only was there a greater willingness to take risks, but the risks themselves were reduced by measures taken prior to and during the period. The fruits were now being reaped of the tax incentives for exports introduced in 1956, the grants for industrial development first introduced in 1952 and greatly extended in 1956 and 1959, and the work of development bodies such as the Industrial Development Authority, Bord Fáilte and Coras Tráchtála which had commenced in the early 1950s. The gradual emergence of new attitudes to the use of foreign capital meant that there was less concern about a current balance of payments deficit that could be covered by an inflow of foreign investment. In 1966, for example, the authorities borrowed extensively abroad to minimise the cut-back in the Public Capital

Programme—an approach that would not be considered in the 1950s given the official attitudes then prevailing.

The changes in the structure of the economy that had taken place throughout the 1950s also helped to make for greater stability. The shift, in both output and exports, from agriculture to industry reduced the impact on the economy as a whole of the considerable fluctuations in price and volume to which agricultural production was subject throughout the entire post-war period. In particular, the rapid expansion of manufactured exports since 1950 tended to reduce export instability once such exports became a significant share of the total. While manufactured exports are not immune to fluctuation, they have not been subject to the large short-term instability in price and volume that has characterised agricultural exports.

THE RECESSION OF 1966

The only serious set-back to the expansion of total output occurred in 1965–66. The recession was caused, partly at least, by deflationary measures taken to correct the adverse balance of payments position that developed in the first half of 1965. A large increase in money incomes in 1964, combined with liberal expansion of consumer credit led to a considerable rise in consumption. The rise in consumption coincided with, and was also partly stimulated by, an exceptionally large rise in investment, led by public capital spending. Fiscal policy was highly expansionary in 1964. As well as the rise in capital spending, there was also a large increase in current public expenditure, and the public borrowing requirement increased by almost a third. Prices rose rapidly due to the effects of the incomes increase on costs, the large rise in indirect taxes imposed partly to finance the income increases in the public sector, the general buoyancy of demand, and a rise in the export price of cattle that also affected domestic meat prices. Imports, however, did not rise (seasonally corrected) in the course of 1964, but began to increase substantially in the first half of 1965.

At about this time there was also a number of other unfavourable developments. The British authorities imposed a surcharge on imports of 15 per cent in the autumn of 1964. Though this was partly offset by the Irish authorities' action in compensating exporters in respect of one-half of the surcharge, it contributed to a marked slowing down in expansion of industrial exports. The more important cause of the reduction in industrial export expansion, however, was probably the slowing down in expansion of demand in the U K. There was a fall of £8 million in the value of cattle exports in 1965, but this was a temporary factor and was much more than offset by a rise in cattle stocks. The net capital inflow, which was unusually large in 1964, declined substantially in 1965. The decline reflected, partly at least, the effect of measures by the British and U S A governments to limit capital exports. The seasonally corrected trade deficit rose from £32.5 million in the fourth quarter of 1964 to £44.9 million in the second quarter of 1965, and the external reserves fell by almost £40 million (about one-sixth) between December 1964 and July 1965.

Action to check demand was initiated about the middle of 1965. In May 1965 the Central Bank advised that the rate of credit expansion should be decelerated and that priority should be given to loans for productive purposes, especially exports. In July 1965 the government announced a package of measures including a reduction in the Public Capital Programme already fixed for 1965, restraint on current government spending, hire-purchase restrictions and price control. The White Paper on public capital spending issued in October 1965 indicated that the planned cutback on the announced Public Capital Programme would be £3½ million.

In retrospect, it appears doubtful whether a cut-back in public investment was necessary. The large incomes increase in 1964 was negotiated for a 2½-year period, and it is likely that the consumer boom would have tapered off anyway, especially once credit was restricted. Even before credit restriction began to bite and retail sales turned down in the fourth quarter of 1965, the trade deficit (seasonally corrected) had begun to fall from the peak of £44.9 million in the second quarter of 1965 to £33.9 million in the third quarter. It fell further to £31.8 million in the fourth quarter. This reduction in the trade deficit could have owed little to the cutback in public investment, which would only begin to take effect late in 1965 or early in 1966. Much of the steam was taken out of the economy by the depressed conditions in the U K and by the import surcharge. The volume of output in transportable goods fell in the fourth quarter of 1964 and advanced only slowly during

1965. It would have been reasonable to regard the U K situation and the decline in cattle exports (more than matched by a rise in cattle stocks) as the sort of temporary externally determined disturbance that would justify using external reserves.

However, the cut-back in government spending in 1965 was in relation to the budget level, not in relation to the actual 1964 level. The outturn for the year shows that the volume of public capital expenditure was about the same as in 1964, while the overall public deficit rose slightly. Moreover, because of difficulties in raising finance from normal sources, the government, in effect, borrowed £20 million directly from the Central Bank to maintain a reasonably high level of public expenditure. Such an approach on this scale would not have been contemplated in the 1950s and the action indicates the greater determination to avoid the adverse consequences of a large reduction in public investment.

It is more difficult to defend the intensification of deflationary measures in 1966. At the end of 1965 the external reserves had recovered by over £20 million from the low point reached in July 1965. In the first quarter of 1966, the trade deficit (seasonally corrected) had fallen to £28.7 million, the lowest figure since the third quarter of 1963, and the volume of output in transportable goods was declining. The government did not wait, however, for the first quarter figures, but introduced an early budget in March 1966. A wide range of taxes were increased, including income tax and duties on petrol, tobacco, beer, spirits and motor vehicles. The value of public capital expenditure was reduced below the 1965 level, representing a substantial decline in volume terms. Later, in June 1966, taxes on petrol and tobacco were further raised and a new selective wholesale tax at the rate of 5 per cent was announced to take effect from October. The outturn for the year in national accounts terms clearly illustrates the deflationary nature of fiscal policy in 1966. The surplus on current account rose by £13.2 million from £12.0 million to £25.2 million, public capital expenditure fell by just over 5 per cent in current values and the borrowing requirement (excluding redemption of securities) was reduced by £18.9 million from £56.7 million to £37.8 million. The deflationary measures contributed to a substantial improvement in the balance of payments; the current deficit of £42 million in 1965 was reduced to £16 million in 1966 —despite a large fall in cattle prices and a decline in tourism due mainly to the shipping strike—and was converted into a surplus of £15 million in 1967. But building activity in 1966 declined, the rise in industrial output was the lowest for many years and real GNP grew by only 1½ per cent.

The considerations underlying the deflationary fiscal policy in 1966 appear to have been strongly related to financial constraints.[3] Difficulties in borrowing were experienced by the government in the financial year 1965–66 due to the lack of adequate support for direct government borrowing from the public through the small savings and national loan media. The authorities were anxious both to limit total bank credit expansion and to avoid monopolising bank credit to such an extent as to deprive the private sector of all access to bank borrowing. The government resorted to significant direct foreign borrowing, amounting to £25 million in the calendar year 1966, and also, in effect, financed part of the capital programme by a larger current surplus (on a national accounts basis). While, in retrospect, fiscal policy in 1966 seems unnecessarily deflationary, it must also be recognised that the use of substantial direct foreign borrowing to avoid a more serious reduction in public capital expenditure indicates a greater determination to support the level of domestic demand than in the 1950s.

Paradoxically, the deflationary measures taken in June 1966 served initially to give a significant boost to recovery in the economy. The reason is that the announcement then of a wholesale tax, applying mainly to consumer durables and not due to come into effect until October, encouraged immediate large-scale purchases of consumer goods. This rise in consumption was further stimulated by the Tenth Round wage increase in the middle of 1966 and by an unplanned expansion of credit during the bank strike from May to August 1966. The retail sales index (seasonally corrected) in the third quarter of 1966 rose by 9 per cent in value terms compared with the preceding quarter, representing a volume rise of about 7½ per cent, and this contributed to a strong rise in industrial production. Although retail sales and industrial output fell back somewhat in the fourth quarter, the basis of recovery was established and was sustained by renewed rapid expansion of industrial exports and later by reflationary fiscal policy in 1967.

CONCLUSIONS ON DEMAND MANAGEMENT

The argument of this and the previous two chapters is most forcefully summarised in Chart 23, where gross domestic expenditure (or domestic demand), exports of goods and services (or foreign

CHART 23: FINAL EXPENDITURE, GROSS DOMESTIC EXPENDITURE AND
TOTAL EXPORTS (CONSTANT PRICES) 1947 – 1968

£ million
(log scale)

A : Final Expenditure
B : Gross Domestic Expenditure
C : Exports of Goods and Services

I

demand), and total final expenditure (or total final demand) are plotted at constant (1958) prices. In the years 1947 to 1951 there was a strong and steady growth of total final demand, which depended to a considerable extent on expansion of home demand through fiscal policy. In the years 1952 to 1958 total final demand was relatively stagnant. There was little by way of increased stimulus from fiscal policy or domestic private investment in these years, and only in 1955 and 1956 was the level of home demand above the 1951 level. The deflationary policies of 1957 and 1958 contributed to a substantial cut-back in home demand, which in 1958 was 2 per cent below the level of 1951 Thus any stimulus to increased activity in this period came mainly from exports, and total exports were growing relatively slowly. The third phase (1959–68) was one of strong expansion in both domestic demand and exports. Three years of the period (1959, 1962 and 1965) were marked by negligible expansion or slight decline in volume of exports. In the first two of these years a high growth of total final demand was maintained with the help of expansionary fiscal policy. The falling off in exports in 1965, among other factors, led to deflationary measures which resulted in 1966 in the only reduction in domestic demand, and the smallest growth in total final demand, in the period.

In Table 44 we show the average annual growth rates of volume of total final demand, divided into home demand and foreign demand, for the periods 1947–51, 1951–58 and 1958–68. Final demand is met either from domestic production (i.e. G N P) or from foreign supply (i.e. imports of goods and services) and the growth rates of volume of G N P and total imports are also given in the table. The second part of the table shows how much the growth rates of each of the components contributed to the growth rate of final demand (or supply). We do not attach as much importance to Table 44 as to the annual figures in Chart 23, since the years 1951 and 1958 were disturbed, and the data in the chart give a fuller picture of developments in each of the periods. Nevertheless, the figures in the table are revealing.

Table 44 shows clearly that in the period 1947–51 almost all of the expansion of total demand was due to rising home demand. There was, indeed, a sizeable contribution from visible exports, but this was substantially offset by falling invisibles. In the period 1951–58 the only expansionary element was visible exports,

Table 44: Growth rates of major components of total final demand and supply (at 1958 prices), 1947–51, 1951–58 and 1958–68

	Average annual growth rate of components			Contribution of components to growth rate of total*		
	1947–51	1951–58	1958–68	1947–51	1951–58	1958–68
	%	%	%	%	%	%
Demand:						
Gross domestic expenditure	4.0	—0.3	4.7	3.0	—0.2	3.3
Exports of goods and services	1.3	2.7	7.3	0.4	0.7	2.2
Visibles	9.1	5.6	8.6	0.9	0.7	1.5
Invisibles	—3.4	—0.2	5.5	—0.5	0.0	0.7
Total final demand	3.4	0.4	5.5	3.4	0.4	5.5
Supply:						
GNP	3.0	0.9	4.3	2.2	0.6	3.0
Imports of goods and services	4.1	—0.7	8.1	1.2	—0.2	2.5
Total final supply (=Total final demand)	3.4	0.4	5.5	3.4	0.4	5.5

*This was measured by weighting the average annual growth rates for each period by the average of the component shares in total final demand (or supply) in the first and last year of each period. See also note to Table 6.
Source: As for Table 12.

domestic demand being a negative factor, and invisible exports contributing a negligible fall. In the final period the growth rate of final demand of 5.5 per cent per annum was made up of a contribution of 3.3 per cent from home demand, 1.5 per cent from visible exports, and 0.7 per cent from invisible exports. The contrast between the first and the third periods in the role of invisible exports is quite striking, as is the fact that in all periods visible exports made a significant contribution.

It is our contention that in the Irish circumstances of the post-war period—and, indeed, until the levels of unemployment and emigration are further substantially reduced—a high and steady growth of final demand is essential to the achievement of a high growth rate of output. We would suggest further that an expansionary fiscal policy must form an important part of the overall expansion in demand. The close relationship between changes in fiscal policy and in domestic demand show clearly the important role of public spending, particularly public capital spending, in maintaining the growth of demand and stimulating private investment.

It might be argued that a domestically induced rise in aggregate demand is not sustainable due to the pressure it puts on reserves. However, while not in the least wishing to minimise the importance of exports, we do not accept the view that, in the post-war Irish economy, demand expansion could only be successfully initiated by increased exports in order to maintain external balance. The view mentioned frequently claims support from the experience of the period 1947–51, which exemplifies an attempt to increase demand rapidly by domestic measures, an attempt that is regarded as having ended in failure because of the pressure it put on the balance of payments. However, our view is that the attempt was abandoned too soon due to excessive financial prudence and panic engendered by unfavourable external circumstances that were not, in the main, a consequence of the expansionary policies. The growth record of these years suggests that a good deal was achieved within the period and that a basis for further growth was laid without serious loss of reserves. Had greater priority been attached to employment and growth rather than financial prudence (as exemplified by unwillingness to tolerate a decline in the high level of external reserves and the negative attitudes to the use of foreign capital inflows), it would have been feasible to sustain an expansionary policy long enough to give time for measures designed to raise exports to take effect.

The period of stagnation that followed was due largely to the failure to use fiscal policy to stimulate demand at a time when tourism and important categories of agricultural exports were in difficulties. True, the authorities may also be justly criticised for failure to act more decisively in export development. Nevertheless, important measures to encourage exports were introduced, and the more serious fault seems to us to lie in the failure to use expansionary fiscal policy, since export development would take time even with the most effective measures. In the period 1959-68 fiscal policy and export growth provided a relatively strong growth of demand. Moreover, when the growth of exports slowed, the authorities were willing (except in 1966) to maintain the growth of overall demand by the appropriate use of fiscal policy. Clearly, expansion through a balanced growth of home demand and exports is to be preferred. But the structure of the early post-war economy was such that it was unilkely to be achieved. Even if measures to expand exports had been more vigorously pursued, it is likely that adequate expansion of final demand would have depended largely on the direction of fiscal policy.

It would also appear that the stagnation in home demand in the 1950s did not aid exports at all. The post-war period does not provide any evidence to show that export growth was greater when domestic demand pressures were restrained. It is more likely that the stagnation of the home economy was unfavourable to exports in that it adversely affected manufacturing investment, company profits, savings and possibly the capital inflow. Moreover, a more rapid growth of manufacturing output might have been accompanied by a more rapid growth of productivity and an improvement in competitiveness. Furthermore, the lack of confidence in the economy, associated with falling employment and population, created an atmosphere unfavourable to the enterprise required for successful entry into export markets.

PART V

CONCLUSIONS AND IMPLICATIONS

CHAPTER 16

An Overall View

THE central question, providing the unifying theme for this study, may be stated simply: why was economic growth in Ireland much greater in the 1960s than the 1950s? An outside observer, familiar with European post-war experience, would be likely to approach this question more in terms of why the growth rate of the Irish economy was so poor in the 1950s, rather than why it was reasonably high in the 1960s. In a European context, the unique feature of the performance of the Irish economy since the war was the slow rate of expansion in the 1950s, when the Irish growth rate was one of the lowest in Europe, and even with substantial emigration the growth rate of real *per capita* income was well below the average European experience. The slow growth rate cannot be explained simply by the close links with the UK economy. Although the UK had a slower growth rate in this period than other European economies, it was higher than that achieved in Ireland. Yet Ireland was not constrained by some of the factors that probably retarded growth in the UK. Two of the main reasons frequently advanced for the relatively slow growth rate in the UK are inadequate supply of labour for manufacturing industry, and insufficient foreign reserves, relative to the pressure on sterling, to permit sustained expansion of demand. Neither of these two factors applied in Ireland with anything like the same force. There was no scarcity of labour in general—although there were shortages of certain types of skilled workers, accentuated by emigration in the 1950s—and the reserves position was much less tight than in the UK. Moreover, in the 1960s, when the economic relationship between the two countries was, if anything, closer, a faster rate of growth was achieved in Ireland despite continued slow growth in the UK.

We have discussed in detail the possible causes of the slower growth in the 1950s. The chief factor seems to us to be the failure to secure a satisfactory rate of expansion in aggregate demand. On the export side, the authorities can, to some extent, be blamed for slowness in coping with the problems posed by the weak structural composition of exports. But even more serious was the failure to maintain expansion of the Public Capital Programme from 1952, despite the very considerable progress that had been achieved in this way from 1947 to 1951. More particularly, the massive cut-back in public investment in 1957 and 1958 unnecessarily deepened and prolonged the depression in the economy. It could be argued in opposition to this view that, given the slow expansion of total exports, it was impossible to have a faster growth of domestic demand without taking undue risks with the balance of payments and external reserves. The choice between these two views depends on a number of judgments on which there is room for legitimate difference of opinion. It depends, for instance, on the emphasis placed on the risk to reserves as against the costs of stagnation. In the 1960s, as we have shown, a less restrictive view was taken of the reserves constraint even though the problems of idle capacity, unemployment and emigration were then somewhat less acute. It depends also on whether one could regard the taking of such risks as a means of buying time to support the level of activity until progress had been made on the export side, or whether, in fact, in the end the country would be left with little or no reserves and in no better position to export. There can be no doubt that, at the time, a pessimistic view was taken of the progress made in expanding exports. In retrospect, however, we see that a fair measure of progress had been made. In the 1950s manufacturing exports had begun to expand, the decline in tourism was arrested, and even on the agricultural side there had been some progress in expanding the potential for cattle exports.

Even in the 1960s, with a rapid rate of growth of exports, the maintenance of a high rate of growth of production required a strong fiscal stimulus to the growth of demand. And it is certain that in the earlier post-war phase, even had the authorities been more industrious in promoting exports, the achievement of a satisfactory growth rate would have required relatively greater dependence on demand from domestic sources. We do not claim that the slow growth rate of the 1950s was solely due to the absence of a sufficiently expansionary fiscal policy, or that it would necessarily have been feasible then to maintain a rate of growth of demand sufficient to secure as good a growth rate of output as in the 1960s. But a reasonable rate of growth of demand led by an expansionary fiscal policy could have been safely sustained had there been a less restrictive view of the balance of payments constraint and less concern about increasing the national debt. Moreover, the unwillingness to take risks with the balance of payments in the interests of maintaining a more satisfactory growth of demand led the economy into a vicious circle. The authorities felt that it was impossible to expand investment because of insufficient saving. This held back expansion of demand and capacity and led to a low growth of output and real income *per capita* as well as to declining population and high dependency ratio—these factors being, as we have shown, adverse to personal savings. There is also evidence that the lack of profitable investment opportunities, consequent on the slow growth of demand, reduced company savings, and it may also have reduced foreign capital inflows for direct investment. Moreover, the continued fall in employment and population had widespread depressing effects on confidence and initiative as well as increasing the burden on the remaining population of providing infrastructural facilities.

It might also be argued, in opposition to our views, that the cutback in social investment in 1957–58 was a necessary, though painful, measure to open the way for more immediately productive investment and that had attempts been made to do this more gradually it would not have been done at all.[1] However, this line of argument, as it pertains to 1957–58, does not altogether fit the facts. As Finola Kennedy (1970) pointed out, the trend in the share of social investment in total public investment was downwards from 1951—long before the large reductions in 1957 and 1958—whereas it was upwards in the period 1959–66. Faster growth in the second period was therefore achieved in the context of a rising social capital share. It is quite true, as she also pointed out, that for the period 1959–66, on average, the social share was lower than for the period 1949–58 because of the low base in 1958. It might, therefore, be claimed that faster growth was due to the fact that a larger proportion of public investment was devoted to immediately productive activities. But of far greater importance, in our view, was the fact that in the second period the volume of both social and productive investment expanded rapidly within the context of a steeply rising Public Capital Programme. We would even go further and question whether it would have been possible to maintain a rapid growth of productive investment in this period if the volume of social investment had not risen also and if the large amount of social and infrastructural investment had not been undertaken earlier.

In summing up, we may say that the major difference in the period since 1958 compared with the preceding years has been high and steady growth of aggregate demand. A high rate of growth of exports of goods and services was achieved through a range of measures for the development of export-oriented industry and because a more balanced structure of exports existed than at the start of the earlier period. The size of the incentives for the development of tourism and manufactured exports was greatly expanded. Also important to the development of exports was the emergence of new attitudes towards the use of foreign enterprise and capital. Hand in hand with the rapid growth of exports went a high and relatively stable growth of investment and consumption, stimulated by an expansionary fiscal policy and a rapidly increasing Public Capital Programme, as well as by rising export earnings. The growth of aggregate demand could proceed more safely because of the satisfactory growth of exports. But there is evidence also that a greater priority was given to output and employment in the later period and that a less restrictive view was taken of the balance of payments. It would thus appear that the authorities were more willing to maintain output and employment and allow reserves to decline in the face of temporary set-backs in the growth of exports. The emergence of more liberal attitudes in relation to national debt was also important.

The 1960s, in contrast with the 1950s, offer us an example of the virtuous circle where growth feeds on growth—at least up to near full employment. Faster growth of exports and expansionary fiscal policy created adequate pressure of demand, rapid growth of output, a rising investment ratio, a faster growth of real income *per capita,* reduced emigration and a rising savings ratio. In turn, the rising savings ratio permitted an increasing investment ratio without unduly large balance of payments problems, thereby increasing capacity and the potential for further growth. A great deal of prominence has been accorded to the rise in manufactured exports, and, indeed, this was very important; but equally striking, in our view, was the expansion in tourism and building. In Ireland there are three major industries which exert a particularly strong influence on the overall level of domestic activity by reason of their low import content and the degree to which they rely on domestic resources. These are agriculture, tourism, and building and construction. For most of the 1950s all three were depressed or expanding only slowly. In the more recent period, agriculture continued to grow slowly and erratically, but from 1957 in the case of tourism and from 1958 in the case of building there was a radical reversal of the preceding situation of decline and stagnation.

In understanding why the rate of economic growth was much lower in the 1950s, however, it would be wrong to place all of the blame on policy, and to neglect the fact that conditions in many respects were less conducive to growth then than later. Serious structural problems existed at the start of the post-war period. Massive protection in the 1930s had helped establish an industrial base, but production for export markets was negligible. The main component of merchandise exports was agricultural exports which were liable to considerable short-term instability. Moreover, agricultural exports were concentrated in the U K market where policy changes in the early 1950s caused severe short-run problems and weakened longer-term prospects. The major category of agricultural exports, cattle, that could be sold at reasonably favourable prices was among the least labour-intensive of agricultural products. This probably contributed further to the rural exodus. Tourism declined considerably after the post-war boom ended and, while well-managed development efforts could have at least mitigated the size and duration of the decline, an initial fall was almost inevitable as the continental market opened up again for British tourists. In areas like housing, health, education, transport, power and communications, serious deficiencies in infrastructural facilities existed. These and other structural problems constrained the effectiveness of policies aimed at achieving sustained growth. And however harshly the policies pursued in the 1950s may be judged, by the end of the decade many of the problems had been overcome or considerably reduced.[2] The decline in tourism was reversed, manufactured exports had a more important weight in total exports and were growing rapidly, and a considerable amount of infrastructural facilities had been provided.

Apart from the structural problems in the economy, there were also major disturbances in the first period that were wholly or largely outside the control of the authorities. The impact of these disturbances was all the greater because of the structural weaknesses in the economy. We have mentioned the difficulties caused by changes in U K agricultural policies at a time when agricultural exports represented a large proportion of total exports, and tourism—the other major export category—was declining. During the 1950s the terms of trade were adverse and fluctuated considerably. There were serious disturbances caused by the 1949 sterling devaluation, the Korean War and the Suez crisis. Of course, one must avoid special pleading since many other economies faced the same problems and recovered fairly quickly. Moreover, the period of the 1960s was not without its own adverse external factors. However, it would appear that the disturbances in the earlier period were larger in scale and more disruptive in impact.

Thus structural weakness and external factors combined to make the successful implementation of economic policies rather more difficult than in the later period. Moreover, domestic policymakers had less experience of dealing with the problems that were to emerge after the war. By the end of the 1930s, protection had been pushed close to the limit, and there was no clear idea about what further measures might be adopted to secure sustained industrial development. While the need to expand exports was evident to the authorities, the concrete measures for achieving this goal were less evident. Indeed, it would be demanding a lot to expect that the right policies would be selected and implemented immediately on the required scale without the benefit of testing their suitability for the Irish economy. Delays were likely to occur if only because the successful implementation of new measures of any significance usually requires the mobilisation of public opinion and the creation of a consensus in favour of the new approach.[3] In fact, many of the measures that were later important for the development of exports were initiated early on, though often somewhat timidly at first. Examples of this include the establishment of such bodies as the Industrial Development Authority, Coras Tráchtála and Bord Fáilte, the introduction of tax incentives to manufactured exports and the extension of the scope of industrial grants. More generally, the major policy innovation of the whole post-war period—the launching of the Public Capital Programme—was begun very soon after the war; and while we consider that the retreat from expansion in public investment in the period 1951–58 was the most costly policy error of the post-war period, nevertheless, even in these years a considerable amount of valuable capital investment was undertaken that facilitated subsequent development.

Thus, in our opinion, the post-war period up to the end of the 1950s should not be seen in the conventional terms as a period in which little or nothing was done to develop the economy. While we have been critical of many aspects of policy in this period, we could not agree fully with the conclusion of FitzGerald (1968) that

> What was achieved after 1958 could have been secured a decade earlier with a better organisation of the economy, a greater will to develop its potentialities, sounder economic policies and adequate leadership.[4]

This view does not, we feel, give due regard to the magnitude of the structural deficiencies of the immediate post-war economy and the large external shocks of the early 1950s. It also fails to allow for the interdependence between the two periods and the degree to which growth in the 1960s depended on, for example, the provision of infrastructure in the 1950s. But, most important of all, it ignores what may be referred to as the 'learning process' that applies to policy formation and execution.

The work of Arrow (1962) and of other writers has made economists familiar with the concept of 'learning-by-doing' in relation to technical progress. The general idea is that the acquisition of technological knowledge, which is termed learning, is a product of experience, and learning takes place in an attempt to solve a problem. A similar notion can validly be applied to the formulation and execution of new policies. The basic knowledge underlying the policies may not be new—indeed, it may have existed for a long time—but the translation of the ideas into practical policies in a given environment represents a new creative process. And, as in the case of technical change, the underlying ideas are likely to be improved and the methods of implementation perfected as experience is gained of their use. It appears to us that the process of trial and error is an essential component of the dynamics of policy change, and that it is necessary to take this into account in order to achieve an adequate understanding of the course of economic policy over time. We have given several examples of policy measures that were tried on a small scale at first and were later extended as experience of their use grew and confidence developed in regard to their merits.

It would be wrong, of course, to idealise this process, since it would then degenerate into a *Candide*-type world where 'everything is for the best in the best of all possible worlds'. We do not claim that the process represents a smooth and unbroken progression of ideas. It is easy to find examples both of substantial forward leaps and significant back-tracking on previous advances. Nevertheless, the impression remains of some progress towards a keener understanding of the requirements of growth in the Irish context. Thus, in our view, the dichotomy between the 1950s and the 1960s should not be exaggerated. Many developments that took place in the earlier period facilitated growth in the later period. It is undeniable that the quality of economic policy towards development improved greatly after the publication of *Economic Development* (Whitaker, 1958). But it in no way detracts from the originality of this study to say that it benefited from being able to survey the range of development efforts tried since the war. Thus it could evaluate actual experience in relation to various policies, rejecting those that were failures and emphasising those that seemed to be successful. One might say that the study was revolutionary in the degree to which it accelerated evolution.

However, the importance of *Economic Development* was not just due to its evaluation of previous policies. Firstly, unlike many previous official studies, it attempted a comprehensive exploration of all development possibilities. No single panacea, no unique elixir, was offered as the source of economic growth. In contrast with the view of many commentators at the time that agriculture represented *the* source of future growth, *Economic Development* maintained that 'a dynamic of progress awaits release in agriculture, fisheries, industry and tourism'.

Secondly, the report attempted to be specific about the opportunities for development and how they could be realised. This, again, was in contrast to most previous advice offered to the government which was cast in generalities, upon which it was easy to agree but difficult to act.

A third important feature of *Economic Development* was that it adopted a flexible approach and allowed for changing economic conditions. Thus, in the course of the first programme, as we have seen, the public capital investment targets were substantially exceeded, and both the total and the social component were allowed to expand quite rapidly. As we have indicated, this was crucial in ensuring that aggregate demand expanded in line with the potential output of the economy.

Fourthly, the study secured official blessing for the view that the balance of payments constraint should be interpreted more liberally and that the use of foreign capital should be encouraged. Although this had occurred in the period 1947–51, it had not received a coherent justification so that there was no authoritative resistance to the conservative financial pressures for deflationary measures following the balance of payments crisis of 1951. While *Economic Development* stressed the need to increase external reserves, the urgency of this was tempered by the emphasis on achieving a more rapid rate of growth. The study showed both a greater willingness to take risks and a greater drive to reduce the risks by policies to expand exports.

Fifthly, and perhaps most important of all, *Economic Development* adopted a confident stance at a time when there was profound gloom about the future of the Irish economy. The degree of pessimism then prevailing may be difficult to comprehend since our analysis shows that though the 1950s emerges as a period in which there was a poor growth rate of output, falling employment and large emigration, a slowness in adopting measures on the scale required, and some major mistakes in policy, it also emerges as one in which much of the groundwork was laid for faster growth in the later period. Granted that economic performance within the period was poor, it may still seem surprising that it should give rise to a 'national *malaise*' and 'symptoms . . . resembling the "death wish" of a society'.[5] We can try to account for this in terms of an analogy with the construction of a building. Laying the foundations appears to most of us as an untidy process that takes a disproportionate amount of time and during which little progress is seen to be made. Add to this the absence of a clear view of what the final structure might be and, indeed, the lack of a general assurance that any structure would emerge at all, and we get a deeper insight into the mood of the time. Thus, while many individual and useful development measures were implemented, there was little coordination of these measures and no comprehensive vision of the final shape of things. It appears to us that it was this absence of an overall sense of direction, even more than the inadequate performance in the period itself, that generated so much gloom. And the overwhelming achievement of *Economic Development* was in dissipating the prevailing pessimism, even before recovery from the economic depression had begun. The immediate boost to national morale consequent on the publication of that document arose from the recognition by the public at large that it provided an overall sense of direction in government economic policy and welded the many isolated measures into an integrated development programme.

CHAPTER 17

The Economy from 1968 to 1972

I N the main body of this study, the analysis has been confined to the post-war period up to 1968. It is desirable, however, before concluding to examine the course of the economy since then, as we do in this chapter. However, it must be stressed that the data, especially for the years 1971 and 1972, are subject to revision, which in some cases could be substantial.

There are advantages in considering the 1968–72 period separately after the analysis has been completed for the earlier periods. It provides an opportunity to examine the extent to which the conclusions of the earlier analysis hold up in relation to a new period when new factors are likely to be influential. One of the dominating features of the years 1969 to 1972 has been the marked acceleration in inflation. In addition, the economy has been considerably affected since 1969 by the Northern Ireland conflict which, among other things, has led to a substantial decline in tourist revenue in the Republic. Moreover, an economy is a dynamic entity in which the priorities of economic policy must change if policy is to respond adequately to present and future problems. These problems can be brought into sharper focus by considering recent experience in relation to past experience.

Our study of the 1968–72 period, then, will be a miniscule version of the main study in which we explore the similarities with the earlier post-war period as well, of course, as the differences.

ECONOMIC GROWTH 1968–72

Aggregate Growth

Table 45 sets out the average annual growth rates from 1968 to 1972 of real G N P, population and employment, together with the growth rates of real G N P *per capita* and per worker. The

Table 45: Average annual growth rates of real G N P, etc. 1968–72*

	Average annual growth rate
	%
G N P	3.7
Population	0.9
Employment	—0.4
G N P *per capita*	2.8
G N P per worker	4.1

*In *National Income and Expenditure 1972* emigrants' remittances and pensions from abroad are no longer counted, as formerly, as part of G N P. For comparability with earlier periods, however, we have throughout this chapter added them back to total invisible exports and G N P.

Sources: *National Income and Expenditure 1972*; Department of Finance, *Review of 1972 and Outlook for 1973*; and *Trend of Employment and Unemployment 1972*.

growth rate of G N P, 3.7 per cent per annum, was somewhat less than the growth rate of 4.1 per cent from 1961 to 1968. Indeed, if we omit 1969, when there was a growth rate of 5½ per cent, the average rate from 1969 to 1972 was 3.2 per cent, while in each of the years 1970 and 1971 the growth rate was below 3 per cent. There was, however, a further remarkable improvement, especially in 1972, in the terms of trade, the importance of which, as already demonstrated, was considerable in the period 1961–68. Thus, if we add to G N P the external trading gain—and this is justified in considering changes in living standards as distinct from physical production—the growth rate for the period 1968–72 rises to 4.8 per cent per annum, compared with a corresponding growth rate of 4.6 per cent from 1961 to 1968, and 3.2 per cent from 1947 to 1968.

Population rose at nearly 1 per cent per annum, rather faster than the annual growth rate of ½ per cent from 1961 to 1968, and substantially different from the post-war period up to 1961 when population was declining. Thus the annual growth rate of G N P *per capita* from 1968 to 1972 (2.8 per cent) was well below the rate from 1961 to 1968 (3.6 per cent) and slightly below the rate for the whole post-war period from 1947 to 1968. However, when allowance is made for the external trading gain resulting from the improvement in the terms of trade, the growth rate of real income *per capita* from 1968 to 1972 was 3.9 per cent per annum, much the same as from 1961 to 1968. The faster rate of growth of population was mainly due to a substantial decline in emigration. In the years 1961 to 1968 net emigration averaged 16,000 per annum, and this dropped to an annual average of 5,000 in the four years 1969 to 1972. Indeed, in the years 1971 and 1972 there was a small net inflow. The decline in emigration was probably largely due to rising unemployment in the U K.[1]

Total employment declined from 1968 to 1972 by 0.4 per cent per annum, compared with a rise of 0.2 per cent per annum from 1961 to 1968. Thus the small gain in total employment made after 1961 was reversed, and the 1972 level of 1,046,000 at work was the lowest ever recorded. The decline in employment, combined with the reduction in net emigration, involved a considerable rise in unemployment. The non-agricultural unemployment rate rose from 6.7 per cent in 1968 to 8.1 per cent in 1972. The average annual growth rate of productivity was 4.1 per cent, compared with 3.9 per cent from 1961 to 1968.

Clearly the performance of the economy after 1968, and especially in the years 1970 and 1971, has not been as impressive as in the preceding decade. There was a reduction in the growth rate of aggregate production. While the big improvement in the terms of trade prevented a decline in the growth of average real income *per capita*, there was a fall in total employment. It is important to examine the reasons for the slower growth of output and employment, and in particular to determine whether it represented a temporary phenomenon due to exceptional and (hopefully) transitory factors, or whether it suggests a reduction in the longer-term growth prospects of the economy.

Sectoral Growth

Table 46 shows the growth rates of real G D P, employment and productivity in the three main sectors of the economy: agriculture, industry and services. The figures for the services sector are broadly similar to those for 1961–68. The volume of agricultural output rose much faster than formerly, due mainly to live-stock—in particular, cattle—and, to a lesser extent, livestock products, while crop production continued to rise slowly. Agricultural employment declined at a greater rate, so that the absolute decline in numbers (10,750 per annum, on average) was larger

Table 46: Average annual growth rates of sectoral real product, etc.,
1968–72*

Sector	Real G D P	Employment	Productivity
	%	%	%
Agriculture	2.7	—3.7	6.6
Industry	4.9	0.7	4.1
Services	3.9	0.9	2.9
Total	4.0	—0.4	4.4

*It may be noted that the figures in this table relate to G D P at factor cost. Since net factor income from abroad declined from 1968 to 1972, the growth rate of total G N P at factor cost was 3.6 per cent.

Sources: *National Income and Expenditure 1972*; *Trend of Employment and Unemployment 1972*.

than from 1961 to 1968 (9,100 per annum) despite the big reductions that had already taken place in the agricultural work force. Thus agricultural productivity rose considerably faster (6.6 per cent per annum) than the relatively constant rate of about 4 per cent attained in the preceding post-war periods. The higher growth rate of productivity was no doubt due, in part at least, to the more rapid growth of the less labour-intensive forms of agricultural production and the greatly increased use of fertilizers.

The industrial sector fared poorly compared with the period 1961–68. The growth rate of industrial G D P fell from 6.4 per cent to 4.9 per cent. Industrial productivity rose at about the same rate as in the previous period, so that the decline in the growth of industrial output involved a similar decline in the growth rate of industrial employment—from 2.4 per cent from 1961 to 1968 to 0.8 per cent from 1968 to 1972.

Major Demand and Supply Components

Table 47 shows the growth rates of the major components of total final demand and supply from 1968 to 1972. Two factors stand out immediately as substantially different from the period 1961–68. The first is the far higher rate of growth of all prices. Thus, for example, the rate of growth of the personal consumption price (8.2 per cent) was more than twice the rate in the period 1961–68. This difference was not peculiar to Ireland, as

Table 47: Average annual growth rates of total final demand and supply, 1968–72

	At current prices	At constant prices	Implied price
	%	%	%
DEMAND			
Gross domestic expenditure	14.7	5.3	9.0
Personal consumption	12.3	3.7	8.2
Government consumption	21.1	8.7	11.4
Gross domestic physical investment	18.3	7.9	9.6
Of which: fixed investment	(17.2)	(7.3)	(9.2)
Exports of goods and services	12.4	4.5	7.6
Visibles	16.2	7.2	8.4
Invisibles	5.2	—0.4	5.6
TOTAL FINAL DEMAND	14.0	5.0	8.6
SUPPLY			
Gross National Product	14.3	3.7	10.2
Imports of goods and services	13.3	7.9	5.0
Visibles	13.2	7.9	4.9
Invisibles	13.9	7.8	5.6
TOTAL FINAL SUPPLY (=TOTAL FINAL DEMAND	14.0	5.0	8.6

Source: *National Income and Expenditure 1972.* See notes to Tables 12 and 45.

most developed countries experienced a marked rise in the rate of inflation at about the same time. Undoubtedly, Ireland would find it difficult to isolate itself from such developments in these countries. It is nevertheless of interest to look more closely, as we do later in this chapter, at the sources of the acceleration in inflation in Ireland and its impact on the economy.

A second major difference compared with 1961–68 was the substantial fall in the growth rate of volume of total exports from 6.5 per cent to 4.5 per cent. Since the volume of visible exports grew at much the same rate as previously, the decline in the growth of the total was almost entirely due to the substantial adverse change in invisibles. From 1961 to 1968 the volume of invisible exports rose by over 5 per cent per annum but from

1968 to 1972 declined by ½ per cent per annum.[2] Even in current values, despite a much faster rate of price increase, the rate of growth of invisible exports was only 5.2 per cent per annum. from 1968 to 1972 compared with 7.8 per cent from 1961 to 1968. On the other hand, since visible exports maintained much the same volume growth in the two periods and had a much higher rate of price increase from 1968 to 1972, the rate of growth of value of visible exports in the latter period (16.2 per cent per annum) was substantially higher than from 1961 to 1968 (10.2 per cent). Thus from 1968 to 1972 there was an acceleration in the decline in invisible relative to visible exports, which characterised the whole post-war period but had been significantly slowed down from 1961 to 1968. In 1947 the value of invisible exports amounted to more than twice the value of visible exports; the ratio fell to 71 per cent in 1961 and to 61 per cent in 1968, while in 1972 the ratio was down to 41 per cent. The major component of the fall in the growth of invisibles was tourism, which we examine in detail later in this chapter.

The volume of gross domestic expenditure (GDE), on average, rose somewhat faster than from 1961 to 1968—5.3 per cent per annum as against 4.6 per cent. However, the average for the period 1968–72 conceals the fact that nearly half the total rise took place in 1969, when GDE rose by 9.7 per cent. In the following two years, 1970 and 1971, GDE rose at more modest rates of 1.9 per cent and 3.4 per cent respectively, while in 1972 the growth rate rose to 6.2 per cent. A similar pattern appears in the growth of volume of gross physical capital formation which rose by no less than 25.3 per cent in 1969, followed by a decline of 0.9 per cent in 1970 and increases of 2.7 per cent and 6.3 per cent in 1971 and 1972 respectively. The average annual rate of growth of fixed investment, in volume terms, was 7.3 per cent from 1968 to 1972, rather less than the growth of 8.9 per cent per annum for 1961–68. Again, a substantial part of the increase took place in 1969 when the volume of fixed investment rose by 19.7 per cent. Variations in the volume rate of growth of personal consumption, though less extreme, followed a similar pattern, the percentage increases in each of the four years from 1968 to 1972 being 5.4, 2.1, 2.1 and 5.4 respectively.

Thus the sequence emerging in relation to the growth of volume of home demand shows that, following a large rise in

1969, growth was slow in 1970 and 1971 and was followed by a pick-up in 1972. There can be little doubt that this pattern was strongly influenced by policy in relation to public investment. In volume terms, the Public Capital Programme rose by 15.0 per cent in 1969, but by only 2.0 per cent in 1970 and 3.3 per cent in 1971, while there was a rise of 6.6 per cent in 1972. We consider this aspect later in discussing short-term movements in the economy.

The volume of total consumption, personal and government combined, rose by 4½ per cent per annum or somewhat faster than the growth of G N P, while the volume of investment also rose faster than G N P. There was thus a substantial rise in the volume ratio of consumption and investment to G N P. This would have implied a fall in the ratio of savings to G N P and a substantial rise in the ratio of total net foreign disinvestment (i.e. the current balance of payments) to G N P in current values, were it not for the fact that the terms of trade improved so substantially. In fact, the savings ratio in current values rose from 19.4 per cent to 21.2 per cent, while the balance of payments deficit in current values rose only from 1.2 per cent of G N P in 1968 to 2.5 per cent in 1972. Had 1968 prices prevailed in 1972, the balance of payments deficit in 1972 would, *ceteris paribus*, have amounted to over 7 per cent of G N P.

Even with the benefit of improved terms of trade, however, the amount of foreign disinvestment was on average considerably greater than that for the period 1961–68. In 1969 the current balance of payments deficit rose to £69 million from £16 million in 1968. The 1969 deficit was the largest ever in absolute terms, and relative to G N P (4.5 per cent) was the highest since 1955 (6.5 per cent). Although the deficit remained at about the 1969 level in the three following years, it declined as a proportion of G N P. Nevertheless, on average for the four years 1969 to 1972, the deficit amounted to 3.6 per cent of G N P compared with 1.6 per cent in the years 1961 to 1968 and 3.2 per cent in the years 1949 to 1960.

Capital Inflows

The deficits on the current account of the balance of payments in the years 1969 to 1972 were more than covered by substantially increased capital inflows, and the external reserves rose by £150 million to a level of £432 million at end-1972. The net capital inflow in each of the years 1969–72 was substantial and on average amounted to just over £100 million per annum, far larger than anything previously experienced. The major source of the increased net capital inflow was through changes in the net external assets of the banks, especially the Non-Associated Banks, but also, in 1972, in the Associated Banks.[3] In fact, this accounted for nearly half of the total net inflow. Much of the inflow through the Non-Associated Banks may have been essentially direct investment. The other major form of capital inflow was borrowing abroad by the public sector (both the central government itself and state-sponsored bodies) at an average annual figure of over £30 million, far in excess of the average of about £6 million per annum in the period 1961–68. The remainder of about £20 million represented private net flows of various kinds and was roughly in line with experience in the preceding period.[4] Therefore the broad picture is that, despite relatively large deficits on the current account of the balance of payments, the reserves were more than maintained chiefly by means of greatly increased capital inflows through the banks and of borrowing abroad by the public sector.

However, as we suggested in Chapter 8, it was unlikely that increased foreign indebtedness could continue on the same scale as up to 1968, let alone at the much higher rate in the years 1969 to 1972, without adversely affecting the surplus on investment in the current account of the balance of payments. Up to 1968 the inflow of investment income had risen at much the same rate as the outflow, but, as we suggested in Chapter 8, this position was likely to change as a result of the substantial amount of direct investment and public borrowing abroad during the 1960s. In fact, from 1968 to 1972, while the inflow of investment income rose from £51.0 million to £71.8 million, the outflow rose at a much higher rate from £27.4 million to £60.9 million. It appears to us that the traditional surplus on investment income is soon likely to become a substantial deficit item, even if the rate of capital inflow is substantially lower than in the years 1969 to 1972.

Summary

In the period 1968–72 the economy had a poorer performance in regard to the growth of output and employment than in the period 1961–68. This was so despite much more favourable conditions for agriculture, and was associated largely with a reduction in industrial growth. At the same time, the rate of inflation was far higher than previously. This substantial acceleration in inflation calls for further examination, not only because its sources are of interest, but because it may have affected industrial growth through reduced competitiveness. On the demand side, the decline in tourism would appear, on past experience, to be a significant factor in restraining growth. Moreover, the considerable reduction in the growth of public investment after 1969 is another probable cause of the slow growth of home demand, and the poor overall growth performance, experienced in the years 1970 and 1971. We now consider these factors in greater detail.

THE ACCELERATION IN INFLATION

The average annual rate of increase in the consumer price index from 1968 to 1972 was 8.3 per cent. This was about double the rate of increase in the earlier post-war periods, 1949–61 (3.5 per cent) and 1961–68 (4.2 per cent). The only comparable rates of increase previously were in 1951 (7.9 per cent) and 1952 (8.7 per cent), which were clearly due to special factors (the 1949 devaluation and the Korean War) and were quickly reduced to more tolerable levels when the upward movement of import prices slackened and reversed. The highest previous rate of price increase in the 1960s was in 1964, when prices rose by 6.4 per cent.

Table 48: Annual percentage changes in various prices, 1968–72

	1967 –68	1968 –69	1969 –70	1970 –71	1971 –72	1968 –72*
	%	%	%	%	%	%
Consumer price index	4.7	7.4	8.2	8.9	8.7	8.3
Import unit value index	8.3	4.0	6.8	6.0	2.9	4.9
Export unit value index	7.3	6.1	6.6	7.7	13.5	8.4
Agricultural price index	10.3	2.8	4.7	7.0	21.5	8.7
Unit price of cattle and beef exports	19.2	7.6	8.9	9.7	29.6	13.8

*Annual average
Source: *Irish Statistical Bulletin*, various issues.

Table 48 gives details of the annual changes in various prices in recent years as well as the annual average for 1968–72. As may be seen by comparing this table with Table 17 of Chapter 3, the rate of increase in import, export and agricultural prices has risen even more than in the case of consumer prices. We show in Table 48 the price changes in 1968 because it was then that the general rise in prices began. A major initial impetus was the sterling devaluation of November 1967 which was an important cause of the substantial rise in import prices in 1968. In the first quarter of 1968 the import price index (seasonally corrected) rose 6.7 per cent above the level of the fourth quarter of 1967, and for the year 1968 as a whole, import prices were 8.3 per cent above the 1967 level. Because of the high import content of production and domestic consumption in Ireland, such a large rise in import prices was bound to have a significant impact on both consumer and export prices. In addition, the agricultural price index rose substantially in the fourth quarter of 1967 and the first quarter of 1968 due to rising export prices of livestock. This affected the consumer price of meat, etc., since the domestic consumer must pay a price competitive with that offered to farmers by foreign buyers. The consumer price index rose by 3.8 per cent between the fourth quarter of 1967 and the second quarter of 1968 (equivalent to an annual rate of about 8 per cent).

Thus external factors in the form of rising import and livestock prices gave the first thrust to the acceleration in domestic prices, and were undoubtedly among the major factors leading to the large rise in the scale of wage demands from about the end of 1968. The maintenance men's settlement early in 1969 has come to be regarded as a landmark, involving an increase of roughly 20 per cent over eighteen months and leading to a very large general Twelfth Round increase.[5] Subsequently, the scale of wage demands reached chaotic proportions, with increases of 50 per cent and even 100 per cent being sought in some occupations, until the National Pay Agreements of December 1970 and July 1972 restored a considerable degree of order, though at the price of high overall settlements relative to previous post-war experience. Resistance to wage demands involved major industrial disputes in 1969 and 1970, notably the maintenance men's strike in 1969, the cement strike in the first half of 1970, and a prolonged bank dispute which involved closure of the Associated

Banks from 1 May to 17 November 1970 and curtailed banking services for nearly a year. The number of man-days lost as a result of industrial disputes in 1969 and 1970 was 936,000 and 1,008,000 respectively, compared with an average of 398,000 in the years 1961 to 1968.[6] Disputes of this nature and scale had a serious adverse effect on production in 1969 to 1970.

Apart from the rise in import and livestock prices in 1968, a number of other factors may have contributed to the more inflationary wage settlements. One such factor was the enormously high growth of demand in 1968 and 1969. The volume of gross domestic expenditure rose by 10.8 per cent in 1968 and by 9.7 per cent in 1969, while the volume of total final expenditure rose by 10.5 per cent and 7.8 per cent respectively. Increased demand on this scale did not take place in any previous year of the post-war period, let alone for two years running: the highest previous rise in gross domestic expenditure was 6.9 per cent in 1959, and in total final expenditure 7.2 per cent in 1961. It would be surprising if the rate of growth in demand on the scale of 1968 and 1969 did not have some impact on the size of wage demands and wage settlements. However, the effect should not be exaggerated, since the high growth of demand did not succeed in significantly reducing the unemployment rate below the relatively high level caused by the 1966 recession. One would expect demand to influence wage rates through labour scarcities. While there may have been scarcities in particular occupations,[7] the unemployment figures do not suggest that there were widespread labour shortages. Moreover, despite the cut-back in expansion of demand after 1969, the size of wage increases continued at a very high rate.

Another possible factor leading to higher wage demands was the substantial rise in indirect taxation. In the supplementary budget of November 1968 the rate of wholesale tax was raised, with effect from 1 January 1969, from 5 per cent to 10 per cent. The rate was further raised, in the case of certain items, to 15 per cent in the 1969 budget and to 20 per cent in the supplementary budget of October 1970. Turnover tax was doubled to 5 per cent in the 1970 budget. In addition to these tax increases, there were also increases in the rates of duty on petrol, alcohol and tobacco. Overall, the increases in indirect tax rates imposed in the years 1969 and 1970 seem far greater than in most post-war years.[8]

This helped to raise the rate of inflation in two ways. Firstly, the indirect tax rates directly affected the consumer price index, and secondly, the resulting price increases influenced the scale of wage demands.

It might be claimed that the rise in indirect tax rates was a response to, rather than an independent cause of, inflation. This argument is presumably based on the view that inflation raises government expenditure more than government revenue at existing tax rates. As regards expenditure, it is generally true that the price element in public expenditure tends to rise relative to the price of G N P because there is no measured productivity increase in public sector activity. Thus maintenance of a given volume ratio of public expenditure to G N P will generally imply a rise in the ratio in current values. But this would happen whatever the rate of inflation, and even if there were no inflation, so long as average earnings of public sector employees, social welfare benefits, etc. rise at the same rate as average earnings in the rest of the economy. It is not obvious that inflation as such induces any relative change in this position. On the other hand, as regards government revenue, there is some reason to expect that a higher rate of inflation will raise the ratio of government revenue to G N P.[9] It is, then, improbable that inflation causes an increase in government expenditure relative to government revenue at existing tax rates: rather, it is more likely to raise revenue relative to expenditure. Therefore the rise in tax rates cannot be justified as necessary on that basis.

It should also be noted that the different possible ways of securing a given increase in government revenue may have different implications for inflation. An increase in direct taxes could possibly have similar *secondary* effects on inflation as a rise in indirect taxation, since the reduction in take-home pay can generate increased wage demands. This factor was probably also operative in this period, since tax allowances did not keep pace with the very large increases in money incomes, so that the disparity in gross and take-home pay widened.[10] However, the *primary* effect is quite different in that an increase in indirect taxation generally involves an immediate mark-up on prices, whereas direct taxation does not. A decision to increase tax rates, and the choice between direct and indirect taxes, obviously involves many considerations. Indirect taxes may even be raised to curtail demand as a means of *curbing* inflation. This should not, however, obscure the fact that an increase in indirect taxation also tends to be an independent source of inflation on the lines mentioned above, and this to a greater extent than in the case of a corresponding rise in direct taxation.

As already mentioned, the inflation of the early 1950s declined when the rapid rise in import prices terminated. The same might well have happened in this period had import prices fallen, but, in fact, they continued to rise rapidly due to worldwide inflation. While there was a considerable fall in the rate of increase in import prices in 1969 to 4 per cent, this rate was well above the average for the period 1961–68. It was followed in 1970 and 1971 by increases of 6.8 per cent and 6.0 per cent respectively. On a quarterly (seasonally corrected) basis, import prices were steady from the second quarter of 1971 to the second quarter of 1972, helped no doubt by the dollar devaluation of December 1971. However, in the third and fourth quarters of 1972 import prices again began to rise rapidly, partly due to the downward float of the pound. Thus, though the average rise for the year 1972 was only 2.9 per cent, import prices in the fourth quarter of 1972 were 6 per cent higher than in the same period of 1971.

The rise in export prices of cattle, which was partly responsible for the initial rise in the rate of inflation, also contributed to maintaining the pace of inflation in 1971 and 1972. Cattle prices began to increase rapidly in the fourth quarter of 1971 and continued to rise throughout 1972 due to the world shortage of beef. As may be seen from Table 48, the increases in the agricultural price index in 1971 and 1972 were 7.0 per cent and 21.5 per cent respectively.

It has been argued by Nordhaus (1972) that the major independent cause of the rise in the inflation rate in most of the developed countries—the U S A being the most important exception—was the impact of rising trade prices. This would seem to be borne out for Ireland, with the additional point that larger increases in indirect tax rates have also been of some consequence.[11]

The rise in the rate of inflation was greater in Ireland than in most other countries, though not substantially greater than in the U K, where the rate of increase in consumer prices rose from 3.6 per cent from 1961 to 1968 to 7.1 per cent from 1968 to 1972, as against the rise in the Irish case from 4.0 per cent to 8.3 per cent. Typically, however, the increase in other countries between these two periods was smaller. To give some examples: in the U S A the rate rose from 2.2 per cent to 4.7 per cent, in Canada from 2.7 per cent to 3.9 per cent, in France from 3.7 per cent to 5.4 per cent, in Germany from 2.6 per cent to 4.3 per cent, in the Netherlands from 4.2 per cent to 6.8 per cent, and in Japan from 5.6 per cent to 5.9 per cent. The relatively faster rate of increase in consumer prices in Ireland would tend to dis-improve the competitive position of tourism, a factor which we consider in discussing the decline in that industry.

Moreover, the much faster rate of increase in money incomes would appear to have made for a substantial deterioration in the price competitiveness of manufacturing industry. The vastly greater rise in money incomes compared with 1961–68, which was accompanied by some decline in the rate of growth of manu-facturing productivity, resulted in an average annual growth rate of unit wage cost in manufacturing of 11.0 per cent from 1968 to 1972, compared with 3.9 per cent from 1961 to 1968. In the U K, Ireland's main trading partner, unit wage cost rose by 8.8 per cent per annum from 1968 to 1972.[12] In other countries, such as the U S A, Germany and France, unit wage cost rose still less. Exchange rate changes, on balance, helped to mitigate the deterioration in our position relative to these countries. Neverthe-less, it is significant to note that the export price of Irish manufac-tured exports rose by 6 per cent per annum, well above the rise of only 3 per cent in the U K import price of manufactures, and also well above the rate of increase in the export prices (converted to sterling) of most other contries with which Ireland competes. We examine next whether the deterioration in manufacturing wage costs and prices affected the growth of manufactured exports and competing imports.

COMPETITIVENESS, EXPORTS AND COMPETING IMPORTS

Domestic exports in current values rose by 16.7 per cent per annum on average from 1968 to 1972. This was a much faster rate of growth than from 1961 to 1968, but allowing for the much greater rise in export prices, the volume rate of increase was of the same order of magnitude. The most remarkable feature of the rise in exports was the sustained rapid rate of growth in manufactured exports. In value terms, manufactured exports rose by 23 per cent per annum as against 19½ per cent from 1961 to 1968, but the rate of increase in price was greater (6.0 per cent per annum from 1968 to 1972 compared with 3.6 per cent from 1961 to 1968), so that the volume rates of increase were similar in both periods. In 1972 manufactured exports accounted for 41 per cent of domestic exports as against 33 per cent in 1968; they were substantially greater than exports of livestock and meat and even approached total food exports in importance.

The value of food exports, however, also rose strongly—by 13.7 per cent per annum, while cattle and beef exports, the largest component, rose by 12.0 per cent. The rise in cattle and beef exports, however, was entirely attributable to price increases. Only in 1971 was the volume above the 1968 level, and for the four years 1969 to 1972 the volume was 1,123,000 per annum on average, compared with 1,194,000 for the five years 1964–68. In 1972 the volume was 6 per cent below the 1968 level, while prices were up 67.6 per cent. This represented an annual average rate of increase in price of 13.8 per cent per annum, far above anything previously experienced by Irish farmers. While the price rose in every year, by far the largest increase was the rise of nearly 30 per cent in 1972, which was the major reason for the very large external trading gain in that year. Although export volume did not rise, output volume expanded in every year. On average for the four years 1969 to 1972, output was 12 per cent above the 1964–68 average, and in 1972 the volume was 21 per cent above the 1968 level. Differences in the movements of output and exports are due mainly to stockbuilding. Additions to stock for the four years 1969 to 1972 amounted, on average, to 206,000 per annum, representing a sustained rise in stocks greater than in any previous post-war period. The substantial addition to stocks was due to the high prices of milk and calves and the belief that E E C entry assured relatively high and stable prices of beef and dairy products for the future. Farmers therefore considered it worthwhile to invest in increased productive capacity for the future rather than, as often in the past, run down stocks while beef prices were high.

K

Manufactured Exports

In view of what we saw earlier of the behaviour of Irish prices and wage costs relative to those abroad, the sustained high growth of manufactured exports seems remarkable, especially as the growth of manufactured imports in two of the main markets, the U K and the U S A, was far less than from 1963 to 1968.

U K manufactured imports rose by 62 per cent from 1968 to 1972, but Irish manufactured exports to the U K rose by 107 per cent. Thus the Irish share of U K imports rose substantially, from 1.82 per cent to 2.34 per cent. In Chapter 6 we broke down the rise in Irish manufactured exports to the U K for various periods into three components: the changes due to (*a*) the growth of total U K imports, (*b*) changes in competitiveness broadly defined; and (*c*) changes in the commodity composition of U K imports. A similar exercise has been done for the period 1968–72. This shows that, of the total rise of £74 million in Irish exports to the U K, £42.5 million can be attributed to the overall growth of the U K market. Changes in the commodity composition of U K imports were, on balance, favourable to Irish exports and accounted for a net rise of £11.5 million. This still leaves a substantial increase of £20.1 million due to competitiveness, representing 27 per cent of the total rise in exports and much the same proportion as in the preceding period analysed in Chapter 6 (1963–68).

Irish manufactured exports to the two next most important market groups, North America and the E E C, rose substantially faster than to the U K and, what is more relevant here, they rose faster than total manufactured imports in these areas. A share analysis to distinguish composition and competitive effects in these areas would not be likely to be meaningful because of the small share of Irish exports in their total imports. The probability is, however, that competitiveness would account for part of the rise in exports to these areas. A similar statement holds good in relation to the balance of Irish manufactured exports to all other areas, taken together, which only accounted for about one-tenth of the total.

How can these results be reconciled with the evidence on relative wage costs and prices? We have discussed this issue thoroughly in Chapter 6, and it is necessary to add only a few points here of relevance to the period 1968–72. The Anglo-Irish Free Trade Area Agreement (A I F T A A) became operative in July 1966, involving the removal of the remaining tariffs on Irish exports to the U K. This improved Ireland's competitive position in the U K market for certain goods, but the full effect of this might not be felt immediately since they might take some time to be realised. This effect might have been operative in a significant way from 1968 to 1972. However, the A I F T A A benefit applied only to a limited range of manufactured exports, chiefly clothing and textiles. Examination of the figures shows that, of the relevant categories, only in S I T C item 65 (textile yarn, fabrics, etc.) was there a competitive gain. In that case the gain was substantial, amounting to £8½ million. However, given that the total competitive gain in the U K was much larger, and that there were probably significant gains in markets other than the U K, it does not seem that A I F T A A alone can explain the apparent contradiction.

It is possible that A I F T A A may have encouraged exports in another respect suggested by McAleese (1971), who argued that Irish import tariffs created a bias against exports by increasing the rate of return on home sales relative to exports. He calculated a 'bias against exports' coefficient showing the percentage by which tariffs (or export subsidies) raised (lowered) the rate of return per unit of value added on production for the home market relative to production for export in the mid-1960s. For the twenty-eight industries considered, he found a positive bias in all but three, ranging to as high as 142 per cent and with a median value of over 60 per cent. Thus, as Irish tariffs were progressively lowered under A I F T A A, the relative rate of return from exports would tend to rise, and this may have encouraged export growth. However, it should be noted that while this factor would make exporting relatively more attractive, it would not make it any easier since it would not raise the absolute rate of return.

Another possibility is that the deterioration in wage costs and prices might be reflected, not in a fall in exports, but in the domestic value added content of exports. As mentioned earlier, the import content of manufactured exports rose from 1964 to 1968. However, there are no figures after 1968 to show whether this trend continued or accelerated and, if so, whether this was due to price competitiveness or other influences such as changes in the composition of exports.

Even taking account of these factors, however, it seems likely that the sustained rapid rise in manufactured exports was due to the industrial incentive schemes and the efforts of the Industrial Development Authority in attracting new export industries—what we described in Chapter 6 as the exploitation of the competitive potential. No doubt, a boost was given to these efforts by the prospect of entry into the E E C, with eventual free access to the markets of all the other eight members.

Competing Manufactured Imports

A deterioration in price competitiveness could also show up in increased imports at the expense of home production for the domestic market. Indeed, one might expect that the effect would be greater here following McAleese (1971) who stresses the duality of Irish manufacturing. His thesis is that on the one hand there is a strong export sector made up mainly of new firms, many with foreign enterprise and techniques, and, on the other hand, a weak import-competing sector of older firms established behind tariff barriers.

The Department of Finance's annual review of the economy gives data for total manufacturing and some broad sub-divisions in respect of gross output, exports, competing imports and domestic use (i.e. output plus competing imports less exports) covering all years since 1960.[13] The figures show that while competing imports as a proportion of domestic use were relatively constant from 1960 up to 1967 at about 22 per cent, the ratio began to rise sharply thereafter reaching 31.6 per cent in 1972. This would suggest that competing imports began to rapidly increase their share of the Irish home market at the same time that inflation began to accelerate.

To examine this matter further we have divided the rise in competing imports into three components, analogous to the analysis of exports. These are (*a*) the change due to the growth of total domestic use, (*b*) the change due to changes in competitiveness in the widest sense (and measured by the change in the import share of domestic use in each of the manufactured groups considered), and (*c*) the change due to changes in the composition of domestic use.[14] Since the rise in the import share of domestic use began after 1967, we decided to compare the two five-year periods 1962–67 and 1967–72. The figures are given in Table 49.

Before commenting on the figures, it is necessary to draw attention to the fact that some competing manufactured imports

Table 49: Sources of growth in competitive manufactured imports, 1962–67 and 1967–72

	1962–67		1967–72	
	(i) Domestic Use	(ii) Final Use	(i) Domestic Use	(ii) Final Use
Changes in imports due to:	£ million current values			
Growth of total	28.0	33.9	72.9	88.3
Changes in competitiveness	5.8	0.2	73.3	58.3
Changes in composition	—0.1	—0.3	—1.0	—1.5
Total change	33.7	33.7	145.2	145.2

Source: The calculations are based on figures in Department of Finance, *Review of 1972 and Outlook for 1973*, Appendix 2, Table (i) (pp. 101–4), using the eight manufacturing groups that correspond roughly to S I T C items 5–8. The method used has been described in Chapter 6, except that there we related Irish exports to U K imports, whereas here we are relating imports into Ireland to Irish domestic and final use.

are, in fact, intermediate goods that go into the production of domestic manufactured output, whether produced for export or the home market. In such circumstances, the fact that exports were rising much faster than domestic use in Ireland would involve a rise in the ratio of competing imports to domestic use even if there were no change in competitiveness. In other words, if the ratio of imports to domestic use and exports combined were unchanged, the ratio to domestic use alone would rise because of the faster growth of exports. In fact, while the ratio of competing imports to domestic use rose from 22.0 per cent in 1967 to 31.6 per cent in 1972, the ratio to final use (domestic use plus exports) rose rather less, from 18.3 per cent to 24.1 per cent. In Table 49, therefore, we also distinguish the components of the import rise in relation to final use as well as domestic use. Of course, once it is admitted that some competing imports are subject to further processing in the manufactured sector, there is a double counting problem in adding output and imports to arrive at domestic and final use. However, the problem is not so severe as to prevent us getting a broad picture of the components of the rise in imports. Since non-competing imports are excluded, much of the problem is avoided because the greater part of the intermediate imports used for further production in manufacturing would fall into the non-competing category.

It may be seen from Table 49 that whether imports are related to domestic use or final use, the period 1967–72 witnessed a large rise in imports—of the order of £60–70 million—due to changes in competitiveness. From 1962 to 1967 the change in imports due to changes in competitiveness was only a small proportion of the total change in manufactured imports, whereas from 1967 to 1972 it represented 40–50 per cent of the much larger overall rise.

Part of the large gain in the competitiveness of imports may be explained by factors other than relative rates of inflation. The rise in the ratio of imports to domestic use beginning in 1968 may have been partly due to the devaluation of 1967. Competing imports and similar products produced at home may not be perfect substitutes. If substitutes could not be found readily on the home market, and the import price rose by nearly the full amount of the devaluation—as is likely for a small country like Ireland—then the ratio of imports to domestic use would tend to rise. Since the UK devalued at the same time, devaluation also might induce a switch, not to higher-cost domestic products, but to higher-cost products in the UK.

Another important influence was the progressive lowering of import protection under the A I F T A A. McAleese and Martin (1973) have estimated the rise in UK imports up to 1969–70 (compared with 1964–65) due to A I F T A A at £17 million, of which £5 million was at the expense of exports from other countries and £12 million at the expense of home production. As tariffs continued to fall in 1971 and 1972, the loss to imports due to this factor might be expected to rise further.

There remains, however, a large rise in competing manufactured imports that can probably be attributed mainly to the deterioration in relative costs and prices outlined earlier. Thus, even if the rate of inflation of costs and prices in Ireland did not seriously affect the growth of manufactured exports, it had a major adverse impact on manufacturing production for the home market.

TOURISM

One of the most serious adverse features of the years 1969 to 1972 was the decline in tourism. Some commentators have suggested that the decline preceded the Northern Ireland troubles beginning in 1969. There was indeed a decline in tourism in 1966, recovery from which was not complete until 1968. However, that reverse would appear to have been a temporary set-back rather than indicative of a secular decline. In 1966 the British dock strike severely affected car tourists, while the outbreak of foot-and-mouth disease in Britain restricted tourist movement towards the end of 1967. Moreover, if tourist receipts from the U K are viewed in terms of their share of U K total tourist spending, it emerges that the decline in share was confined to 1966, recovery was complete in 1967, and there was a significant rise in share in 1968 (see Table 33). In the case of U S A tourism, the share rose steadily from 1965 to 1968 (see Table 34).

After 1968, however, there was a substantial fall in tourist receipts from the U K, measured either in absolute terms or as a share of U K total tourist spending. In current money values, Irish receipts from U K tourists declined in every year from £60.3 million in 1968 to £46.9 million in 1972, implying a far greater decline in real terms. Since U K tourist spending abroad grew significantly in this period, the Irish share fell substantially from 16.3 per cent in 1968 to 7.5 per cent in 1972. If Ireland had maintained its 1968 share of U K tourist spending, receipts in 1972 would have been £104 million, compared with the actual figure of £47 million.

It is impossible to account for so great a decline other than in terms of the Northern Ireland conflict. Admittedly, the relatively more rapid rate of inflation in Ireland than in other European markets for British tourists probably played some part, but with any reasonable price elasticity, relative price changes would account for no more than a fraction of the total loss of tourist revenue. Some indication of the impact of price alone may be given as follows. The consumer price index is the price used in the Irish national accounts to estimate the volume of tourist receipts. While not altogether appropriate, it provides a rough approximation to the price rise facing U K tourists in Ireland, since exchange rates are stable between the two countries. This price rose on average by 8.3 per cent per annum from 1968 to 1972. In the British national accounts, U K total spending abroad is deflated by an appropriately weighted index (adjusted for exchange rate changes) of goods and services likely to be bought by British tourists in the different countries visited. From 1968 to 1972 this price rose by 6.5 per cent per annum. Had the Irish share of U K total spending remained at the 1968 level, the value of Irish tourist receipts from the U K in 1972 would have been £104 million, The relative price deterioration alone would, if we assume an elasticity of 3, reduce this figure only to £91 million. But, in fact, the actual figure for 1972 was a mere £47 million. Thus only a comparatively small part of the decline in the Irish share of U K tourist spending can reasonably be attributed to the rise in the Irish relative price level.[15] Of course, if the price elasticity were, in fact, greater than we have assumed, the reduction attributable to the relative price deterioration would be greater, but the assumed elasticity of 3 is a comparatively high figure in the light of studies for other countries.

In the case of tourist receipts from the U S A, while there was some rise in revenue in current values, the Irish share of total U S A tourist expenditure in Europe declined, and there was an even greater decline in the share in numbers of visitors. The size of decline in U S A tourism could possibly be explained by the deterioration in price competitiveness, but there can be little doubt that tourism from the U S A was also adversely affected by the Northern Ireland situation.

The decline in tourism seriously affected the overall growth rate. Total tourist receipts in current values fell from £75.7 million in 1968 to £70.4 million in 1972, representing a fall in constant (1968) prices to £51.2 million, or a decline of 9.3 per cent per annum on average. This compares with a rise of 3.9 per cent per annum from 1961 to 1968. If the latter rate had continued from 1968 to 1972,[16] then tourist receipts in 1972 would have been £88.3 million at 1968 prices. Allowing for a direct and indirect import content of 25 per cent, this would have raised the average annual growth rate of G N P to 4.2 per cent compared with an actual 3.7 per cent. If, further, we take into account multiplier effects resulting from increased tourist demand, then it is not too much to say that, had the experience of the tourist industry been similar to that from 1961 to 1968, the growth rate of G N P would, *ceteris paribus*, probably have been at least 4½ per cent.

DEMAND MANAGEMENT

The two years 1968 and 1969 witnessed highly expansionary fiscal policies. In volume terms, the Public Capital Programme rose by 23.3 per cent in 1968 and by 15.0 per cent in 1969. Taking the two years together, the overall borrowing requirement rose by over 50 per cent (from £61 million in 1967 to £93 million in 1969). Fiscal policy, therefore, contributed to the record growth rates of total home demand in these years. Even had fiscal policy been non-expansionary, however, it is likely that demand would still have expanded rapidly in these years, particularly in 1968. In the initial recovery in 1967 from the 1966 depression, stock levels had not been restored, so that there was very substantial re-stocking in both 1968 and 1969. As the recovery proceeded, it also put pressure on fixed capital, so that substantial increases in fixed investment were likely even apart from the stimulus of public investment. The very large growth in volume of consumer expenditure in 1968 (8.4 per cent) represented, in part at least, the type of bunching of consumer purchasing suggested in Chapter 14. The rise came after three years of moderate increase in volume of consumer expenditure, following the previous consumer boom of 1964. The rise was only 0.9 per cent in 1965, 1.8 per cent in 1966 and 3.8 per cent in 1967. With recovery proceeding at a rapid rate and credit freely available, it is not too surprising, on past experience, that there was a consumer boom in 1968.[17] This was associated particularly with durable goods purchases, the most notable increase being the volume rise of one-third in purchases of transport equipment, following three years in which purchases were below the 1964 level.

It might therefore reasonably be argued that a much more moderate fiscal policy would have been appropriate, especially in 1968 when there were so many other autonomous or semi-autonomous factors stimulating demand. In 1969 some of these factors had ceased to operate. The maintenance men's strike early in 1969 involved an estimated loss of one-third of normal industrial production for a period of one month, equivalent to a loss of nearly 3 per cent for the whole year.[18] Although some of this was made good in subsequent quarters, nevertheless the loss of output and incomes was substantial. The consumer boom seems to have been exhausted by the middle of 1969, and for more than a year afterwards the seasonally corrected quarterly volume of retail sales was close to or below the level of the second quarter of 1969. New car registrations levelled off and declined. The growth rate of manufactured exports was relatively low in volume terms due to demand conditions abroad, while the drop in tourism affected demand significantly. Thus the high growth rate of total home and final demand for 1969 as a whole was partly due to the carry-over effect of rising demand in the course of 1968, as well as the lagged response of investment to increased output and the expansionary fiscal policy. The expansionary policy in that year can be more readily justified than in 1968, but it would have been much easier to provide strong fiscal stimuli in 1969—and, more important, in the following years—had greater moderation been exercised in 1968.

The high rate of growth of demand may, as suggested earlier, have contributed to the acceleration in wage inflation. It undoubtedly contributed to the exceptionally large rise in the volume of total imports (15.5 per cent in 1968 and 13.5 per cent in 1969) and the deterioration in the current account of the balance of payments. In 1968 there was a swing of £31.5 million from a surplus of £15.2 million in 1967 to a deficit of £16.3 million in 1968, and a further rise of £52.8 million in 1969 to a deficit of £69.1 million.[19] Thus budgetary policy in 1970 had to be decided in the unenviable conditions of depressed demand and slow growth, high current balance of payments deficit and rapidly rising prices and wage demands. On a quarterly basis, output in transportable goods industry had not risen since the second quarter of 1969, while a strike in the cement industry was seriously affecting output in building and related industries. A fiscal stimulus to demand need not have been ruled out on balance of payments grounds since, despite the large deficit in 1969, the reserves were maintained by large capital inflows. However, in the light of the wage situation, the authorities no doubt wished to avoid adding further fuel to inflation.

In the event, the 1970 budget provided for a much smaller rate of increase in the Public Capital Programme than in the previous two years—from £173.4 million to £194.5 million—representing a rise of 12 per cent in current values and a much lower rate of increase in real terms. In fact, as a result of the effects of the cement dispute on public building and deliberate budgetary policy, as outlined in the supplementary budget of October 1970, the actual rise was only to £189.7 million, or 9.4 per cent in value terms. Had there been more prompt and effective action by the authorities on the incomes front, as was later secured in the National Pay Agreement, a more expansionary budgetary policy would have been possible and justified in the light of demand conditions. Given the desirability of securing wage restraint, it is all the more difficult to understand the reasons for the large increases in indirect taxation in 1970, which directly raised prices and added further to wage pressures. The turnover tax rate was raised from $2\frac{1}{2}$ per cent to 5 per cent in the budget while the wholesale tax on certain items was raised from 15 per cent to 20 per cent in the supplementary budget. For the year as a whole, the outturn of the current budget balance, on a national accounts basis, was a surplus of the same order as in 1968 and 1969. These were years of much higher pressure of demand, which would lead us to expect, if current budget policy were the same, a big reduction in the current budget balance. The overall borrowing requirement of public authorities rose from £92.8 million to £109.3 million, but when allowance is made in both years for redemption of securities, which were exceptionally large in 1970, the rise was only from £77.1 million to £81.3 million.

Since a National Pay Agreement was concluded in December 1970 covering a period of eighteen months, it was unlikely that an expansionary fiscal policy in 1971 would add to wage inflation. On the other hand, it might well make for a lowering of unit costs in so far as it helped to raise output and productivity. Certainly, demand conditions argued strongly for an expansionary budget in 1971. The unemployment rate rose significantly above the 1969 level in 1970, from 6.4 per cent to 7.3 per cent. Although manufacturing output rose substantially in the third quarter of 1970, this was due largely to the conclusion of the cement strike, and there was no further advance in the next four quarters. We explained earlier in this study the importance of building and construction in maintaining demand. In 1970 the volume of fixed investment in building declined slightly. The 1970 bank dispute, unlike that of 1966, probably had a restrictive effect as businessmen were cautious in issuing credit by accepting cheques.[20] The volume of retail sales in the first quarter of 1971, though it had recovered from the depressed level of the second quarter of 1970, was only 3 per cent above the level of the second quarter of 1969. Tourism was depressed and likely to continue so in 1971. Admittedly, the balance of payments situation placed a constraint on expansionary policies. The deficit in 1970 fell slightly to £65 million, but when account is taken of the timing of aircraft purchases, the deficit was, in effect, slightly greater than in 1969. However, given the depressed demand conditions and the wage settlement arrived at, this was scarcely a sufficient reason for failing to stimulate renewed expansion, especially as the external reserves were maintained by capital inflows.

In fact, the budget of 1971 continued the restrictive fiscal policy. The planned size of the Public Capital Programme was £193.4 million as against an outturn of £189.7 million for the previous year. Even allowing for the timing of purchases of ships and aircraft, the planned increase was only $6\frac{1}{2}$ per cent, implying no change (or even a slight fall) in volume. Total public expenditure was planned to rise by only $9\frac{1}{2}$ per cent in current values, again implying little or no volume increase. The restrictive budgetary policy was somewhat reversed later in the year in a supplementary budget introduced in October 1971. The original provision for public capital expenditure was raised by £20 million. In addition, company taxation was reduced and restrictions on hire-purchase were removed. However, even given these relaxations, the outturn of the current budget balance was a slight increase in the surplus to £35.0 million compared with £31.1 million in 1971. The overall borrowing requirement rose from £81.3 million to £97.7 million (excluding redemption of securities). This indicates that, had public capital spending remained as in the original 1971 budget, the borrowing requirement would have fallen. The volume increase in the Public Capital Programme was only 3 per cent, and in the building and construction component there was a decline of 1 per cent following a decline of 3 per cent in the previous year.

The expansionary policy initiated in the supplementary budget of 1971 was strengthened in the 1972 budget. The Public Capital Programme was planned at £251.3 million, compared with an outturn of £213.9 million in the previous year. For the first time ever, the authorities budgeted for a deficit on the current budget.

On the traditional accounting basis, a deficit of £27.8 million was envisaged, compared with an actual deficit of £2.2 million in the previous year. In the outturn for the year 1972–73, however, the deficit was only £5.5 million, partly due to the pick-up in activity and partly due to overestimation of the size of the deficit. However, on the national accounts classification, the current surplus of public authorities fell from £35 million to £19 million, while the overall borrowing requirement rose substantially. The actual rise in the Public Capital Programme was 6½ per cent in volume terms, which was mainly made up of a substantial volume rise of 16 per cent in the building component, the first rise of any consequence in this component since 1968. Demand and production in the economy were somewhat slow to rise, the pick-up during most of 1972 being moderate. Substantial recovery became evident only in the fourth quarter of 1972 and continued into 1973.

In the main body of this study we stressed the role of public investment in maintaining demand, output and employment, laying particular emphasis on 'social' investment (i.e. the building of houses, schools, hospitals, etc.). It is interesting, then, to compare the position in this regard from 1968 to 1972 with the period 1961–68. The volume growth of the Public Capital Programme fell from 10.1 per cent per annum in the earlier period to 6.6 per cent per annum. Excluding the social element, the growth rate was similar in both periods—8.9 per cent from 1961 to 1968 and 8.3 per cent from 1968 to 1972. Practically all of the fall was therefore due to the slow growth of the social component which rose, in volume terms, by only 3.0 per cent per annum—all of the rise occurring in 1972—compared with an annual average rise from 1961 to 1968 of 12.8 per cent. Admittedly, the 1961 level was low because of the cut-back enforced earlier from 1956 to 1958. Nevertheless, the very substantial reduction in the growth of public social investment must be seen as a significant factor in explaining the decline in the growth of output and employment from mid-1969 to mid-1972.

CONCLUSIONS

We have discussed the reasons why the rate of progress achieved in the 1960s up to 1968 was not fully maintained in the following years despite the much more favourable conditions for agriculture.

The major factors were the decline in tourism, the loss to competing imports of manufacturing sales on the home market, and the disruptive effects of major strikes. It might have been difficult to compensate adequately for these factors by demand management policies, but more appropriate fiscal policies would have been easier to implement had fiscal policy not been excessively expansionary in 1968, and perhaps to a lesser extent in 1969. Even so, more determined efforts to get to grips with the wage situation in 1969 and 1970 through incomes policy would have placed the authorities in a stronger position to respond to the weak demand conditions existing from the middle of 1969. Moreover, following the conclusion of the National Pay Agreement at the end of 1970, the authorities delayed too long in stimulating renewed expansion. The absence of any increase in volume of public social investment in the three years 1969, 1970 and 1971 tended to depress activity. The substantial increases in indirect taxation also tended to aggravate the inflationary situation.

Economic experience in this period bears out many of the earlier conclusions. In particular, it confirms the importance of building and construction and tourism in maintaining adequate growth of demand, output and employment. Although a rapid growth of volume of merchandise exports, and manufactured exports in particular, was achieved, this on its own did not suffice.

The major new influence in the period was the greatly accelerated rate of inflation and the associated large increase in industrial strife. Our examination of the causes of the rise in the rate of price increase suggests that the primary stimulus was the rise in import prices and in export prices of cattle. This is not to say that the economy was necessarily completely helpless in controlling inflation as a result of these external factors. But what we are saying is that, given much the same sort of responses on the part of trade unions as formerly, the rate of inflation was bound to accelerate. In other words, keeping the rate of inflation at its previous level would have required far greater moderation in wage demands than formerly, whereas, not surprisingly, the level of wage demands rose in response to the effects of higher trade prices.

In the light of this analysis, can we say whether the reduced rate of progress represents a permanent set-back in Ireland's growth prospects? Our analysis suggests that some of the important factors restraining growth arose from external forces, largely beyond domestic control. This does not mean that they are necessarily temporary, but neither, however, does it mean that the economy does not have the capacity to respond to external factors and counter, to some extent, their adverse effects. In regard to tourism, the decline in which we attributed mainly to the Northern Ireland conflict, recovery depends to a large extent on securing a political settlement that will end the violence. Domestic political repercussions of the Northern crisis also appear to have adversely affected the capacity to manage the economy effectively in 1970 and subsequently, in a way which is unlikely to recur. No significant abatement of the rate of inflation seems likely if prices abroad continue to rise rapidly. However, the National Pay Agreements have so far been effective in countering the loss of output occasioned by major industrial disputes. E E C entry holds out the prospect of considerable long-term gains for agriculture and perhaps also for manufactured exports, and the possibility of receiving investment resources from the Regional Fund. Hence, barring some major set-back in the international environment, as could now be threatened by reaction to the oil situation, the early years of the 1970s may come to be regarded as a temporary, though rather prolonged, reduction in the rate of progress achieved during the 1960s.

In the next and final chapter we discuss in greater detail some of the major problems and opportunities affecting future growth prospects.

CHAPTER 18

Problems and Prospects for the Future

I N this chapter we look to the future and discuss what seem to us to be the important factors influencing future growth prospects. We do not claim any special qualification as seers, nor have we developed an explicit forecasting model. Rather, we wish to highlight major policy issues on which fresh thinking may be required.

EMPLOYMENT AND GROWTH

There would probably be general agreement that the major economic and social problem facing Ireland over the next decade, as in the five decades since independence, is the provision of full employment. In 1972 the unemployment rate was 8 per cent, and in the post-war period it never fell below 5½ per cent in any year, while much higher rates were experienced in pre-war years. Moreover, given the employment situation in the post-war period, unemployment rates would have been even higher except for substantial emigration.

We showed in Chapter 1 that the rise in the growth rate of G N P between the periods 1949–61 and 1961–68, from 1.9 per cent to 4.1 per cent, was accompanied by nearly as large a turn-around in employment, from a fall of 1.3 per cent per annum to a rise of 0.2 per cent per annum. Likewise, the fall in the output growth rate to 3.7 per cent from 1968 to 1972 was accompanied by almost a similar swing in employment to a decline of 0.4 per cent per annum. These results show that employment growth is clearly related to output growth, and we may reasonably presume that the former is the dependent variable. The implication is that one way of raising the growth rate of employment and reducing unemployment is to raise the G N P growth rate. Put crudely, past experience shows that a *sustained* rise in the growth rate of G N P to 6 per cent could be expected to raise the employment growth rate to 1½–2 per cent. All of this may appear very obvious, but it conflicts with many statements that Irish unemployment represents essentially a structural problem on the supply side that can only be solved by measures such as education, retraining, relocation of workers, etc. Our view is that, while such structural problems are important, their overall significance can be exaggerated, and that maintenance of buoyant labour demand is of crucial importance in reducing unemployment to more acceptable levels.[1] It would not necessarily be sensible, however, to raise the general level of demand without regard also to its composition. Because unemployment rates differ considerably by sector, occupation and area, consideration might be given in the short term to selective measures (e.g. through the Public Capital Programme) to raise the demand for labour relatively more in what Geary and Hughes (1970) have described as the 'depressed occupations'.[2]

Walsh (1975) has estimated the growth of employment required to achieve full employment by 1986, based on population projections and assumptions about the changes in participation rates in the period 1971–86. Full employment is taken to be consistent with 4 per cent of the labour force unemployed, and only a low level of net emigration. His results show that the achievement of full employment would require an average annual growth rate in total employment of 1¼ per cent over the period 1971–86.

To raise the employment growth rate to such a level would require sustaining a much higher growth rate of G N P or altering the character of growth substantially towards more employment creation. While the latter should certainly be considered, it is likely that the possibilities are limited, given the openness of the Irish economy. In addition, the decision to join the E E C rules out some policy options (e.g. selective tariff protection) that might otherwise be considered. The implication of securing faster employment growth with the same growth rate of G N P would be a lower rate of growth of national productivity. The implied reduction in the growth rate of real income per person employed is unlikely to be acceptable to the Irish people, given that earnings are already much lower than in the other E E C countries.

Thus, even if some measures can be adopted to encourage a greater employment-giving bias in economic growth, these are unlikely to be sufficient, and a higher rate of economic growth would also be necessary to meet the goal of full employment over the next decade or so. In turn, this would require a high rate of growth of demand. Our earlier analysis suggests that stimulation of home demand, as well as rapid export growth, would be necessary for this purpose. This raises questions about industrial strategy, the outlook for exports, the growth of public expenditure and the resources needed to finance such a faster growth of demand and output.

INDUSTRIAL STRATEGY

On past experience, industry is the sector likely to be the spearhead of any drive to raise employment. Despite the better long-term outlook for agricultural output and incomes as a result of EEC entry, it is probable that the numbers engaged in agriculture will continue to decline. Indeed, since EEC agricultural policy will tend to encourage less labour-intensive production in Ireland (i.e. livestock rather than tillage) and may seek to rationalise production into larger holdings, the percentage rate of decline might even increase, though the absolute decline in numbers must ultimately fall. Assuming that the decline in numbers engaged in agriculture continues at much the same percentage rate as in the past, then the overall employment growth rate required to achieve full employment by 1986 ($1\frac{1}{4}$ per cent per annum) would imply an average annual growth rate of about $2\frac{1}{4}$ per cent in non-agricultural employment. The services sector is capable of contributing significantly to employment growth, but such growth will depend a good deal on industrial growth. Moreover, within the services sector there are substantial numbers engaged in low productivity occupations, as in the retail trade, which are likely to decline.

Can the present industrial development strategy be improved to secure a faster growth of employment and output? There are a number of features of present policy that require reconsideration. Much of the growth of manufacturing experienced in the past decade has come from foreign enterprise attracted notably by capital grants and tax concessions. The evidence available suggests that these industries have a low domestic value added content, import most of their raw materials and have few backward or forward linkages with domestic industries. This implies that the direct and indirect contribution of each new enterprise to employment has been relatively small. Furthermore, given also that the profits can ultimately be repatriated, their contribution to the balance of payments is relatively limited. It might be argued that these criticisms suggest merely the need for many more such enterprises to raise employment adequately. However, the absence of linkages with the rest of the economy may retard development in various ways. It implies a failure to build on the country's natural advantages in activities like food processing and mineral processing, which would secure a greater regional diffusion of the benefits of industrial development. Greater linkages would help to develop a larger pool of native entrepreneurs. These would be far more likely to expand and diversify their activities in Ireland rather than in some other part of the world, as in the case of the multi-national enterprises. The low level of technology required for assembly and processing operations means that relatively few resources are devoted within Ireland to research and development, which may have undesirable implications for future growth prospects.[3]

It is also questionable whether the industrial incentives are not excessively directed towards export enterprises relative to import-competing firms. The latter contribute substantially to the balance of payments and employment. However, they do not receive the industrial grants and their profits are subject to the relatively high rates of company tax prevailing in Ireland. It was understandable that initially the incentives should be directed primarily towards exports, at a time when there was little tradition or experience of exporting, and when tariffs abroad were a serious impediment. The latter problem has now been substantially removed as a result of A I F T A A and entry into the E E C, while the range of services by Coras Tráchtála provides much more information about possible export opportunities. On the other hand, import-competing firms are under increasing pressure from imports, facilitated by the reciprocation of the tariff cuts that favour exports.

There is also a case for examining whether the existing range of incentives do not discriminate against labour-intensive enterprises. The scheme of grants would appear to have a bias towards capital-intensive production, a tendency that may be increased by generous depreciation allowances and tax relief on export profits.

Moreover, in the administration of grants, although the Industrial Development Authority undoubtedly consider the *projected* employment figures, there is no assurance that these projections will be met. There is no incentive for an enterprise to meet or exceed the employment targets once the plant is established and the grant received. There is, in fact, evidence that new grant-aided firms are more effective in achieving their output and export projections than their employment projection.[4] Labour subsidies would encourage labour-intensive enterprises and methods of production. This is a complex area in which we wish only to emphasise the urgent need for re-examination and for the initiation of research to throw light on these questions.

Responsibility for industrial development in the public sector need not be limited to the efforts of the Industrial Development Authority. Encouragement might also be given to the state-sponsored bodies to initiate industrial development by diversifying their activities. Some of the state-sponsored bodies are already doing so, but many appear to view their role solely in relation to the particular function for which they were established. This may lead to considerable curtailment of potential enterprise. The state-sponsored bodies are large-scale employers of engineers, accountants and other professional workers, who in private enterprise would be encouraged to seek out new opportunities for expansion and diversification.[5]

Continued heavy reliance on foreign enterprise for industrial development may also have adverse repercussions that could prejudice economic growth. It is not an expression of crude nationalism to assert that severe social tensions could be aroused by a situation where the bulk of the industrial work force was employed by foreign-owned companies whose production and employment decisions were based on the requirements of their parent companies. It is not clear that sufficient efforts have been made to secure the benefits of foreign technology for development, through licensing arrangements, etc., without the potentially undesirable consequences of foreign ownership and enterprise— a strategy pursued with such success in initiating Japanese industrial development.[6]

EEC ENTRY

Ireland's entry into the European Economic Community, which took effect on 1 January 1973, is the single most important change in the economic environment in the post-war period. Under the terms of entry, trade restrictions affecting industrial products will be abolished gradually over a five-year period, and the adjustment of farm prices covered by the Common Agricultural Policy will likewise take place over five years. EEC entry also involved acceptance of a body of regulations and legislation concerning such matters as the free movement of labour, standardisation of products, financing Community institutions, etc. The Irish Treaty of Accession included a special protocol recognising the under-developed nature of the Irish economy and the need for EEC resources to reduce the disparity in living standards *vis-à-vis* the rest of the Community. Under the treaty, the industrial incentives granted by the Irish government can be continued within the Community for the time being; and although the EEC Commission may later require replacement of some of the incentives by other measures, it has been accepted that any revised incentives should be such as to be equally effective in promoting industrial development.

The most significant benefit to the economy from EEC entry will be from the operation of the Common Agricultural Policy (CAP). McAleese (1975) has estimated that had Ireland been a full participant in CAP in 1972, this would have added £26 million in exports of cattle and beef, even at the very high world price levels then prevailing, and nearly £20 million in exports of dairy products. More important is the fact that in times of excess world supply, the CAP is designed to put a floor on the downward movement in beef and milk prices. Producers of finished cattle and of milk are likely to continue to secure far higher and more stable prices than in the absence of the CAP. Thus there is likely to be a substantial longer-term rise in agricultural output and exports.[7] However, since the intervention system for beef provides only a floor for prices of finished cattle, there may still be large fluctuations in prices of store cattle and calves, involving major shifts in the distribution of income among Irish farmers. It is also possible that the CAP will be modified, particularly under pressure from the U K, in a manner unfavourable to Ireland. However, in any such modification Ireland will have a more effective say than in the past.

It is not at all obvious, however, that membership of E E C will reduce the decline in numbers engaged in agriculture. Indeed, for the reasons already suggested, the rate of decline could increase. Moreover, the realisation of the gains through increased output is likely to require substantially increased agricultural investment. This may initially exceed increases in agricultural savings and thus add to the pressures of financing total investment. The increased agricultural prices are also likely to be inflationary, both in directly raising the consumer price index and in influencing wage claims and wage settlements in the rest of the economy.

With regard to manufactured exports, the removal of the common external tariff against Irish goods will lead to increased exports to the original six members of the E E C. On the other hand, Ireland will lose its preferential position *vis-à-vis* these countries in the U K market. The analysis of McAleese (1975) indicates that this loss will just cancel out the benefit from the reduction of the common external tariff, with little or no change in the total. This is, admittedly, a comparative static analysis based on estimates of export price elasticities and nominal tariff averages, and does not take into account some important factors. Firstly, the growth of demand for imports in the original six E E C countries has been much more rapid than in the U K. If this trend continues, then the shift from the U K to the E E C would imply a somewhat faster overall rate of growth of Irish exports without any further improvement in competitiveness. Secondly, the analysis does not include the so-called 'dynamic', or long-term, benefits. In particular, tariff-free access to such a large market is likely to increase Ireland's attraction as a location for foreign investment. It may also provide greater encouragement for investment by Irish entrepreneurs, in that the E E C market has been much less affected by 'stop-go' policies characteristic of the British economy since the war.

The E E C will, however, involve a major loss on the home market to competing manufactured imports. McAleese (1975) puts the figure at £106 million—almost as great as his estimate of the gain in agricultural exports. However, in looking at the implications of these figures for the balance of payments and national income, it is important to take account of differences in import content. The increased agricultural exports have a low import content relative to the manufactured goods that will be displaced by competing imports.

Thus, while the E E C holds out the prospect of considerable net gains for the economy, some sectors of the economy stand to suffer considerably. Since there is no automatic way in which the gainers can compensate the losers, this situation contains the seeds of considerable social tension unless resolved by suitable policy measures. However, Ireland, unlike the U K, is in the fortunate position that E E C entry is likely to have a net favourable effect on the balance of payments, so that restrictive economic policies need not ensue. It is much easier to realise the 'dynamic' gains, and to provide alternative employment opportunities for those rendered redundant, in conditions of buoyant demand.

However, maintenance of adequate demand buoyancy and sufficient investment to move rapidly towards full employment, could create a strain on the balance of payments unless resources are forthcoming from the Regional and Social Funds. Ireland can expect to be a net recipient of resources from both of these funds. At present, we do not know the magnitude of these funds for the next few years. However, the indications are that some other member countries may be unwilling to contemplate funding on anything like the scale that Ireland would require for the attainment of such Community objectives as full monetary union. It would therefore be unwise to rely too heavily on the development of large-scale unrequited transfers from the E E C to Ireland. The prospects of receiving substantial aid would, however, be enhanced by presentation of a well-documented and specific programme of development, giving estimates of the resources needed to achieve those aims to which the E E C is committed, in particular full employment and reduction of disparities in living standards among the regions of the Community.

An important aspect of E E C membership which may not be discernible in economic statistics or other quantifiable measures will be the effects of exposure to a wider range of ideas and institutions. The close historical, political and economic ties between Ireland and the U K have meant that the legal and institutional structures of the two countries are quite similar. Irish policy-makers have tended to examine and adopt British policies much more than policies pursued by other countries. In so far as Ireland and the U K share common problems, this tendency could be justified by the advantages of maintaining an economic and trading environment similar to that in the U K. Moreover, Ireland could learn from British experience, without the need for costly experimentation. But, given the different economic structure of the two countries, there are obvious dangers in imitating British solutions too closely. Accession to the E E C will bring greater exposure to different types of institutions and greater awareness of the economic policies of other member states. One cannot help noticing already the increased interest, as demonstrated, for example, through media coverage, in European ideas and policies. Even at this early stage it would seem safe to assert that entry into the E E C has had a considerable effect on Irish attitudes, an effect which appears to be far greater than in the U K. While this need not necessarily be of benefit to the Irish economy, it should be noted that the U K has experienced the lowest growth rate of all member states in the 1960s. The experience of France or Italy, for example, in encouraging and maintaining rapid economic growth may be more relevant to Irish circumstances than that of the U K.

PUBLIC FINANCE

Public expenditure has grown rapidly over the last decade. Between 1961 and 1972 total expenditure (current and capital) of public authorities rose at an average annual rate of 13.8 per cent in current prices. This compares with a growth rate of 10.9 per cent in G N P at current prices, so that the ratio of public spending to G N P rose substantially from 31 per cent in 1961 to 42 per cent in 1972. This rapid growth of public expenditure has been in many ways an important contributor to economic and social progress. We have argued, in particular, that the growth of public investment provided a necessary stimulus to demand and helped to create the infrastructural and other forms of capital formation required for growth.

Ireland is not exceptional in experiencing a rate of growth of government expenditure faster than G N P. As Garin-Painter (1970) has shown in an O E C D study, this has been the experience in all O E C D member countries for the period 1955–65. Indeed, the ratio of government expenditure growth to G N P growth for Ireland of 1.3 is not much different from the ratios experienced elsewhere. For most O E C D countries studied, it was found that increases in expenditure on education, health and social security were mainly responsible for the rising ratio of government expenditure.

Nevertheless, a sustained rise in the ratio of public expenditure to G N P could not continue indefinitely at this rate. If, indeed, it were possible to maintain the relative growth rates mentioned, the ratio of public expenditure to G N P would be about 60 per cent in 1980, and 100 per cent only twenty-five years from now! While theory does not suggest what is the upper limit to the ratio of public spending to G N P in a mixed economy, it seems fairly certain that as the ratio continued rising it would give rise to considerable resistance that could be adverse to economic growth. It is safe to say that, in practice, the ratio will not rise indefinitely. However, what seems to us important is whether the rise tapers off in a planned fashion, which minimises adverse side-effects, or is allowed to go on rising until curtailed by crises in public finance.

Obviously, if the ratio of public expenditure to G N P is not to rise indefinitely, then either the rate of growth of public spending must slow down, or the *real* rate of growth of G N P must rise. Examination of the likely future trend of public expenditure in Ireland, which we discuss further below, indicates that there are strong pressures making for a continued rapid rise in public expenditure over the next five to ten years. Furthermore, we believe that this rise is not only desirable in many ways, but necessary, in order to aim at full employment and to alleviate social deprivation. This being so, if serious difficulties in public finance are to be avoided, then the growth of public expenditure should be planned either in such a way that a tapering off will eventually become possible without reducing economic growth or in a way that will bring about a rise in the economic growth potential. Either way, this calls for careful examination of the categories of public spending and their effect on economic growth. Moreover, given that the authorities are already encountering problems in securing resources to finance the present level of public spending, such planning should also have regard to acquiring the required resources in ways that minimise the adverse effects on growth.

In examining the likely future trend of public expenditure, it is

Table 50: Growth of public authorities' expenditure classified by
function, 1963–70

	Average annual growth rate 1963–70	Share in total 1963	1970
	%	%	%
Public debt	16.8	11.3	13.3
Health	16.8	8.5	9.9
Education	16.3	10.5	11.9
Other community and social services	14.1	2.5	2.4
Social security and welfare	14.0	17.5	17.3
Agriculture, forestry and fishing	13.4	13.1	12.5
Mining, manufacturing and construction	13.3	4.8	4.5
Housing	12.4	6.5	5.8
General government services (excl. defence)	12.3	8.4	7.5
Transport and communications, other economic services	12.1	13.0	11.4
Defence	10.8	3.9	3.2
Total expenditure	14.2	100.0	100.0
Current	14.4	76.7	77.8
Capital	13.4*	23.3	22.2
Capital (excl. debt redemption)	12.0*	20.9	18.3

*These figures do not include the capital expenditure of state-sponsored
bodies except to the extent that it is financed through the exchequer. The
Public Capital Programme, which includes nearly all capital expenditure
of these bodies and excludes debt redemption, grew in current values by
13.4 per cent per annum in this period.

Source: *National Income and Expenditure 1972* and earlier issues.

helpful to look at the past growth rates of the major categories
classified by function. Such a functional classification is available
back to 1963, and in Table 50 we show the shares of the main
categories and their average annual growth rate from 1963 to 1970,
the latter being the latest year for which figures are available. As
in other European countries, the growth rate of expenditure for
social purposes has been relatively rapid, but the fastest growing
category was public debt,[8] arising from the sustained borrowing

by public authorities. However, it is remarkable that all categories increased relative to G N P in current values, which rose by 10.6 per cent per annum from 1963 to 1970. Thus, while there were variations in the growth rates among different categories—reflecting changing priorities, notably the greater commitment to social needs—nevertheless all components contributed to the overall rise relative to G N P. The figures, combined with other knowledge, give little reason to suppose that the relatively high growth rate of public expenditure was a once-for-all effort to meet important social and economic needs, or that the growth rate can now taper off relative to that of G N P.

The tendency for *all* categories of public expenditure to rise reflects the nature of the political process, in that programmes once established are extremely difficult to terminate. On the contrary, they tend to rise by at least as much as the rise in prices. Since some of these programmes may have outlived their usefulness, this is a major source of inefficiency. Moreover, it may tend to crowd out some new programmes that would be highly desirable for economic and social progress. In order to make room for projects responsive to new economic and social needs within an acceptable total of public expenditure, it would seem that any plan for the public sector would need to do more than operate on the margin in relation to existing programmes. Indeed, it would be necessary to review the continued existence of some of the latter. The recent introduction of programme budgeting and the establishment of a new Department of the Public Service could make an important contribution in this regard to ensuring efficient utilisation of public resources.

However, even assuming that these efforts are successful, the demand for increased public expenditure is likely to be such that the growth rate must continue to rise relative to G N P for some years to come. In Chapter 11 we suggested that the substantial public resources committed to social and infrastructural investment in the 1950s provided a measure of spare capacity which was utilised in the 1960s. The additional capital requirements of the economy in the last decade may therefore have been lower than would otherwise be warranted by the growth of output and population. It would now seem that any excess capacity in infrastructural facilities has been used up. The growth of output and population, with increased urbanisation and industrialisation, has led to a considerable rise in the demand for housing, hospitals, roads, power supplies, telephones, etc. Large capital projects are already under consideration in these areas, notably in nuclear power and hospitals.

Even allowing for transfers from the E E C Regional and Social Funds and for the possibility of financing some capital expenditure out of current revenue, public borrowing is still likely to grow considerably, so that interest on public debt is also likely to go on rising rapidly. To bring the social welfare services into line with those prevailing in the E E C would require large increases in social welfare spending. The very high dependency ratio in the younger age groups is likely to persist for some considerable time, so that it is difficult to see any slowing-down in the demands on the public sector to help provide educational and health services. State expenditure in relation to agriculture is one of the few areas in which it is possible to foresee relief for the exchequer, as a result of the operation of the C A P.

Granted then that there are no obvious indications, except possibly in agriculture, of a slowing down in the demands imposed on the public sector on the expenditure side, what are the prospects of finding the increased resources without undue strain? Doherty and O'Neill (1973) have shown that, relative to other E E C countries, the ratio of taxation to G N P is quite low in Ireland. Furthermore, there is a greater dependence on indirect taxes than elsewhere so that the ratio of direct taxes to G N P for Ireland for the years 1967 to 1969 was less than half that of the next lowest E E C member. However, several qualifications must be made in regard to such figures. Firstly, the agricultural sector is largely exempt from income tax in Ireland. Secondly, the dependency rate per worker is far higher than in other E E C countries. Thirdly, average earnings per worker are lower in Ireland, although in some occupations wage and salary rates are higher. And fourthly, profits on manufactured exports above the 1956 level are exempt from tax. Fifthly, as pointed out by Finola Kennedy (1975), social security in Ireland is financed to a large extent out of general taxation, whereas in many E E C countries it is financed mainly by social insurance contributions, the greater proportion of which is paid by the employer; with social insurance excluded, the ratio of direct taxes to G N P is very similar in Ireland to other E E C countries. When these qualifications are taken into account, the burden of income tax on those who are liable is already substantial.

These considerations suggest the need to widen the existing tax base. Whatever the merits of excluding all farm incomes from income tax in the past, the long-term benefits to agriculture from E E C entry now provide a strong case for taxing income from agriculture on the same basis as other income.[9] In considering the extension of the income tax base in this way, regard should be had, of course, to the burden of local authority rates on property. The latter may be relatively heavier in the case of farm enterprises, which necessarily use a greater area of land than corresponding industrial or commercial enterprises.[10] Consideration might also be given to providing investment incentives to encourage farmers to raise production and reap the potential offered by the C A P.

Another possible way of widening the tax net is to tax capital gains, which at present are exempt from all taxation.[11] In an inflationary situation with high marginal income tax rates there is a strong incentive to substitute capital gains for income. Indeed, one might say that the traditional distinction between the two has largely broken down. It may be noted that the effectiveness of taxation on farm incomes and capital gains in raising total revenue should not be judged solely in terms of what these taxes themselves yield. As long as they are exempt from taxation, they tend to be used as a 'bolt-hole' to avoid income tax. Once the bolt-hole is effectively closed, the incentive to switch is diminished and part of the increased tax revenue accrues in the original forms.

The tax concession for profits on manufactured exports might also be reconsidered. Admittedly, in this case the tax concession is directly related to the need to generate industrial development and employment. Given, however, the low domestic value added contributed by these enterprises, as well as the substantial gain that will accrue to those exporting to the E E C as a result of the removal of the common external tariff, there may well be a case for somewhat less generous tax concessions. Moreover, if it were possible to relate the tax concessions to the domestic value added directly and indirectly created by these export enterprises, this would be more effective in increasing both employment and exchequer revenue. These points apply with even greater force to the tax concessions for mining, where use of an exhaustible asset is involved and where, in fact, the government has already indicated its intention to reduce the tax concessions.

A further issue deserving of greater public concern is the amount of tax evasion. Although there is little or no hard evidence about its overall extent, few with knowledge of the practice in some industries (such as building) and professions would deny that the problem of income tax evasion exists on a larger scale than the Revenue Commissioners would be prepared to admit. It is also common knowledge that evasion was widespread in the case of the wholesale tax, though this has largely been eliminated, following its replacement by value added tax. The staff of the Revenue Commission is heavily overburdened with its existing workload and is not sufficient to deal effectively with many forms of income tax evasion. It should be noted that the revenue recovered directly by increasing the staff for this purpose is not the only benefit that would arise.[12] The elimination of bolt-holes, as mentioned earlier, increases other forms of revenue. Moreover, the existence of tax evasion gives rise to a strong sense of injustice among tax-payers generally, something that is of no small consequence in relation to incomes policy and the control of inflation.

If current revenue can be raised significantly by widening the tax net, it may conceivably be possible to allocate a somewhat larger proportion of such resources than in the past to finance the large amount of public capital expenditure likely to be required over the next five to ten years. Even so, however, the borrowing requirements of public authorities would still probably have to grow substantially in absolute terms. E E C funds can be expected to finance part of this, but, as mentioned earlier, the amounts likely to be forthcoming from these sources may be small relative to the needs involved. Given that the traditional sources of financing public investment are already encountering difficulties, there is, then, a need for a thorough reconsideration of the methods of financing public investment. The national loan, once a major source of funds, now yields only a small proportion of the required resources. The attraction of such long-term, fixed interest stock is likely to diminish even further if present inflation rates continue. Borrowing from the commercial banks has become a much more important source. However, as the share of government in total bank lending has risen, this has created difficulties for the private sector, which has traditionally relied heavily on this source. In recent years the government has had to resort increasingly to borrowing abroad.

A reconsideration of the financing of public investment should, on the one hand, seek to secure greater efficiency and lower cost in public borrowing, whether at home or abroad, and, on the other hand, aim to increase the total of domestic finance. In regard to the former, the Post Office savings media might be improved to compete more effectively with the commercial banks for deposits. At present they provide only a small proportion of the finance for public investment relative to the amounts borrowed from the banks, even though potentially they represent a cheaper source from the exchequer viewpoint. Equity participation in the commercial state-sponsored bodies is a possible way of attracting more domestic funds.

The need for efficiency in public expenditure, revenue collection and borrowing has assumed greater importance, given that the proportion of total resources allocated by the public sector has increased so much and is likely to increase further in the next decade. The role of the public sector in the decade ahead is particularly crucial in solving the employment problem. Success in that regard would, in fact, greatly alleviate the strains of public finance subsequently, both by increasing government revenue and by reducing some of the calls on the exchequer. Careful forward planning of public expenditure now could help to avoid many future problems. Experience of economic planning in Ireland in the past indicates that the public sector was the one in which the plans were least adhered to. The success of economic planning in the future would seem to us, however, to depend crucially on how effectively the public sector is planned.

INFLATION, ECONOMIC GROWTH AND POVERTY

Little is known about the effect of economic growth on the distribution of income and wealth in Ireland. What we do know is that, despite the relatively rapid economic growth achieved in the 1960s, the extent of poverty is still considerable.[13] Economic growth alone cannot solve the problem of poverty—the single experience of the U S A is enough to dispel any such illusions. Yet it would seem that continued growth is a necessary, though insufficient, condition of effectively alleviating much of the poverty and social deprivation in Ireland.[14]

The very high rate of inflation in recent years can seriously aggravate the position of the existing poor and create new classes of poor. A weak bargaining position is one of the characteristics of poverty, so that the poor may find it particularly difficult to maintain the real value of their sources of income. Those who retired on a fixed pension find the purchasing power of their income going down at a rapid rate. The savings of those who invested in government securities have suffered a severe fall in capital values and yield interest far less than the rise in prices. Inflation, through its effect on competitiveness, can also lead to unemployment, one of the most serious sources of poverty in Ireland.

Our analysis in Chapter 17 of the acceleration in inflation suggests that the major cause was rising external trade prices, followed by the acceleration in the growth of money incomes, partly, at least, in response to price increases. Although export prices of beef and dairy products may not continue rising so rapidly, there is no indication of a slow-down in import prices. On the contrary, the indications are that in the immediate future import prices may rise even faster due to the oil situation. Rapid inflation is therefore likely to continue at least for some time into the future. To attempt to control the resulting pressure for higher money incomes through restraint in demand would impose a disproportionately high cost, and could in any event be fruitless. The consequent cut in the growth of *real* income would tend to aggravate the pressure for higher *money* incomes, while the likely reduction in productivity growth would be adverse to competitiveness.

What *can* be attempted in the face of external inflationary pressures is to try, by agreed limitations on money incomes increases, to ensure that inflation in Ireland is no worse than in competing countries, and to take steps to alleviate social distress, including that caused by inflation. These two objectives are closely tied together. An attempt to secure and maintain sufficient restraint on money incomes is unlikely to succeed in a climate of unrest in regard to social inequality. Consequently it may prove difficult to maintain an incomes policy unless it can have three components: (*a*) an economic programme to raise the growth rate of real incomes and employment; (*b*) a policy to reduce inequalities in the distribution of income and wealth; and (*c*) agreed limitations on the rate of increase in money incomes.

This would represent a much wider concept of incomes policy than that implicit in the recent National Pay Agreements. These agreements deal essentially with only the third component, though they have sought to favour the lower-paid workers through proportionately larger increases at lower scales of pay. However, it remains doubtful whether nationally negotiated changes in incomes represent an effective way of dealing with poverty and inequality. The task is likely to prove too complex, given the intricate repercussions of changing wage differentials. Besides, the national wage agreements do not deal with many categories of income (such as dividends, professional earnings, etc.) and cannot deal directly with those who have no income. Government tax and expenditure policies could provide much more flexible and sensitive instruments for the purpose. There is a lot to be said for not overburdening national pay agreements with tasks for which they may not be suited, and to limit their scope to securing general pay increases that will not be unduly inflationary. At the same time, the unions, together with other representative bodies, might be brought much more into the discussion of the type of tax and expenditure programmes that could command general acceptance on grounds of social equity. Moreover, the cooperation of these interests might be sought in devising policies aimed at full employment.

This would envisage a much more participative form of economic policy-making than in the past. The National Industrial and Economic Council in the 1960s provided a possible forum in this regard. However, its views evidently did not have much impact on policy and it eventually lapsed. Nevertheless, past failures need not necessarily deter future efforts. The government, through its recent establishment of the National Economic and Social Council, appears favourably disposed to an enlarged form of participative policy formulation. Moreover, the idea is in keeping with other concepts of participation current in the E E C, such as industrial democracy.

L

CONCLUDING REMARKS

The analysis in this chapter suggests the need now to re-think some aspects of the policies that have been successful in the past in generating economic growth. This is not to suggest that the policies were necessarily wrong. On the contrary, very considerable progress has been made, and the lessons emerging from past experience provide an excellent basis for evaluating which features of the present strategy require reconsideration. But it is scarcely to be expected that the strategy that was successful in one decade should continue unchanged in the next. This is so both because new problems emerge and because old problems are viewed in a new light as circumstances and values alter. A general re-evaluation of economic policy is called for both by reason of E E C entry and because of the likely repercussions of the oil situation, but it would in any event be necessary. This is not to imply any need for despondency in the face of the problems we have outlined. Our study indicates that Ireland has shown a considerable capacity for solving its problems in the past. The confidence derived from past successes should improve the capacity to deal with present and future problems.

List of Works Cited

K. J. Arrow (1962): 'The Economic Implications of Learning by Doing', *Review of Economic Studies*, XXIX, (Jun. 1962)

T. J. Baker (1969, I): 'An Analysis of Industrial Exports', *Quarterly Economic Commentary* (Jan. 1969)

T. J. Baker (1969, II): 'Commentary' and 'A Study of Imports, Part 1', *Quarterly Economic Commentary* (May 1969)

T. J. Baker and J. Durkan (1970, I): 'A Study of Imports, Part 2', *Quarterly Economic Commentary* (Sep. 1969)

T. J. Baker and J. Durkan (1969, II): 'A Study of Imports, Part 3', *Quarterly Economic Commentary* (Dec. 1969)

T. J. Baker and J. Durkan (1970, I): 'A Study of Imports, Part 4', *Quarterly Economic Commentary* (Mar. 1970)

T. J. Baker and J. Durkan (1970, II): 'Commentary', *Quarterly Economic Commentary* (Jun. 1970)

T. J. Baker and J. P. Neary (1971): 'A Study of Consumer Prices, Part 1', *Quarterly Economic Commentary* (Mar. 1971)

W. Beckerman (1962): 'Projecting Europe's Growth', *Economic Journal*, LXXII (Dec. 1962)

W. Beckerman (1965): 'Demand, Exports and Growth' in W. Beckerman and Associates, *The British Economy in 1975*, Cambridge (Cambridge University Press) 1965

W. Beckerman (1966): 'The Determinants of Economic Growth' in P. D. Henderson, ed., *Economic Growth in Britain*, London (Weidenfeld and Nicolson) 1966

K. Bieda (1970): *The Structure and Operation of the Japanese Economy*, Sydney (John Wiley) 1970

J. B. Broderick (1960): 'An Analysis of Government Revenue and Expenditure in Relation to National Accounts', *Journal of the Statistical and Social Inquiry Society of Ireland, XX, 3* (1959–60)

J. B. Broderick (1968): 'Problems in Measuring the Growth Rate', *Journal of the Statistical and Social Inquiry Society of Ireland,* XXI, 6 (1967–68)

S. Burenstam-Linder (1961): *An Essay on Trade and Transformation,* New York (John Wiley) 1961

Capital Investment Advisory Committee (1957, I): *First Report,* Dublin (Stationery Office) 1957

Capital Investment Advisory Committee (1957, II): *Second Report,* Dublin (Stationery Office) 1957

Capital Investment Advisory Committee (1958): *Third Report,* Dublin (Stationery Office) 1958

Richard E. Caves (1968): 'Market Organisation, Performance and Public Policy' in Richard E. Caves and Associates, *Britain's Economic Prospects,* Washington (The Brookings Institution) and London (Allen and Unwin) 1968

Richard E. Caves (1970): 'Export-led Growth: the Post-war Industrial Setting' in W. A. Eltis, M. F. Scott and J. N. Wolfe, ed., *Induction, Growth and Trade: Essays in Honour of Sir Roy Harrod,* Oxford (Clarendon Press) 1970

F. B. Chubb and P. Lynch, ed. (1969): *Economic Development and Planning,* Dublin (Institute of Public Administration) 1969

C. Cooper and N. Whelan (1973): 'Science, Technology and Industry in Ireland', *Report to the National Science Council,* Dublin (Stationery Office) 1973

R. A. Cooper, K. Hartley and C. R. M. Harvey (1970): *Export Performance and the Pressure of Demand: A Study of Firms,* London (Allen and Unwin) 1970

J. H. Doherty and J. P. O'Neill (1973): 'Recent Trends in Public Finance', in Central Bank of Ireland, *Annual Report 1972–73*

L. Donaldson (1966): *Development Planning in Ireland,* New York and London (Frederick A. Praeger) 1966

J. C. R. Dow (1964): *The Management of the British Economy 1945–60,* Cambridge (Cambridge University Press for National Institute of Economic and Social Research) 1964

B. R. Dowling (1970): *Post-War Tourism in Ireland and Western Europe* (Unpublished M.A. thesis, University College, Dublin, 1970)

G. A. Duncan (1939): 'The Social Income of the Irish Free State,

1926–38', *Journal of the Statistical and Social Inquiry Society of Ireland*, XVI (1939–40)

G. A. Duncan (1941): 'The Social Income of Éire, 1938–40', *Journal of the Statistical and Social Inquiry Society of Ireland*, XVI 1940–41)

Garret FitzGerald (1968): *Planning in Ireland*, Dublin (Institute of Public Administration) and London (Political and Economic Planning) 1968

Michael P. Fogarty (1958): 'Ireland's Angry Young Men', *The Commonweal* (Jan. 1958)

Michael P. Fogarty (1974): *Irish Entrepreneurs Speak for Themselves* (Economic and Social Research Institute Broadsheet No. 8), Dublin 1974

H. G. Foster (1971): 'Ireland's Trade with Britain' in I. F. Bailie and S. J. Sheehy, ed., *Irish Agriculture in a Changing World*, Edinburgh (Oliver and Boyd) 1971

Mary Garin-Painter (1970): 'Public Expenditure Trends in O E C D Countries', *O E C D Economic Outlook* (O E C D Occasional Studies, Jul. 1970), Paris 1970

R. C. Geary (1961): 'Introduction to Part One' and 'Productivity Aspects of Accounts Deflation: Data for Ireland' in P. Deane, ed., *Studies in Social and Financial Accounting* (International Association for Research in Income and Wealth, Income and Wealth Series IX), London (Bowes and Bowes) 1961

R. C. Geary and J. G. Hughes (1970): *Certain Aspects of Non-Agricultural Unemployment in Ireland* (Economic and Social Research Institute Paper No. 52), Dublin 1970

R. C. Geary and J. L. Pratschke (1968): *Some Aspects of Price Inflation in Ireland* (Economic and Social Research Institute Paper No. 40), Dublin 1968

E. W. Henry (1972): *Irish Input-Output Structures, 1964 and 1968* (Economic and Social Research Institute Paper No. 66), Dublin 1972

George B. Henry (1970): 'Domestic Demand Pressure and Short-run Export Fluctuations', *Yale Economic Essays*, X, 1 (Spring 1970)

Ursula Hicks (1957): 'Discussion' following James Meenan 'The Political Economy of Development', *Journal of the Statistical and Social Inquiry Society of Ireland*, XX, 1 (1957–58)

J. G. Hughes (1971): 'Output, Prices and Productivity in Irish Sheltered and Exposed Transportable Goods Industries', *Economic and Social Review*, II, 2 (Jan. 1971)

J. G. Hughes (1972): 'Some Aspects of Inequality in Income, Wealth and Educational Opportunity in Ireland' (Paper read to Social Study Conference, Falcarragh, Aug. 1972)

Charles W. Hultman (1967): 'Exports and Economic Growth: A Survey', *Land Economics*, XLIII, 2 (May 1967)

N. Kaldor (1955): *An Expenditure Tax*, London (Unwin University Books) 1955

N. Kaldor (1966): *Causes of the Slow Rate of Economic Growth of the United Kingdom*, Inaugural Lecture, Cambridge (Cambridge University Press) 1966

Finola Kennedy (1970): 'Social Expenditure of Public Authorities and Economic Growth, 1947–66', *Economic and Social Review*, I, 3 (Apr. 1970)

Finola Kennedy (1975): *Public Social Expenditure in Ireland* (Economic and Social Research Institute Broadsheet No. 11), Dublin 1975

Kieran A. Kennedy (1968): *Labour Productivity in Irish Industry* (Unpublished Ph.D. thesis, Harvard University, 1968)

Kieran A. Kennedy (1969): 'Growth of Labour Productivity in Irish Manufacturing, 1953–1967', *Journal of the Statistical and Social Inquiry Society of Ireland*, XXII, 1 (1968–69)

Kieran A. Kennedy (1971, I): *Productivity and Industrial Growth: The Irish Experience*, Oxford (Clarendon Press) 1971

Kieran A. Kennedy (1971, II): 'The Mixed Economy in Western Europe', *Christus Rex*, XXV, 3 (Jul. 1971)

Kieran A. Kennedy (1972): 'The Irish Economy in 1972' (Paper read to First National Economic Conference of the Confederation of Irish Industry, Dublin, Jan. 1972)

Kieran A. Kennedy and B. R. Dowling (1970): 'The Determinants of Personal Savings in Ireland', *Economic and Social Review*, II, 1 (Oct. 1970) (Reissued in E S R I Reprint Series as Reprint No. 26)

Alfred Kuehn (1961): *Short-Term Economic Forecasting and its Application in Ireland* (Economic Research Institute Paper No. 2), Dublin 1961

Alfred Kuehn (1962): *Prospects of the Irish Economy in 1962* (Economic Research Institute Paper No. 6), Dublin 1962

Simon Kuznets (1968): 'Notes on Japan's Economic Growth' in L. Klein and K. Ohkawa, ed., *Economic Growth: The Japanese Experience since the Meiji Era*, Illinois (Richard D. Irwin Inc. for the Economic Growth Center, Yale University) 1968

A. Lamfalussy (1963): *The United Kingdom and the Six*, London (Macmillan) 1963

C. E. V. Leser (1963, I): *Imports and Economic Growth in Ireland, 1947-61* (Economic Research Institute Paper No. 14), Dublin 1963

C. E. V. Leser (1963, II): *The Irish Economy in 1962 and 1963*, (Economic Research Institute Paper No. 15) Dublin 1963

C. E. V. Leser (1964): *The Irish Economy in 1963 and 1964* (Economic Research Institute Paper No. 21), Dublin 1964

C. E. V. Leser (1965, I): *Seasonality in Irish Economic Statistics* (Economic Research Institute Paper No. 26), Dublin 1965

C. E. V. Leser (1965, II): *The Irish Economy in 1964 and 1965* (Economic Research Institute Paper No. 27), Dublin 1965

C. E. V. Leser (1967): *A Study of Imports* (Economic and Social Research Institute Paper No. 38), Dublin 1967

P. Lynch (1969): 'The Irish Economy since the War, 1946-51' in Kevin B. Nowlan and T. Desmond Williams, ed., *Ireland in the War Years and After, 1939-51*, Dublin (Gill and Macmillan) 1969

Alfred Maizels (1965): *Industrial Growth and World Trade*, Cambridge (Cambridge University Press) 1965

Alfred Maizels (1970): *Growth and Trade*, Cambridge (Cambridge University Press) 1970

Dermot McAleese (1970): *A Study of Demand Elasticities for Irish Imports* (Economic and Social Research Institute Paper No. 53), Dublin 1970

Dermot McAleese (1971): *Effective Tariffs and the Structure of Industrial Protection in Ireland* (Economic and Social Research Institute Paper No. 62), Dublin 1971

Dermot McAleese (1975): 'Ireland in the Enlarged E E C, Economic Consequences and Prospects' in John Vaizey, ed., *Regional Policy and Economic Sovereignty*, Dublin (Gill and Macmillan) 1975

Dermot McAleese and J. Martin (1973): *Irish Manufactured Imports from the United Kingdom in the Sixties: the Effects of A I F T A* (Economic and Social Research Institute Paper No. 70) Dublin 1973

James Meenan (1970): *The Irish Economy Since 1922*, Liverpool (Liverpool University Press) 1970

C. Mulvey and J. A. Trevithick (1970): 'Wage Inflation: Causes and Cures', in Central Bank of Ireland, *Quarterly Bulletin* (Winter 1970)

National Industrial Economic Council (1965): *Report on the Economic Situation 1965—Report No. 11*, Dublin (Stationery Office) 1965

W. D. Nordhaus (1972): 'The Worldwide Wage Explosion' *Brookings Papers on Economic Activity*, No. 2 (1972)

Séamus Ó Cinnéide (1972): 'The Extent of Poverty in Ireland', *Social Studies*, I, 4 (Aug. 1972)

Robert O'Connor (1970): 'An Analysis of Recent Policies for Beef and Milk', *Journal of the Statistical and Social Inquiry Society of Ireland*, XXII, 2 (1969–70)

T. J. O'Driscoll (1955): 'Coras Tráchtála Teo.', *Administration*, III, 1 (Spring 1955)

John O'Hagan (1972): 'Export and Import Visitor Trends and Determinants in Ireland', *Journal of the Statistical and Social Inquiry Society of Ireland*, XXII, 5 (1972–73)

Report of the Committee on the Working of the Monetary System (1959) (Radcliffe Report) London (H M S O, Cmd 827) 1959

Report of the Store Cattle Study Group (1968) Dublin (Stationery Office) 1968

L. Ryan (1972): 'Fiscal Policy and Demand Management in Ireland, 1960–1970', *Economic and Social Review*, II, 2 (Jan. 1971) (Reprinted in A. A. Tait and J. A. Bristow, ed., *Ireland: Some Problems of a Developing Economy*, Dublin (Gill and Macmillan) and New York (Barnes and Noble) 1972)

Charles Schultze (1959): *Recent Inflation in the United States*, Study Paper No. 1, U S A Congress, Joint Economic Committee, Washington (Government Printing Office) 1959

Miyohei Shinohara (1962): *Growth and Cycles in the Japanese Economy*, Tokyo (Kinokuniya Bookstore) 1962

Staff of the Economic Research Institute (1966): *The Irish Economy in 1966* (Economic Research Institute Paper No. 33), Dublin 1966

Staff of the Economic and Social Research Institute (1967): *The*

Irish Economy in 1967 (Economic and Social Research Institute Paper No. 39), Dublin 1967

Survey of Grant-Aided Industry (1967) Dublin (Stationery Office) 1967

A. Dale Tussing (1973): 'Poverty Research in the United States' *Economic and Social Review*, V, 1 (Oct. 1973)

Besim Üstünel (1972): *Growth, Trade and Technology: from 'Trade-Generated Growth' to 'Growth-Generated Trade' and the Cases of Sweden, Japan, Turkey* (Institute for International Economic Studies, University of Stockholm, Seminar Paper No. 18, Jun. 1972), Stockholm 1972

Brendan M. Walsh (1968): *Some Irish Population Problems Reconsidered* (Economic and Social Research Institute Paper No. 42), Dublin 1968

Brendan M. Walsh (1972): *Poverty in Ireland: Research Priorities* (Economic and Social Research Institute Broadsheet No. 7), Dublin 1972

Brendan M. Walsh (1974): *The Structure of Non-Agricultural Unemployment in Ireland* (Economic and Social Research Institute Paper No. 77), Dublin 1974

Brendan M. Walsh (1975): *Population and Employment Projections: 1971-86* (National Economic and Social Council Report No. 5), Dublin 1975

T. K. Whitaker (1949): 'Ireland's External Assets', *Journal of the Statistical and Social Inquiry Society of Ireland*, XVIII (1948-49)

T. K. Whitaker (1955): 'Why We Need to Export Overseas' *Administration*, III, 1 (Spring 1955)

T. K. Whitaker (1956): 'Capital Formation, Savings and Economic Progress', *Journal of the Statistical and Social Inquiry Society of Ireland*, XIX (1955-56) (Reprinted in F. B. Chubb and P. Lynch, ed., *Economic Development and Planning*, Dublin (Institute of Public Administration) 1969)

T. K. Whitaker (1958): *Economic Development*, Dublin (Stationery Office) 1958

G. D. N. Worswick (1970) 'Trade and Payments' in Alec Cairncross, ed., *Britain's Economic Prospects Reconsidered*, London (Allen and Unwin) 1970

Notes

Chapter 1

1. The year 1968 is used here—and elsewhere throughout the book —as the terminal year because at the time the research for this study was undertaken it was the latest year for which all the data used in the analysis were available. The years 1969–72 are dealt with in a separate chapter in Part V, using the most up-to-date data at the time of going to press.

2. A logarithmic scale for G N P is used. Thus a change in the slope of the line indicates a change in the *rate of growth*. On arithmetic graphs a rise in slope would merely indicate a rise in the absolute change, which does not neccessarily imply a rise in growth rate.

3. This is also true for regression trend lines which, although less sensitive to beginning and end year observations, can be affected by cyclical fluctuations in the economy. If an economy can be characterised by cycles of long periodicity, then trend growth rates fitted on observations between the peak (trough) and trough (peak) of the cycle will be lower (higher) than the overall trend.

4. This judgement is based on the C S O index of volume of G N P in 1938 (at 1953 prices) in the *Irish Statistical Survey 1957,* and on the index of real income for various years 1926–40 given by Duncan (1939) and (1941).

5. The growth rate of real income from 1931–39, based on Duncan's estimates, was 0.7 per cent per annum. The year 1931 is chosen here because it immediately precedes the transformation in the economy in the 1930s associated with the switch to an autarkic economic policy, while 1939 is the year with the highest pre-war volume of national product.

6. It may be noted also that the 1955 level of total non-agricultural employment was again reached for the first time only in 1963. However, this fact is indicative of the longer-term change of trend that took place in the economy rather than of recovery from depression, since the trend of total non-agricultural employment was downward even before the 1956–58 depression.

7. In this connection, it is of interest to note that if one projects

forward from 1939 the actual growth rate of total real income achieved in the longest pre-war period for which figures are available (viz. 1.46 per cent per annum from 1926 to 1939), we find that the actual level matched the projected level for the first time in 1961; and since the rate of growth since 1961 has been substantially above the longer-term pre-war and post-war rates, this gives added support to our contention that substantial improvement on all previous long-term trends was established from about the beginning of the 1960s.

8. For many purposes we treat 1949–61 as a single period and contrast it with 1961–68. However, where it is appropriate to the purpose in hand, we shall also from time to time mark off different periods. Moreover, although we exclude the years 1947 and 1948 in many instances, we shall include them where this helps the exposition.

9. The annual percentage changes in these variables in all post-war years are given in Table A.1 at the end of this chapter.

10. Agriculture includes forestry and fishing as well as farm activities. Industry covers mining, manufacturing, building, electricity, gas and water. Services cover the remainder of domestic economic activity, e.g. distribution, transport and communications, public administration and defence, banking and finance, professional and personal services, etc.

11. GDP differs from GNP in that it excludes factor income from abroad.

12. In an appendix to this chapter we consider why there has been only a small rise in productivity growth in the industrial sector as a whole, whereas there has been a significant rise in productivity growth in industry as covered by the CIP.

13. For an excellent discussion of the methods of estimating changes in real product in the Irish national income accounts, see Broderick (1968). A discussion of this issue is also given in Kennedy (1968).

14. For further explanation of this term, see Kennedy (1969) and (1971, I).

15. As measured here, the intra-sectoral component also includes an 'interrelations' effect due to the fact that sectoral productivity and employment shares are both changing in practice. The interrelations component is, however, usually small. See Kennedy (1971, I).

16. Kennedy (1971, I).

17. For a full description of the coverage of the CIP, see Kennedy (1971, I), Appendix I.

18. For consistency, we include in the non-CIP part certain building workers that have only been included in the CIP since 1966.

Chapter 2

1. This item includes the consumption of local authorities as well as the central government, but it refers only to government current purchases of goods and services and therefore excludes such major items of government expenditure as current transfers and capital expenditure.

2. There was a large rise in the savings ratio between 1958 and 1959, from 11.9 per cent to 15.5 per cent, but the 1958 level was very depressed and the rise in 1959 simply raised the savings ratio to the highest level previously attained in the post-war period (i.e. 15.5 per cent in 1953).

3. By foreign disinvestment here we mean the total net capital inflow both on private account and through changes in official reserves. It is therefore equal to the current balance of payments deficit.

4. The balance of payments deficit in constant prices is here measured as the difference between imports and exports deflated, respectively, by import and export price indices. As is shown in Chapter 10, a different picture emerges if the balance of payments in current values is directly deflated by some appropriate price index.

5. It may be noted that even if exports of the Shannon Industrial Estate were included gross in the visible export category, the conclusion would still hold that the chief contrast in the growth rates as between the two periods was in regard to invisible, rather than visible, exports.

6. It might be objected that the growth rate of visible exports from 1949 to 1961 is inflated by the rapid rates of growth that occurred in 1960 and 1961, and that the growth rates in these two years mark the beginning of a longer-term rise in the growth of visible exports. However, it should be noted that the rapid growth rates in 1960 and 1961 followed two years in which visible exports were stagnant or declining, and that the growth rate from 1961 to 1968 was not significantly higher than from 1949 to 1957.

7. Thus the contrast in the growth of invisibles in the earlier years compared with later years is even more pronounced if account is taken of the fact that the longer-term change in the growth of invisibles seems to have taken place from about 1957. The average annual growth rate of volume of invisibles from 1949 to 1957 was −1.9 per cent as against 5.5 per cent from 1957 to 1968. The comparable figures for volume of visible exports are 6.8 per cent and 7.4 per cent respectively.

8. Baker (1969, II); Baker and Durkan (1969, I), (1969, II) and (1970, I); Leser (1963, I) and (1967); and McAleese (1970).

9. Although the figures are not shown here, the same holds true for invisibles, the category of Irish exports whose performance improved most.

Chapter 3

1. The term 'net capital inflow' is defined here as the difference between the change in external reserves and the current account balance. It would be appropriate in the present context to exclude 'hot moneys' from net capital inflow, since they have only a temporary and highly unstable influence on reserves, but no data are available in Ireland for making this distinction.

2. Like Geary and Pratschke (1968) we regard the price deflator of gross domestic expenditure (G D E) as the most suitable comprehensive internal price index. As pointed out by Geary and Pratschke, the price of G D E varies very closely with the price deflator of G N P including the 'external trading gain' (i.e. an estimate of the real gain or loss due to changes in the terms of trade). This is not surprising as the latter differs from the former only in that it includes the balance of payments directly deflated by some appropriate price (such as the export or import price): since the balance of payments represents only a small proportion of G N P, the price of G N P (including the external trading gain) is bound to move in very close correspondence with the G D E price unless the balance of payments price deflator moves radically differently from the G D E price, and ordinarily this would not be so. No such correspondence is to be expected between the price of G D E and the price of G N P (as ordinarily used, i.e. not counting the trading gain) since the volume of G N P in that case involves separate deflation of exports and imports and results in an implied price of the balance of payments deficit (or surplus) that can fluctuate violently. This can also lead to the position where the average rate of change of the G N P deflator is greater than the average rate of change for any of its components. From Table 17 we can see that this was so for 1961–68.

3. The correlation (r) between the annual percentage changes in the two price indices is 0.80 in the period 1949–61, 0.84 in the period 1961–68, and 0.79 over the whole period 1949–68. All of these coefficients are significant at the 5 per cent level at least. This correlation is not due simply to a tendency for prices generally to change in line with each other; for example, the correlation between the annual percentage changes in the consumer price index and the export price index was only 0.37 in the period 1949–61 and 0.57 in the period 1961–68, neither of which is significant.

4. This may be seen from the figures for the mean deviation in Table 18. Alternatively, in terms of the standard deviation of the annual percentage changes, the variation in the agricultural price index was 4.9 and 4.4 in the first and second periods respectively, and the variation in the export price index was 4.6 and 2.5 in the first and second periods respectively.

5. Agricultural exports (taken here as food and live animals, i.e. Section 0 of the U N Standard International Trade Classification) amounted to 77 per cent of domestic merchandise exports in 1950, and by 1968 had fallen to 51 per cent. On the other hand, manufactured exports (i.e. Sections 5–8 of the U N Classification) rose from 6 per cent in 1950 to 33 per cent in 1968.

Chapter 4

1. Maizels (1970), 222. For similar evidence, see also Shinohara (1962), 44–6.
2. Over the long run, the position might be different if, for example, government spending were devoted to the provision of increased export capacity.
3. See also Beckerman (1962) and (1966).
4. It is generally overlooked that most of the qualifications to the export-led growth theory discussed here were noted by Beckerman himself who applies the theory only to 'fairly advanced economies where foreign trade is a large item in total output', Beckerman (1965), 56 n.
5. For a more detailed discussion of these issues, see Hultman (1967).
6. It should be noted, however, that the fact that the growth rates of output and productivity are highly correlated does not ensure that there will be a strong correlation between export growth and productivity growth (as is required by the export-led growth model), even if there is some correlation between output growth and export growth. The data in Worswick (1970) relating to cross-sections of individual industries in the same country, and to cross-sections for the same industry in different countries, show that while there is a good deal of evidence for the productivity-output correlation, there is less general support for the output-exports correlation, and scarcely any evidence of a correlation between export growth and productivity growth (*op. cit.*, 76–7). However, in the same paper, for data on the growth rates of total G N P per worker and total volume of exports in thirteen developed countries in two post-war periods (1950–62 and 1962–68) the correlation coefficients emerge, on our calculations, as highly significant, viz. 0.86 and 0.80 respectively (*op. cit.*, 74).
7. For a review of this evidence, see Kennedy (1971, I), Chapter 4.
8. See, for example, Kaldor (1966), Kennedy (1969) and Maizels (1970), Chapter 5, Section 5. There is little evidence available on the question whether in the same industry or country over different, reasonably long time periods, the rates of growth of output and productivity are highly correlated. This issue is discussed in Kennedy (1971, I), Chapter 7. However, the cross-

section evidence across countries is more relevant in explaining relative growth performance in different countries in the same time period.

9. This is the view taken by the export-led growth theorists, and also by Kennedy (1971, I) in relation to the correlation across individual industries in the same country. For an opposing view, see Caves (1968) and (1970).

10. On this, see Kennedy (1971, I), Chapter 5, and evidence for different countries cited therein.

11. For evidence on these issues, see Kennedy (1969) and Maizels (1970).

12. See, for example, Üstünel (1972) and Maizels (1970), Chapter 8.

13. Üstünel (1972), 6.

14. Maizels (1970), 222.

15. *Op. cit.,* 21.

16. Burenstam-Linder (1961), 88.

17. See, for example, Henry (1970) and Cooper, Hartley and Harvey (1970), both of which review previous studies as well as providing new evidence.

Chapter 5

1. There is a slight difference between the terms 'merchandise' and 'visible' exports: the latter represents merchandise exports corrected in certain minor ways for balance of payments purposes.

2. As indicated in Chapter 2, these figures include the exports of the Shannon Industrial Estate on a net basis (i.e. exports less imports). If Shannon exports were included on a gross basis, the average annual growth rate of visible exports in current values would be 9.2 per cent from 1949 to 1961 and 10.9 per cent from 1961 to 1968. The corresponding volume figures would be 7.5 per cent and 8.2 per cent respectively. There is considerable justification for treating Shannon exports as rather different from other visible exports, because (a) its determinants may be different, (b) we do not have details of the components or the destination of Shannon exports, and (c) there is a suspicion that a proportion of the exports represents re-exports following minimal processing of imports, though this is not true of all Shannon trade.

3. There was a negative, though non-significant, correlation (r = −0.26) between the annual percentage changes in price and volume for 1949–61, while there was virtually no correlation of price and volume changes (r = 0.07) for the second period.

4. See Maizels (1965), 421.

5. If, however, we include the Shannon Industrial Estate and assume that all of Shannon exports are manufactures, the average annual growth rates from 1950 to 1961 and from 1961 to 1968 are 20.5 per cent and 23.4 per cent respectively.

6. See Kuznets (1968), 406–10.
7. Henry (1972), using input-output data, has estimated the import content of various categories of final demand in 1964 and 1968. For manufactured exports (excluding food, drink and tobacco), the import content in these years was 47.5 per cent and 53.3 per cent respectively; for manufactured food exports, 25.2 per cent and 25.7 per cent respectively; and for non-manufactured agricultural exports (livestock and crops), 11.7 per cent and 10.1 per cent respectively. It should be noted that it is not possible to distinguish, beyond the level of disaggregation in the input-output table, such differences as may exist between the import content of an industry's exports and the import content of its output going to other categories of final demand. In some manufacturing industries there are reasons for expecting the import content of exports to be higher than that of domestic sales; to the extent that this was so, the import content of total manufactured exports may be somewhat understated in the above figures.
8. Under the scheme, which was aimed at increasing beef production, a subsidy of £15 was paid for each additional calved heifer introduced into cow herds. The scheme was terminated in June 1969 and replaced by a beef cattle incentive scheme designed to expand beef production without at the same time encouraging commercial milk production.
9. For a wider discussion of subsidies on dairy exports, see O'Connor (1970).
10. FitzGerald (1968), 11.

Chapter 6

1. The adjusted figures for output were derived as follows. A volume index for output in manufacturing (excluding the food and drink and tobacco groups) was compiled by weighting the published volume indices for the eight remaining manufacturing groups using the net output weights of 1953. In comparing exports with output, the official figure for aggregate gross output is inappropriate since it includes a certain amount of double-counting due to sales within or between the manufacturing groups. From the 1964 input-output table, we estimated that such transactions amounted to about 18 per cent of gross output in that year, the remaining 82 per cent being what we shall call gross value. This is the gross output excluding the duplication that results from double-counting and is the relevant output measure to compare with exports. We applied the 1964 ratio to 1953 gross output to obtain an estimate of 1953 gross value. The gross value figure for 1953 was multiplied by the volume index for each year yielding the volume of gross value in each year. This assumes that the relative degree of double-counting did not change during the period. To measure the volume of manufactured exports the

deflator used was the export unit value index for 'other goods', which are mainly manufactured goods. This index is, however, available only from 1953; and for the three years 1950 to 1952 the deflator used was the implied price of gross output in the manufacturing groups involved. In the manufactured exports data used here, petroleum products have been included since it is not possible to exclude them from the output data.

2. In this context, the term 'direct' refers to imported materials used in manufacturing without further processing, while 'indirect' refers to the import content of materials purchased domestically by manufacturing industries. The figures do not, of course, include expenditure on imports, direct or indirect, from incomes generated by manufacturing activity. The data are based on the 1964 and 1968 Input-Output Tables, and are taken from Henry (1972).

3. Domestic sale could rise more (less) than domestic demand if the former were gaining (losing) in relation to imports. This possibility, however, was not of sufficient consequence in the periods discussed here to affect the argument.

4. Baker (1969, I) using quarterly data carried out an interesting analysis of Irish manufactured exports to the U K over the period 1963 to 1968. He found 'that the Irish share of U K imports of manufactured goods is growing slowly over time', but that 'this secular movement is greatly outweighed by the importance of fluctuations in the growth of total U K manufactured imports'. He concluded that although specific events, such as the Anglo-Irish Free Trade Area Agreement, might have a significant impact, the most important factor determining the level of Irish manufactured exports to the U K is the U K level of total manufactured imports.

5. These figures all exclude Shannon.

6. As pointed out in Baker (1969, I), these export and import figures are not quite compatible, since exports are valued f o b, while imports are valued c i f. The Irish share in all years is therefore somewhat understated.

7. See Lamfalussy (1963).

8. Baker (1969, I) argued that, in so far as the Irish share of the U K market is affected by changes in relative unit wage cost, it is mainly changes in Irish wage cost relative to exporting countries, other than the U K, that is relevant, since changes in U K wage cost relative to the rest of the world are reflected in the level of U K imports. However, this need not always hold. If Irish unit wage costs fall relative to other foreign suppliers of the U K market, its share of U K imports will rise, but not as much as when its unit wage cost has at the same time fallen relative to the U K.

9. Evidence supporting this statement is summarised in Kennedy (1969) and (1971, I).

10. Of course, manufactures of food and drink are also exported in substantial quantities. But many of the major items (e.g. dead meat and dairy produce) are exported under conditions very different from those applying to manufactured exports proper. Unit wage cost in the manufacture of Ireland's most important food exports plays a negligible role in determining the volume of such exports because of (a) the market conditions involved and the special quota, subsidy, etc. arrangements that apply, and (b) the fact that manufacturing value added, let alone wage cost, is a very minor proportion of the value of output of such goods.

11. In a recent study, Hughes (1971) found that productivity growth in 'export-oriented' industries (i.e. those where exports amounted to one-third or more of domestic output) exceeded productivity growth in 'sheltered' industries (i.e. those were exports or competing imports were less than one-third of domestic output). However, he found that productivity growth in 'import-competing' industries (i.e. those that have a low ratio of exports to domestic output but a high ratio of competing imports to domestic production) exceeded that of both export-oriented and sheltered industries. This does not reject our hypothesis, since practically all of the differences in productivity growth could be explained by differences in output growth. It does, however, suggest that it would be wrong to see a necessary association of exports of manufactured goods with industries experiencing relatively rapid productivity growth rates.

12. From 1963–67, before the price of manufacturing output was affected by increased prices of imported materials as a result of devaluation, the export price of manufactures rose by 13.0 per cent. In the same period, unit wage cost in manufacturing industry as a whole rose by 15.4 per cent, compared with a rise of 13.3 per cent in unit wage cost in manufacturing industry excluding food, drink and tobacco.

13. If the profit mark-up for exports was 10 per cent and the effective tax rate was 50 per cent, then abolition of the tax on exports would reduce export prices by $4\frac{1}{2}$ per cent *if* the after-tax profit margin was held constant. However, exporters may have used part of the tax relief to increase after-tax margins.

14. However, this relative improvement occurred due to the devaluation of November 1967, which would affect only 1968 exports, whereas the Irish shares were rising before 1968. This suggests that factors other than relative price changes were also important.

15. McAleese and Martin (1973) estimated that the effect of the A I F T A A on manufactured exports amounted to about £2 million per annum on average for the years 1969–70.

16. See Donaldson (1966) and *Survey of Grant-Aided Industry* (1967).

17. It is arguable, however, that the dominant emphasis on exports,

which was important at the time, involved some neglect of the scope for development of production for the home market, a factor which is likely to assume greater significance as trade barriers disappear.

18. *Survey of Grant-Aided Industry* (1967), 45, Table 2.13. The projects included those established by Irish firms as well as by foreign firms. Some of the projects were undertaken by firms already engaged in manufacturing production in Ireland. The figures given relate to manufacturing industry excluding food, drink and tobacco.

19. The figure is deduced from Tables 2.2, 2.3 and 2.13 of the *Survey of Grant-Aided Industry* (1967).

Chapter 7

1. The figures are shown on arithmetic, rather than logarithmic, scale because it is easier to combine the different series in one chart on the arithmetic scale.

2. For an extensive discussion of the Irish cattle trade with the U K, see the *Report of the Store Cattle Study Group* (1968), and Foster (1971). Ireland's entry into the E E C on 1 January 1973 has substantially changed the marketing situation for the future, as is discussed later in Part V.

3. On the one hand, export values tend to be higher because exports are valued f o b, and therefore beef exports, for example, would include the value added in processing. On the other hand, the farm price figures include certain subsidy payments (e.g. under the Bovine Tuberculosis and Brucellosis Eradication Schemes and under the 1965 Anglo-Irish Free Trade Area Agreement) that do not enter into export prices. On balance, the value of exports in the external trade figures tends to be slightly higher. For example, in 1968 exports at farm prices were valued at £85.9 million, whereas in the external trade figures the value of exports of live cattle, beef, edible cattle offals and undressed cattle hides amounted to £88.9 million.

4. The correlation for 1949–68 is negative (-0.33) but not significant. Neither are changes in net exports significantly correlated with changes in output in the previous year ($r = -0.24$). However, it is interesting to note that there is a significant *positive* correlation (0.57) between changes in net exports and in output lagged by two years. Indeed, this relationship is suggested in Chart 10, in which it may be seen that peaks in export volume generally tend to follow peaks in output volume two years earlier.

Chapter 8

1. Even by 1968 the volume of tourist receipts was still about 4 per cent below the 1948 peak. The figures for 1947 and 1948 are, however, somewhat conjectural.

2. For a discussion on the reliability of balance of payments data, see note 5 of this chapter.

3. In defence of the procedure, however, it may be remarked that Geary, in a comment on Whitaker's paper, noted with satisfaction that Whitaker's estimate of £275 million for net external holdings in 1947 tallied closely with 'the sum of an independently estimated pre-war figure of about £150 million plus a net war-time accrual of £130 million (as shown by the Balance of Payments)', *ibid.*, 215.

4. Of course, devaluation would not reduce the foreign liability in terms of non-sterling currencies in the case of foreign investment in Ireland, where such liabilities were guaranteed in gold or non-sterling currencies. Indeed, in such instances the sterling liability of the nation would be increased by devaluation.

5. The explanation might also lie in the possibility that the net capital inflow is overstated in the official statistics, a view held by some Irish economists. Correspondingly, this school of thought holds that exports of certain services which are difficult to measure (e.g. tourism and emigrants' remittances) are understated. We have no way of establishing the significance of this view. However, if a substantial part of what is regarded as net capital inflow is, indeed, an unidentified current export, this would have consequences for the whole set of national accounts. Not only would the balance of payments table need to be revised, but also the data for national income, expenditure, savings, etc. While not denying that there may be a degree of inaccuracy in the capital inflow figures, we must rely on the official statistics unless and until more definite information is available in support of the view mentioned.

6. It is understood that the C S O has already been giving thought to the adoption of this procedure, which is recommended by the I M F. However, it would seem desirable that such a change should be made in the context of a thorough investigation of the accuracy of the data for invisible exports, which, as mentioned in the preceding note, are considered by some to be underestimated.

7. It should be noted that in discussing tourist revenue we do not include fares received by Irish transport companies for carrying visitors to and from Ireland. In 1968 such receipts amounted to £17.3 million compared with £75.7 million spent by the visitors within the country. See Bord Fáilte Éireann, *Report for the Year ended March 1969.*

8. Bord Fáilte Éireann *Annual Report and Accounts for the Year ended 31st March 1956.*

9. p. 195. We may note that, while we see the force of Professor Lynch's stricture on the use of hindsight, it is surely on the intelligent use of hindsight that we must rely most to improve foresight.

10. See Dowling (1970).
11. The C S O warning about the figures should, however, be noted: 'Classification by reason for journey cannot be considered exact and depends on the interpretation of the various terms by the persons completing the tourist card. This is particularly the case in regard to the distinction between "tourist" and "visit to relatives".' *Irish Statistical Bulletin* (Mar. 1968), 16. See also O'Hagan (1972).

Chapter 9

1. The direct and indirect import content of tourism was about 25 per cent in 1964 and 1968 (Henry (1972)).

Chapter 10

1. Changes in the consumption price may also differ from changes in the G N P price due to differences in the consumption and investment price changes. In practice, however, this does not account for much of the discrepancy. Given that the investment share in G N P is only about one-fourth of the consumption share, increases in the investment price, though generally slightly lower, have not differed so much from increases in the consumption price as to involve a significant divergence between the G N P and consumption prices.
2. This is not to deny that if the price of exports had not risen, the volume of exports might have increased so much as to yield even larger gains. But here we are interested in the correct measurement and analysis of what actually occurred.
3. More generally, the trading gain using the import deflator is given by:

$$X \left(\frac{1}{P_m} - \frac{1}{P_x} \right)$$

where X is the value of exports in year 2 and P_x and P_m are the export and import price indices, respectively, to base year $1 = 1.00$. Using the export deflator, the trading gain is given by:

$$M \left(\frac{1}{P_m} - \frac{1}{P_x} \right)$$

where M is the value of imports in year 2. Geary and Pratschke (1968) have shown that, as in the example above, the size of the external trading gain usually amounts to much the same whichever method is used.
4. It may be mentioned that the concept has not achieved as much

prominence in Irish economic discussion as it deserves. This is so despite the pioneering work of Geary (see Geary (1961) and Geary and Pratschke (1968)) in devising ways of measuring the trading gain and in drawing attention to its magnitude in the Irish context, and despite the fact that the C S O publishes each year a measure of the external trading gain (loss).

5. We are concerned here with the terms of trade between total exports and total imports, and not simply the terms of merchandise trade. In Ireland the overall terms of trade can improve (disimprove) even if there is no change in the terms of trade for either traded goods or traded services, provided the price of services rises more (less) than the price of goods. This is so because exports of services as a share of total exports are far higher than imports of services as a share of total imports. It must be emphasised that such a change in the overall terms of trade is not spurious or a mere statistical peculiarity, provided, of course, the price deflators are satisfactory.

6. The actual size of the external trading gain (loss) in both periods could be substantially altered by taking a base year other than 1958, but the *difference* between the two periods, on which our interest centres here, would not be substantially affected by choice of an alternative base.

7. In making this point about the effect of movements in the terms of trade, we do not wish to convey the impression that the more favourable position in the second period was necessarily entirely accidental and uninfluenced by policy measures. For example, the negotiation of more favourable arrangements for the export marketing of agricultural produce is clearly a way in which policy measures can influence movements in the terms of trade.

8. Revenue and expenditure are classified according to national accounting conventions which differ in important respects from the traditional *Finance Accounts* and *Local Taxation Returns.*

9. Kennedy and Dowling (1970).

10. A selection of thirty-two of the equations is given in Kennedy and Dowling (1970). The equation given here corresponds to Equation 32 in the original paper except that it has been revised in the light of the 1969 *National Income and Expenditure.*

11. For a general discussion of the effect on saving of direct and indirect taxes, see Kaldor (1955).

12. If the dependency ratio rises with income *per capita* held constant, then average income per household must rise. However, reduced saving in households with extra dependants would be likely to outweigh increased saving in households with no increase in dependants.

13. In fact, when the price of agricultural exports rises, the price of agricultural produce consumed at home also tends to rise, thus making for an improvement also in the terms of trade of the agricultural sector *vis-à-vis* the non-agricultural sector.

14. The correlation between changes in manufacturing investment and in company savings in the same year is rather lower (0.52). The relationship is not evident from about 1960 on and the correlation for the nineteen first differences from 1947–48 to 1967–68 is only 0.20, not significant at the 5 per cent level. This is not a surprising finding. The resources available for investment by a company include depreciation and state grants as well as retained earnings. The tax concessions for wear-and-tear allowances were markedly improved at the end of the 1950s and grants for investment purposes were extended. Thus a company planning a particular investment project would have had to rely relatively less for finance on retained earnings.

Chapter 11

1. In this chapter 'investment' refers to fixed investment.
2. Henry (1972).
3. It would also increase imports, with the possibility of balance of payments difficulties—an issue which we consider later.
4. Because of the large increases in building investment in 1950 and 1951, the use of beginning and end year figures may be inappropriate to measure the growth rate over the period 1949–61. However, we have checked that, even on the basis of trend growth rates (using the figures for all years), building expanded more rapidly from 1961 to 1968 than in the period 1949–61, or for that matter, in the earlier sub-period (1949–55) preceding the major cut-back.
5.

$$\frac{I}{\Delta Y} = \frac{I}{Y} \Big/ \frac{\Delta Y}{Y}$$

where I is investment, Y is output and ΔY is the change in output.
6. Analogously, labour productivity is measured as the ratio of output to labour input, without presuming that labour is, in fact, the sole or the main factor determining the level of output.
7. It may be noted that if the period 1949–61 is divided, as in Chapter 1, into the sub-periods 1949–55 and 1955–61, the G I C O R in these sub-periods was rather similar—8.4 for 1949–55 and 7.4 for 1955–61.
8. The balance of the rise in the growth rate, 0.33 per cent (i.e. 2.19—(0.45 + 1.41)), might be called an interrelations effect, showing the residual effect of combined changes in the investment ratio and the G I C O R.
9. The argument is based on Lamfalussy (1963).
10. The depreciated value will—or at least should—tend to reflect the likely remaining economic life of an asset.
11. Indeed, the faster growth of output may lower the ratio of

replacement to output, so that the rise in the net investment ratio would be absolutely, as well as proportionately, greater than the rise in the gross investment ratio.

12. An example may help to illustrate the foregoing point. Suppose that during 1949–61, when the gross investment ratio was 14.8 per cent, about one-third of this, say 5 per cent of G N P, was devoted to replacement of retired assets. It can then be shown that the net I C O R in this first period would be 5.5. Assuming the same net I C O R during 1961–68, and that 5 per cent of G N P continued to be devoted to replacement, the G I C O R in this period would be 7.2 as against 7.8 in the first period. The effect would be reduced if the average length of life of assets fell, while it would be increased if the share of G N P devoted to replacement fell.

13. It should be stressed that this is not the same as changes in the utilisation of capacity due to short-term fluctuations in output. Because of the indivisibilities involved in the construction of infrastructural capital, scope for greater utilisation of such capacity may persist for a long time.

14. In calculating the G I C O R for dwellings, the gross domestic product of dwellings is taken in the usual sense as the value of rent (actual and imputed) plus depreciation. If the G I C O R of 46 for dwellings in Ireland seems very large, it may at least be noted that it compares closely with a G I C O R of 48.5 for the U K in the period 1958–67 (calculated from U N *National Accounts Statistics 1968*, Tables 2 and 5 relating to the U K). In the U S A, however, the G I C O R in dwellings, calculated from the same source and for the same period, was 11, a figure that appears much more realistic. It is difficult to believe that such a vast difference exists in the relation between output and investment in housing in the U S A compared with Ireland or the U K. It is important to note that we are dealing with the factor cost product of housing. Thus a greater degree of rent subsidy in Ireland (or the U K) relative to the U S A should not in principle make any difference in measurement, since the subsidies should be added back to the market price rent to arrive at factor cost. It is true that a greater degree of rent *control,* as distinct from *subsidy,* in Ireland would tend to lower the factor cost value of output, but rent control is hardly on so great a scale in Ireland as to make for so substantial a difference in the G I C O Rs. There are other factors that might partly explain the small increase in product relative to investment in Ireland. However, given that the investment figures are reasonably reliable, the enormously high G I C O R suggests that the authorities might consider whether the product figures are not seriously underestimated in the national accounts. If so, this raises an interesting question. If the product of housing increased more than the present statistics show, the measured growth rate of G N P would be somewhat

higher, especially in the period of relatively high investment in housing from 1949 to 1955. Housing would be seen as contributing more significantly to growth. Would it then be accorded a higher priority from an economic, as distinct from a social, viewpoint?

15. If, in fact, the G I C O Rs in the first period were 46.0 and 10.1 for dwellings and the rest of services respectively, then the change in investment shares alone would have reduced the G I C O R for services as a whole by 1.0, compared with the actual reduction of 5.8.

16.

$$\frac{I}{L} \Big/ \Delta \left(\frac{Y}{L}\right) = \frac{I}{Y} \Big/ \frac{\Delta(Y/L)}{Y/L}$$

where I is investment, L is numbers employed, Y is output and $\triangle$ is the change.

17. As stressed earlier, this statement does not imply that investment is the sole factor raising output or labour productivity. Differences in the productivity of investment may be accounted for by such factors as the rate of technological progress, the degree of utilisation of capacity, etc.

18. See Lamfalussy (1963), 89.

19. At the time, the cut-back in the volume of social overhead investment was also defended on the grounds that it led to an excessive drain on external reserves. This is a separate argument which is examined further in Part IV.

Chapter 12

1. The ratio of public current spending (including transfers) to G N P was 26 per cent in 1947 and 35 per cent in 1968. For most of the post-war period, public capital expenditure (including that of state-sponsored bodies) accounted for well over half of total fixed investment.

2. The direct and indirect import content of public authorities' current expenditure on goods and services is only about 7 per cent. (Henry (1972).) A high proportion of public capital expenditure was devoted to building and construction, which, as we showed earlier, also has a relatively low import content.

3. Since the figures in Chart 18 are included before deduction of depreciation, the current surplus (deficit) is equivalent to gross savings (dissavings) of the public authorities.

4. The figures presented in Chart 18 include an adjustment to the public authorities account as presented in *National Income and Expenditure* in order to make the data more relevant to consideration of the impact of fiscal policy on demand. We have excluded from capital expenditure (and, by implication, from the

overall deficit) government capital payments abroad under the Bretton Woods Agreement Act 1957 and the International Development Association Act 1960. These payments are financed by the Central Bank in a way that secures that such expenditure and borrowing have no impact on the domestic economy. There would also be a case for excluding redemption of securities from capital expenditure, since borrowing for this purpose is likely to have considerably less expansionary effects than borrowing for other forms of public expenditure. While we have not made this adjustment in the chart, we do make it in the text where the figures for redemptions vary considerably from one year to the next.

5. We use 'deficit' here rather than 'deficit or surplus' since at no time from 1947 to the present was there an overall surplus. Thus one might say that, taking the post-war period as a whole, fiscal policy was expansionary throughout. However, in considering the position in any one year, the expansionary or deflationary nature of fiscal policy is best judged by comparing the position with the previous year, since, for example, a reduction in an overall deficit will have much the same deflationary effect as an equivalent rise in an overall surplus.

6. See, for example, Ryan (1972).

7. Although the reserve level of the banks in Ireland was not determined by Central Bank operations, it is true that if the banks' liquidity ratio was sufficiently flexible downwards to meet government borrowing requirements, the expansionary effect of increased borrowing would be similar to that generated by financing a deficit by increasing bank reserves. A deficit wholly financed by bank borrowing would thus be more expansionary than a deficit wholly financed by sales of long-term debt to the non-bank public, although both would tend to stimulate aggregate demand. It is interesting to note that the conflicting views on the expansionary effect of an increased government deficit correspond (albeit against a quite different institutional background) quite closely with the views held by 'monetarists' and 'fiscalists' in the macroeconomic debate current in the USA. The belief in the primacy of bank borrowing would correspond roughly to the monetarist position, while the approach adopted here is similar to that advanced by the fiscalists.

8. The figures in the chart are given in current values, since there is no unique deflator for many of the components. Where the matter is of consequence, however, we give in the text an estimate of the order of magnitude of volume changes.

9. A fuller description of the more important differences between the two classifications is given in *National Income and Expenditure 1963*, 21–2.

10. Since 1971 a national accounts classification of central government expenditure and receipts has been published in connection with

the budget. The figures give the estimated outturn for the previous year and the projections for the current year.

11. Acceptance of the idea of planned imbalance in the current budget came only in 1972 when a deficit of £35 million was planned. This was on the basis of the traditional accounting system. On a national accounts basis, it was equivalent to a planned *surplus* of £14 million *(Budget 1972)*.

12. Of course, as explained in the text of Chapter 12, the obsession with the current account balance, rather than the overall balance on current and capital account, was itself misplaced from a demand management viewpoint.

13. The local authorities' current budgets are fixed separately by each local authority and the details are generally not available to the central government at the time the central government budget is formulated. Considerations of demand management do not enter directly into the setting of their budgets by the local authorities. Such considerations do, however, enter indirectly since a large proportion of the local authorities' expenditure is financed by the central government.

Chapter 13

1. All unemployment rates quoted are from Geary and Hughes (1970).

2. Although a complete public capital budget was first given only in the 1950 budget speech, this simply formalised what had been happening in the previous years.

3. In deriving the seasonal correction factors used in this and other charts in these chapters, the method adopted was that of ratio to moving average. For successive five-year periods the mean ratios to moving annual average for each quarter were calculated and applied as correction factors to the middle year of each period. For the two final years 1967 and 1968 the mean ratios for the five years 1964 to 1968 were used.

4. Admittedly, the reverse would be true of invisibles, where exports far outweighed imports. But prices of invisibles did not rise nearly so much at this time.

5. The fact that the devaluation had adverse effects on the Irish economy does not mean that matters would have been better had Ireland not devalued in response to the sterling devaluation. The Minister for Finance, in his speech on the subject, recognised that Ireland would suffer as a result of the U K devaluation and he regarded the government's decision to follow suit as merely 'the course of least disadvantage'. It may be noted that, prior to legislation passed in 1971, the minister was legally bound to maintain parity with sterling; but, of course, had the government decided otherwise, the law on the matter could have been quickly amended.

6. See Dow (1964), 55–6.
7. We also show in Chart 21 data on money supply each year from 1947 to 1968.
8. Part of the fall in the second quarter of 1952 may have been due to the budget measures introduced on 2 April 1952, but even in the first quarter of 1952 the deficit was down to £24.4 million.
9. By 1947 the volume of output in transportable goods as a whole had recovered from the wartime decline and was 16 per cent above the highest pre-war level. However, in several individual industries the volume of output in 1947 was below the immediate pre-war levels, so that part of the rapid overall growth in the years after 1947 was made up of recovery in these industries. But such industries were by no means the only ones that experienced rapid growth at this time.

Chapter 14

1. Only more than a decade later, as a result of the work of Leser (1965, I) and Baker and Durkan in the E S R I *Quarterly Economic Commentary,* did the use of seasonally corrected data become general practice in evaluating short-term economic trends.
2. In the 1952 budget speech the Minister for Finance stated: 'We shall rely on our own people to provide by their industry and thrift the capital necessary to build up the nation.' *Dáil Debates* (2 Apr. 1952), 1154.
3. *Dáil Debates* (6 May 1953), 1198.
4. The fiscal accounting system may have played some part in the decision. For example, in the 1953 budget the minister made much of the fact that the outturn on the current budget for the previous year involved, despite the deflationary measures taken, a deficit on current account of £2 million. In national accounts terms, there was, in fact, a current surplus in the central government account of £2 million. Moreover, no reference was made to the possible effects of deflationary policies on the size of the current fiscal balance resulting from the impact of the budget on the economy.
5. Though Chart 18 suggests that fiscal policy was deflationary in 1955 in that the value of public capital expenditure and the borrowing requirement both fell, this must be qualified. The capital and borrowing figures are affected by the fact that in 1955 the Electricity Supply Board (E S B) borrowed £10 million directly from the public. Prior to then, the E S B had relied on the government for capital. If the E S B had continued to borrow directly from the government in 1955, the public authorities' capital expenditure figures would have been £10 million greater. Since the Public Capital Programme for 1955 undoubtedly took this change in borrowing patterns into account, it would appear more reasonable to add the £10 million back onto the capital

expenditure and borrowing requirements figures for 1955, as in Table 41. The figures in parentheses in Table 41 include the E S B borrowing. Thus the borrowing figures for 1955 comparable with the figure of £30.6 million in 1954 is really £35.7 million.

6. The Central Bank in its reports, while deploring the excessive credit creation, evidently did not feel that it had the function or the power of limiting the volume and composition of credit creation. It was only following another balance of payments crisis in 1965, again partly associated with substantial credit creation, that the Central Bank began to take responsibility for controlling credit.

7. The fifth of the post-war wage rounds took place in 1955 following two years in which there was no general adjustment in wage rates.

8. This was not known at the time since data on non-agricultural stocks only become available annually about a year after the date to which they refer. The absence of up-to-date quarterly figures on stock changes was, and continues to be, a serious handicap in assessing short-term economic trends.

9. Under trade agreements, tariffs were generally applied at a preferential rate in respect of imports from the U K and Commonwealth countries.

10. Walsh (1968).

11. Another, probably less important, reason was the adverse picture of the government current account balance as shown by the traditional accounting practices compared with that shown by the national accounts classification. The following figures show the surplus (+) or deficit (−) on central government current account (£m) for the years 1955 to 1958.

	1955	1956	1957	1958
Government accounting method	+0.3	−6.0	−5.9	+0.2
National accounts classification	+2.6	+2.5	+5.9	+9.2

12. It may be noted in connection with the improvement in the Irish net capital inflow in 1958 that all resrictions on bank lending in the U K were removed in July 1958 and the capital issues control was eased. See *Report of the Committee on the Working of the Monetary System* (Radcliffe Report), (London: H M S O, Cmnd 827, 1959), 142 ff.

13. A further possibility is that the initiation of the I R A border campaign in December 1956 may have affected the confidence of investors and hindered recovery in the capital inflow.

14. This study was begun in the Department of Finance in 1957 and completed in May 1958. It was published in November 1958.

15. The fact that the actual amount of social investment in 1958 was considerably less than envisaged in *Economic Development*

(published in November 1958) suggests that the actual cut-back in social investment in 1958 was much more radical than intended.

16. *Dáil Debates* (8 May 1956), 30.

17. In this context, the employment criterion of investment (i.e. the degree of employment created by an investment), so beloved by Irish politicians, may be more sensible economically than the experts have allowed.

Chapter 15

1. The interested reader is referred in particular to the following publications: Kuehn (1961) and (1962); Leser (1963, II), (1964) and (1965, II); the staff of the E S R I (1966) and (1967); Baker (later Baker and Durkan), *Quarterly Economic Commentary,* September 1968 and subsequent issues; *Second Programme for Economic Expansion*; *Second Programme: Review of Progress 1964–67*; *N I E C Report on Economic Situation* (1965); Department of Finance, *Annual Review and Outlook*; the greatly expanded *Quarterly Bulletin* and *Annual Report* of the Central Bank; and the O E C D annual *Economic Survey: Ireland.*

2. Paradoxically, another factor aiding recovery in manufacturing production was the setting-up of some new industries under the protective umbrella of the Special Import Levies. As mentioned earlier, these levies were introduced in 1956 on short-term balance of payments grounds, they were not intended as protective instruments, and their immediate impact on industrial production was highly unfavourable. The levies were sufficiently high, however, and lasted sufficiently long, to encourage establishment of some new import-substituting industries. In such cases the levies were subsequently converted to protective tariffs to maintain protection for the firms involved.

3. It is also possible that the large current budget deficit of £8 million that emerged in the government accounts in 1965 on the traditional accounting basis led to a more restrictive policy than if the national accounts basis were in use. The contrast between the two bases of accounting in this period is considerable, as shown by the following figures (£m):

Current Surplus (+) *or Deficit* (−)
on Central Government Account

	1964	1965	1966
Government accounting basis	−4.1	−7.8	+0.8
National accounts basis	+8.9	+8.4	+20.5

Of course, the use of a different method of accounting would not alter the fact that, had the current budget deficit of £8 million in 1965 (on the traditional accounting basis) not been covered by current revenue, it would have had to be met by increased borrowing. Nevertheless, given that the authorities were opposed to the idea of a planned current deficit or surplus, an accounting method that put the position in an unfavourable light may have led to more restrictive action than would otherwise have been taken.

Chapter 16

1. Certainly, Irish economic history is characterised by some sudden and extreme swings in policy that might indicate that this is the only way that major changes can be effected in Ireland. For an interesting discussion of Irish economic policy since independence, see Meenan (1970). The most notable example in the period since independence is the switch to protection in the 1930s. During the 1920s, in spite of public pronouncements in favour of selective protection, the level of protection was very low. With the new Fianna Fáil government in 1932, there was an immediate swing to a policy of widespread protection. Most economists would probably agree now that this was introduced too quickly and on too wide a scale, and that a somewhat more gradual and selective approach would have served better. But defenders of the policy might reply with some justice that a gradual approach would result in nothing at all being done and that it was better to go too far, as in the 1930s, than to do little or nothing in this respect, as in the 1920s. They could argue further that only because of the Economic War and the revival of conflict with Britain was it possible to get the community as a whole and the farming community in particular to accept any such radical change; and that, therefore, the only way of pushing the change through was to do it as quickly as possible.

2. In some cases, though, problems were solved by default rather than by positive action. It was, for example, relatively easier to increase total employment in the 1960s than in the earlier post-war phase because of the decline that had taken place in numbers employed in agriculture. Agricultural employment declined throughout the whole post-war period at a near constant long-term rate of $2\frac{1}{4}$ per cent per annum. At the beginning of the post-war period, this represented a fall of about 15,000 workers in agriculture, and an equivalent amount of new non-agricultural jobs were required to maintain the same overall level of employment. Because of the steady decline in the agricultural work force, the annual fall by 1961 was only about 10,000 workers although the *rate* of decline was unchanged. Thus the critical minimum effort required to sustain total employment was reduced by one-third. This point could be strengthened by including certain service-type activities, like private domestic service, where a secular fall in employment was almost inevitable and where the absolute size of the decline diminished as the numbers remaining contracted.

3. A present-day example may help to elucidate these points,

namely the difficulty of securing a satisfactory incomes policy. While there is a wide measure of agreement on the need for an incomes policy, there is enormous disagreement as to what form it should take, and very few feasible ideas about how it could be implemented in relation to certain categories of income (e.g. dividends).
4. FitzGerald (1968), 13.
5. Chubb and Lynch (1969), 1–2. At the time, however, some outside observers took a less dismal view of the situation than that which prevailed domestically. Replying to Professor Meenan's presidential address to the Statistical and Social Inquiry Society of Ireland in September 1957, Mrs Ursula Hicks remarked that she 'felt that Mr Meenan was perhaps a little pessimistic about the amount of development which had taken place over the last few years, and was currently taking place, in Éire in a number of ways. Re-visiting the country after a few years (and the West after nearly a decade) it seemed to her that progress had been very considerable.' She went on to instance various examples of the type of progress made and added that 'this kind of development, though small in the unit, can in the aggregate be extremely important'. *Journal of the Statistical and Social Inquiry Society of Ireland*. Vol. 20, Part I, 1957–58. And in a percipient article published in January 1958 Michael P. Fogarty, after outlining various developments he had observed during a visit, concluded as follows: 'Much of what I have described is no more than beginnings. But these beginnings, I think, have a solid foundation. There is more than mere talk; something is being done . . . Ireland, I suspect, is about to explode into a new great age of growth.' *The Commonweal* (24 Jan. 1958)

Chapter 17

1. Another factor that may have contributed to the fall in net emigration was the introduction of free secondary education in the school year 1967–68 and the resulting large increase in numbers of secondary students. This could reduce emigration in two ways. The first, a temporary factor, involved some who might have emigrated staying on at school in Ireland. Secondly, as a more permanent influence, those who stayed on might be less willing to emigrate after receiving secondary education, since they might not accept some of the traditional types of work (e.g. as builders' labourers) that many Irish emigrants accepted initially. It might be more difficult for them to find ready employment abroad consonant with their educational attainment.
2. The contrast between the two periods is even greater in regard to net invisibles (exports less imports). The volume growth rate of invisible imports rose, so that the volume of net invisibles declined by 5.4 per cent per annum from 1968 to 1972 compared with a rise of 5.3 per cent from 1961 to 1968.

M

3. Up to 1969 the net external assets of the Associated Banks were counted as part of the reserves. In that year, however, these banks transferred to the Central Bank, in exchange for domestic assets, an amount of foreign assets roughly equal to the value of their net external assets. (At the same time, other changes were made in the definition of reserves.) Since 1969, therefore, any changes in the net external assets of the Associated Banks are regarded as part of the net capital inflow or outflow.

4. Due to changes in the format of the official balance of payments statement, it is not possible to compare precisely with the figures for earlier years given in Table 16. It should also be noted that though the total private net inflow, excluding the public sector and the banks, is similar to the preceding period, the large net inflow through the Non-Associated Banks in the years 1969 to 1972 may have included substantial private direct investment.

5. In Ireland there tends to be a bunching of wage and salary increases at intervals of about $1\frac{1}{2}$–2 years which have become known as wage rounds. The rounds are numbered starting from the first such general increase immediately after the Second World War.

6. The degree of industrial unrest declined greatly in 1971 and 1972, when the number of man-days lost was 274,000 and 207,000 respectively.

7. Excess demand for labour in particular industries or occupations could, of course, push up general wage rates on the lines suggested by Schultze (1959) for the U S A and argued by Mulvey and Trevithick (1970) for Ireland. But, in principle, this form of excess demand could develop even when aggregate demand was low, though it would be less likely to happen then.

8. Baker and Neary (1971) have constructed an index of consumer prices net of indirect taxes. This shows that between November 1968 and November 1970, when the consumer price index rose by 8.8 per cent per annum, on average, the index net of indirect taxes rose by 7.4 per cent per annum.

9. For some indirect taxes levied as a fixed amount of money per unit of volume (e.g. duties on tobacco, alcohol and petrol), inflation tends to reduce government revenue as a proportion of G N P. In the case of indirect taxes levied as a percentage of value, inflation probably does not greatly influence the yield relative to G N P. The income tax yield relative to G N P, however, tends to rise strongly due to inflation since the tax rates are progressive and tax allowances have not kept pace with inflation. Overall, on balance, it is likely that a higher rate of inflation tends to push up the total revenue yield relative to G N P.

10. It remains doubtful, however, whether the secondary impact on inflation of a rise in income tax is as great as a rise in indirect

taxes yielding the same amount of revenue. The latter raises the consumer price index, and price increases have traditionally been the first peg on which pay claims are based. Pay claims have not usually been based on direct tax changes (or, at least, not overtly so. It is obviously more difficult for a trade union to so base a claim since the effect of income tax on different tax payers differs considerably. In addition, trade unions have a traditional preference for direct taxation over indirect taxation because of the generally regressive nature of the latter.

11. In explaining the rise in the scale of wage demands, as distinct from wage settlements, it may be necessary to take wider issues into account. One of the present authors has suggested the possibility that the substantial upward shift in wage demands may be an expression of profound dissatisfaction with the existing distribution of income and wealth. What could be involved is that workers, unhappy about the post-war rate of progress towards income redistribution through governmental tax and expenditure policies, had decided, consciously or not, to try to achieve more radical progress by their own direct efforts. See Kennedy (1971, II).

12. It may be noted, however, that since unit wage cost rose somewhat less in the U K than in Ireland in the 1960s up to 1968, the deterioration in the U K between the two periods was similar.

13. See *Review of 1972 and Outlook for 1973*, Appendix 2, Table (i) (pp. 101–4). The figures used here exclude food and drink and tobacco. For a full discussion of the figures, and in particular the problems of defining competing imports, see McAleese and Martin (1973), 35 ff.

14. Since we can only use a breakdown into eight manufactured groups, we may not adequately measure the effect of changes in composition, and where this is so the effect would be included in (*b*). Also, as McAleese and Martin (1973) have suggested, if the income elasticity of demand for imports is higher than for domestic production, then the ratio of imports to domestic use would rise even if there were no loss of competitiveness, whereas here it could appear in our measure of the competitive effect. However, we do not have evidence on the relative size of the two relevant income elasticities.

15. Moreover, explanation of the decline in terms of the Northern Ireland situation, rather than in terms of prices, receives further support from the fact that receipts from cross-border excursionists declined relatively more than the rest of tourist revenue from the U K.

16. This rate is, in fact, slightly lower than that which would have prevailed had Ireland maintained its 1968 share in value of total U K and U S A tourist spending.

17. In Ireland consumer booms seem to take palce at roughly four-yearly intervals, the years 1955, 1960, 1964 and 1968 all being

years of rapid growth. As suggested on pp. 219–20, this seems to be associated with the bunching of purchases of consumer durables. This semi-autonomous cycle in consumer expenditure cannot be explained solely by current income levels, and is no doubt influenced by such factors as the timing and back-dating of pay increases, credit conditions, etc.

18. Baker (1969, II).
19. Exceptionally large purchases of ships and aircraft contributed about £15 million to the rise in the deficit in 1969. These are purchased abroad and financed by foreign borrowing, and have in the short-term little impact on domestic resources and demand.
20. Baker and Durkan (1970, II).

Chapter 18

1. For more detailed discussion of these questions, see Tussing 1973) and Walsh (1974). We would not wish to go quite as far as the former, however, in diminishing the importance of supply-side measures.
2. These consist of three classes: builders' labourers, contractors' labourers (mainly roadworkers) and general labourers. In 1966, when the total unemployment rate was 6.3 per cent, their unemployment rate was 21.0 per cent compared with 4.0 per cent for all other occupational groups. See Geary and Hughes (1970).
3. These aspects of Irish industrial policy have been discussed at greater length by Cooper and Whelan (1973), who argue for a major reconsideration of industrial development strategy. The I D A claims that the position has changed in recent years towards greater emphasis on domestic value added content and on the establishment of linkages. At the time of writing, however, no data are available to support this claim for the generality of new industry.
4. *Survey of Grant-Aided Industry* (1967), 49–52.
5. For more detailed consideration of this and other aspects of Irish entrepreneurial development, see Fogarty (1974).
6. Bieda (1970).
7. McAleese (1975) has estimated that the total price and volume effect of full application of C A P in 1972 would be an extra £109 million in beef and dairy exports. The volume effect assumes full adjustment to increased prices. Since, however, it has been based on supply elasticities derived from past data when prices were much lower and much less assured, the estimate is probably a conservative one in relation to the new conditions.
8. This includes debt redemptions as well as interest. The growth rate of interest charges alone in this period was 15.6 per cent per annum.
9. In the 1974 budget, after we had gone to press, the government announced that farm incomes would be taxed in future, though

only on a very limited scale and on relatively favourable terms.

10. It should be noted, however, that the central government subsidises rates on agricultural land to the extent of nearly two-thirds of the total involved. The subsidy is at a higher percentage on small farms and a lower percentage on large farms.

11. Since we went to press, the government has issued a White Paper announcing its intention to introduce a capital gains tax and to replace death duties by wealth and inheritance taxes.

12. As well as by increasing staff, evasion can also be partly eliminated by making the system as self-enforcing as possible. For example, the tax concession given for medical expenses ensures that patients will report fees they have paid to consultants, etc.

13. See Ó Cinnéide (1972) and Hughes (1972).

14. For more detailed discussion of these issues, see Walsh (1972).

Index

Agriculture: disguised unemployment in, 16–17; employment, 11–13, 74, 332; fluctuations in, 9, 233; GICOR in, 180–2; investment in, 17, 174, 176, 177, 184–7; import content of, 87, 249; output, 5, 14, 210, 216, 231–2, 233, 257–8, 312; productivity growth in, 16, 17, 184–7. *See also* Exports, Common Agricultural Policy

AIFTAA. *See* Anglo Irish Free Trade Agreement

Anglo Irish Trade Area Agreement (AIFTAA), 58, 89, 119, 274, 287, 318, 320; and manufactured exports, 110–12, 270–1

Arrow, K. J., 251, 303

Austria: growth of exports and imports, 46; growth of GNP, 20, 21

Baker, T. J., 303, 313, 318, 329, 331, 334, 336

Balance of payments: and capital inflows, 54–5, 131, 132; crises, *1950–51*, 203–212; *1955*, 219–20; *1966*, 233; and demand, 67, 68, 202, 216, 218, 232, 235, 240–1, 246, 248, 278, 280; and devaluation, 207; fluctuations in, 35, 36, 49–50, 83, 122–4, 205; relative to GNP, 32, 35, 261; and profits remitted abroad, 77, 80; and terms of trade, 154–7

Banks: Associated, 223, 224, 262, 264; Non-Associated, 262, 334

Beckerman, W., 69, 71, 303, 315

Belgium: growth of GNP, 20

Bieda, K., 303, 336

Bord Fáilte. *See* Bord Fáilte Éireann

Bord Fáilte Éireann, 143, 144, 218, 232, 250, 321. *See also* Fógra Fáilte

Bovine Tuberculosis Eradication Scheme, 118-119, 147, 320

Bretton Woods Agreement Act (1957), 327

British Ministry of Food, 118

Broderick, J. B., 197, 303, 304, 312

Brucellosis Eradication Scheme, 320

Budgets: *1952*, 215–18; *1957*, 221–2; *1970*, 278; *1970* supplementary, 279; *1971* supplementary, 280; *1972*, 280–1. *See also* Fiscal policy, Public Capital Programme

Building and construction: and domestic demand, 187, 228–9, 279, 281, 282; import content of investment in, 171, 249; investment in, 170–2, 173, 227; output, 6. *See also* Investment, Infrastructure

Burenstam-Linder, S., 304, 316

Calved Heifer Subsidy Scheme, 89, 114, 122, 317

Canada: acceleration of inflation in, 268

CAP. *See* Common Agricultural Policy

Capital inflow, 48, 49, 51, 52, 132, 201, 213, 214, 216, 220, 223–5, 253, 314; attitude to, 49, 51, 214, 232, 329; and net external assets, 130; and reinvestment of profits, 132, 261–2; understatement of, 131–2

Capital Investment Advisory Com-